Be Fruitful

The Jewish Pregnancy and Birth Guide

B.J. Woodstein, PhD, IBCLC

Praeclarus Press, LLC
2504 Sweetgum Lane
Amarillo, Texas 79124 U.S.
603-724-7995

www.PraeclarusPress.com

ISBN: 978-1-946665-84-3

Cover Design: Ken Tackett
Copyediting: Kathleen Kendall-Tackett
Layout & Design: Nelly Murariu

Dedication

To my three loves, Fi, Esther, and Tovah, always.

Contents

Acknowledgements

The idea for this book had been brewing for quite some time, but I decided I had to do it for sure in the wake of the attacks on October 7th, 2023. Feeling somewhat isolated as a Jew in the birth world, I was thrilled when another Jewish doula reached out to me after she saw my response to a troubling post in a social media group. She then introduced me to a burgeoning group of Jewish midwives, doulas, doctors, lactation consultants, and others, and the support and fellowship of the MOT Birthworkers' group has been nourishing and vital during these very hard times. A subsection of this group then decided to develop a professional organization both for Jewish birthworkers and also about Jewish birth for non-Jewish birthworkers; this became Shifrah UK. Both groups encouraged me in the belief that now was the right time to write this book, so I want to thank all the members of both MOT Birthworkers and Shifrah for their warmth, knowledge and passion.

Some of the members of these groups, as well as many other Jewish people, chose to share their personal stories of pregnancy, birth, and after with me. I am very grateful to all of them.

Additionally, my thanks to Rabbi Miriam Berger, midwife Laura Godfrey-Isaacs, and midwife Betsy Dwek, who each contributed a short piece to the text that follows below. Their contributions have added another dimension of Jewish information.

At Praeclarus, Ken Tackett is always a delight to work with. Thanks, Ken!

My family is the reason behind everything I do. My wife, Fi, and our daughters, Esther and Tovah, bring a smile to my face each day. Thank you to the three of you for the love, the fun, and the absolute joy.

Introduction

For many people, the experience of parenting is one of the most intense and important occurrences in their life. The step before being parents—that is, actually becoming parents—is likewise incredibly meaningful, and the whole process of fertility, pregnancy, birth, and postpartum can leave folks feeling vulnerable, uncertain, scared, excited, moved, and much more. For lots of us, it's a roller coaster of emotions and events.

The healthcare system, and those employed by it, can all too often treat people as though we're all the same, as though we should all follow the same protocol or treatment plan, or even as annoyances who need to do what the doctor tells us rather than having thoughts and feelings of our own. We need to be seen as the individuals we are, because otherwise we won't feel safe, and we won't have the best outcomes. When you then add in specific cultural or religious beliefs or traditions, this makes it potentially even more important for people to be understood, listened to, and seen, because what's right for one person during their birth isn't necessarily going to work for someone else.

Be Fruitful: The Jewish Pregnancy and Birth Guide has several key aims. The first one is for Jewish people to feel seen, which means, in part, providing information and inspiration specifically for them. For example, a Jewish person considering how long to breastfeed might want to know what other Jews do, or what Jewish religious texts suggest. Or some soon-to-be Jewish parents may wish to know about possible traditions for welcoming their new baby, or they may have a desire to learn about key values for Jewish parents. Although differing levels of religiosity and cultural backgrounds mean that not everything will be applicable to all Jews, at least it may be of interest, and naturally there are some commonalities. And of course, even if a specific Jewish family doesn't use the *mikveh,* or isn't planning on circumcising, they might nonetheless enjoy reading about traditions that their great-grandparents might have partaken in or that their fellow Jews carry on with today.

The second aim of this book is to help educate non-Jews. If you work in healthcare or an adjacent field, especially in a country such as Canada, the UK, the US, France, Australia, or, of course, Israel, you are very likely to come across Jewish patients at some point. You may not have been taught in medical school about Jewish genetic diseases, or you may not have learned during your doula training about Jewish beliefs around the postpartum period. You may not know much about antisemitism or Jewish history. This lack of knowledge, which may be unintentional, means that you might accidentally make a stereotyped remark that offends your client. Or you could get something wrong and encourage them to do something that directly opposes what they need or want to do. So here's a chance for you to increase your knowledge and to improve how you interact with and support the Jews around you, whether they're your patients, colleagues, or friends.

Finally, in this book, I hope to offer ideas for how the birth world can become more inclusive and equitable. This will benefit Jewish staff and applicants, as well as non-Jewish ones. Many of the ideas can be used in other fields and industries too.

In short, the audience of this book is intended to be both Jews and non-Jews, which means that I hope there's something of use to everyone who reads it. What, then, will you find here?

I start off by defining and exploring what Jews actually are, since there is so much misinformation and confusion about this. We look at race, religion, ethnicity, stereotypes, antisemitism, and more. Then I move on to Jewish pregnancy, discussing beliefs and traditions regarding this, followed by Jewish birth practices. From there, I explore Jewish breastfeeding and baby-feeding generally, Jewish postpartum practices, and general ideas around Jewish parenting. Finally, I look at how we can improve the birth world both for Jewish patients, and for Jews who work within the field. Among all the practical and research-based information, I include anecdotes and stories from Jewish people, to illustrate what is being discussed in each section.

"The Jews started it all—and by 'it' I mean so many of the things we care about, the underlying values that make all of us, Jew and Gentile, believer and atheist, tick. Without the Jews, we would see the world through different eyes, hear with different ears, even feel with different feelings... We would think with a different mind, interpret all our experiences differently, draw different conclusions from the things that befall us. And we would set a different course for our lives." (Cahill, n.d., n.p.[1]) Whether or not you believe this, it is certainly true that Jews and Judaism have helped shape the world. It's also true that, if you are not Jewish yourself, you are likely to come across Jews in your work, and it behooves you to know something about them, just as it would about any group of people. Therefore, in this book, I hope to help you understand us/yourself a bit better, and to share information about our birth and parenting practices, so, if you are Jewish, you feel more enabled and empowered, and if you aren't, you will be better able to work with Jewish clients and patients and also to support your Jewish friends.

1 If a reference doesn't have a page number (such as if it's from a website), I'll write "n.p." for "no pagination". Similarly, if it doesn't have a year of publication, I'll write "n.d." for "no date".

A Brief Note

No group of people is homogenous and monolithic, and of course this is as true of Jews as it is of anyone else. Though I am here writing about Jews in general terms, I know that not all Jewish folks will agree with or relate to all parts of this book. Later on in the book, I'll discuss different types and denominations of Jews. It seems obvious to say that there are differences among them, including in regard to belief, behavior, and traditions. So, I apologize in advance if you don't recognize yourself here, or if you disagree with some information or a particular interpretation.

Furthermore, I must point out that traditions and beliefs evolve, and this is as true for Jews as for any other group. One way in which they have been evolving and continue to do so is in regard to listening to women more. "The Talmudic Rabbis, who formulated the basis of traditional Jewish prayer, ritual, and law, were men. Because they were men, they never experienced pregnancy. The Rabbis never felt the disquiet of morning sickness, never endured the discomfort of trying to sleep with a huge belly, and never had their bodies enveloped by labor pains…the Rabbi "skipped" this entire passage of life. If the Rabbis were women, [orthodox Jewish feminist] Blu Greenberg speculates, there would probably be some fantastic birthing rituals" (Falk & Judson, xi-xii, n.p.). However, women are now rectifying this by reading and analyzing traditional Jewish writings from a feminist or feminine lens, and also by creating their own rituals, prayers, and traditions. In other words, Jewish birth practices are in a state of exciting flux.

Also, if you've come to this book to learn how to better serve your Jewish clients or patients, please keep in mind that while it's an excellent idea to educate yourself in broad terms, you should always treat the individual you have in front of you. That means you shouldn't assume that everything in this book is applicable to every Jew you meet or work with, even if it's a useful starting-point. That is to say, if you've met or learned about one Jew, well, you've met or learned about one Jew, not all Jews.

Given the variety you find among Jews, it might be useful for you to know about my own experience and perspective as a Jew. I am Ashkenazi Jewish (I'll explain this shortly!) and I grew up in a secular home in Chicago. Indeed, it was so secular that one of my parents could even be said to have been ashamed of our Jewishness and to almost have disavowed it. We lived in an overwhelmingly Catholic neighborhood, where the local children were taught to not like Jews. They wouldn't allow me in their homes and they spit at me, threw trash at me, stole from me, used antisemitic language to describe me, and called me names. Besides that, I experienced antisemitism in a variety of other forms. For example, I took an entrance exam for a private Catholic school, and was told that despite my incredibly high results, unless I had something else to offer, such as top sporting skills, the school didn't really need yet another Jewish kid (this sort of thing was still legal to say then).

I've also experienced friends and even romantic partners making cruel, stereotyped remarks about Jews, such as that since all Jews were rich, I ought to always pay when we went out for coffee or meals. I've been called awful terms that I've decided not to repeat here (I included them in an early draft and then felt that I didn't need to give such epithets any airspace). Once, I was giving a lecture and during the break, someone I didn't know came over to me and said I ought to change my surname, because no one would want to hire a Jew. That was quite upsetting to hear. Later, I was in fact hired for a job, but I had to deal with colleagues, and even a manager, making antisemitic remarks or telling Jewish "jokes." Unfortunately, people from human resources didn't think this was a big deal and told me to "get over it." These experiences are not unique to me.

Now, as an adult, I live in a small city in England with my wife and our children. I identify as an atheist Jew, and my family and I belong to a synagogue where we enjoy partaking in Hebrew school (also called *cheder*), Shabbat services, and holiday celebrations. I consider it part of my mission to be openly Jewish and to help educate people about Jews and Judaism, so I regularly give talks or write about the subject. I say all this so that it's clear that I am not representing all Jews in this book. I've come to the topic with my own specific Jewish background and trajectory, and I've carried out a lot of research to learn more.

As for my background in the birth world, I'm a doula and an International Board-Certified Lactation Consultant (IBCLC). I've been involved in breastfeeding support for over ten years, and have worked as a birth doula and postnatal doula for a bit less than that. Over that decade, I've seen just how important it is to treat each client as an individual, while never forgetting that the individual is embedded in a particular culture and background, which can persuade them to make certain choices over others, or can sway them to specific beliefs. Therefore, I've made an effort to continue educating myself about groups that I do not belong to so I can understand, to the best of my ability, where my client is coming from and what matters to them.

I hope this book offers you a useful introduction to a fascinating subject. Please feel free to get in touch with me if you want to share your own story about being or supporting a Jewish person through pregnancy, birth, and related periods or rituals.

The Quotes

This book includes quotes from a wide range of Jewish people and families. I put out calls on social media and among my contacts, inviting people to tell me about their distinctly Jewish experiences of fertility, pregnancy, birth, breastfeeding, the postpartum period, and parenting in general. I have anonymized all the quotes so that the families can't be identified. No facts were changed, but I sometimes removed details, such as the location or the gender if it wasn't relevant to the story.

Though I said this in the Acknowledgements, I want to thank everyone who responded to my request for stories for the time and effort they put in. They chose to share their knowledge and their lives in order to help others. I am very grateful for it.

A Comment on Language

Jews live worldwide and thus speak hundreds of languages. Hebrew and Arabic are the official everyday languages of Israel, which is the sole Jewish country on the planet. Hebrew is the language used in prayer by Jews everywhere (however, without getting too technical, I should add that the Mourner's Kaddish, a prayer that is regularly said, is in Aramaic, not Hebrew).

Many people, Jewish or not, tend to believe that Yiddish (based in part on German) is the main Jewish language, but this is an Ashkenormative perspective (i.e., one that privileges Ashkenazi Jews (more on this in a bit), or Jews who lived in Eastern Europe). Other Jewish languages include Ladino (a sort of Jewish version of Spanish), Judeo-Papiamento (a creole from Curaçao), and varieties of Judeo-Arabic. Additionally, Jews have always spoken the languages of the countries in which they lived, such as Dutch, Russian, Chinese, Hindi, Amharic, or English.

Within this book, there will sometimes be words from non-English languages. In most cases they are terms from Hebrew, because they are references to religious or cultural beliefs shaped by the Torah if they are not from Hebrew, I will note that. For the non-Jewish reader, I will explain them as needed. You will notice some varying spellings of Jewish terms, and that is in part because words from, say, Hebrew or Yiddish are transliterated to English and there are multiple ways of doing this. Also, I am quoting from sources that do this differently, sometimes depending on whether they are Ashkenazi or Sephardic, and I didn't want to homogenize the language. At times, what may look like typos or carelessness on my part are, on the contrary, simply me using the spellings and terms that my sources did.

Also, in reference to language, the vast majority of the quotes employed here, whether from books or other resources, or from Jewish people themselves, refer to mothers as the ones who get pregnant and give birth. I am aware that some Jewish birthing parents identify otherwise and use other terms, and although that experience is not really represented in this book, it's always important to try to respect and reflect people's own language for and about themselves.

CHAPTER 1

Defining Jews

Yes, this is a book about birth, pregnancy, and related topics, but before we get into all that, defining Jews is the obvious place to start. Although many people think they know what Jews are, it's actually more complicated than you might initially believe. Also, unfortunately, in these times, antisemitism, antizionism, and anti-Israel sentiments are all on the rise, so it's important to try to understand what people think they are objecting to and whether those beliefs are accurate (spoiler alert: often, the prejudices we see against Jews come from erroneous information and ignorance, as is true for most stereotypes and discriminatory beliefs and actions).

Numbers

Let's start with some fast statistics. There are around 15 million Jewish people in the world. Given the total population on the earth, this means that Jews are only a miniscule 0.2% of the population (see Graph 1). Around half of all Jews live in Israel (i.e., over 7 million Jews), but we must remember that Israel also has around 2 million non-Jewish Arab citizens and another half a million citizens who are both non-Jewish and non-Arab, so although Israel is the sole Jewish country in the world, it is not wholly Jewish by any means. Around 6 million Jews live in the United States, where they make up around 2% of the population; under 400,000 live in Canada, comprising 1% of the population; and around 270,000 live in the UK, where they are 0.46% of the population. The remaining Jewish people are scattered among other countries, such as Russia, Argentina, Australia, France, Hungary, and so on. I've heard the world's Jewish population described as being like a butterfly: one big wing is Israel, the other wing the United States, and the slender head and body the rest of the world.

As is well known, 6 million Jewish people (as well as many non-Jewish people) were killed in the Holocaust. There would be more Jews today if all those Jews had lived and if some of them had reproduced, but "even if the Holocaust hadn't happened, there would still be only about thirty-five million of us, and that's only 0.4 percent of the world's population" (Acho & Tishby, 2024, p. 147). We were never a big group of people, which you might be surprised by, given how much room we seem to take up in the heads of some non-Jews.

As these numbers testify, there aren't that many Jews in the world. If we're going to talk about religion—and believe me, we're going to get into that in just a moment—then I have to point out that adherents of Hinduism add up to over 1 billion people, Muslims account for nearly 2 billion out of the planet's 8 billion people, and Christians for 2.4 billion. If we look at national origin, then there are 1.4 billion Indians on the planet and even more Chinese people. So one could conceivably and understandably ask why such a tiny group of people needs their own book about pregnancy and parenting. Sure, I could make a joke about Jews traditionally being the people of the book and therefore it making sense that they also are the people of this pregnancy and birth guide, but to put it more seriously, Jewish people have a distinct history and culture and this also includes a set of beliefs, which together impacts their approaches to parenthood. Size isn't everything, right?

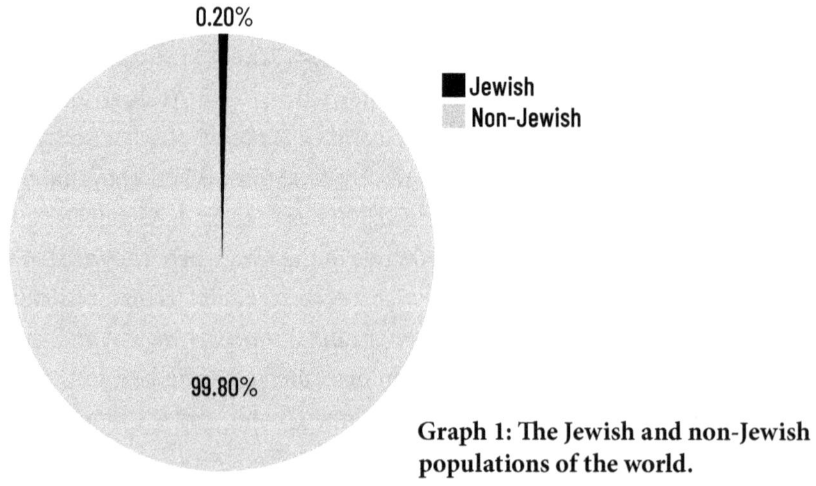

Graph 1: The Jewish and non-Jewish populations of the world.

Origins

You haven't come here for a long history lesson, so let's be brief. Jews traditionally referred to themselves as Israelites. "Ancient Israelites originated roughly in the territory of modern Israel, also known as the ancient Levant or ancient Canaan, sometime before 1000 BCE. These people were united by a sense of shared ancestry, myth, ritual and history. Ancient Israelites believed that they were descendants of three people: Abraham, his son Isaac and his grandson Jacob. Jacob himself is renamed "Israel" in the Bible, which suggests that Israelites had a shared memory of a name change as part of their history" (Ahuvia, 2016, n.p.). While some of the Israelites were expelled from Israel and others chose to leave for various reasons, meaning that there are Jewish people in other countries, there has always been a Jewish presence in Israel. When people use the term Zionism, they mean the belief that Jews have the right to continue to live safely in Israel and determine their own destiny. This hasn't been the case in other countries, where Jews have been forced to live under restrictions and/or have been expelled. In short, Judaism arose in the region of modern Israel thousands of years ago, and there have been Jews there ever since.

Religion, Ethnicity, and Race

All right, we now have to get into what is undeniably a thorny and emotive topic. Are Jews a religion? An ethnicity? A race? All of those? Something else? And yes, we have to explore the question that's been on many people's minds, especially in recent times: are Jews white?

Religion

Religion refers to someone's spiritual beliefs. It tends to be the case that religion is often what people think about first when they consider how to define Jews. Certainly, there are many Jewish people who are religiously observant. There are lots of Jewish women who go to the *mikveh* (the ritual bath) and who cover their hair, Jewish men who spend their days studying the Torah (the bible), Jewish children who study Hebrew from a young age and prepare for their bar and bat mitzvahs, Jewish people who go to synagogue every Friday night and Saturday morning, and so on. There are many people who strictly follow the commandments in the Torah, pray regularly, and keep kosher.

However, there are also many atheist or agnostic Jews (I count myself among them), and, on the whole, research suggests that Jews are less religious than many other groups of people. That might seem confusing, but it's because for lots of us, we have different ways of understanding both the concept of religion as well as what it means to be Jewish. However, over 70% of Jews agree that you can be Jewish without believing in a god. Perhaps surprisingly, more than 40% of very religious Jews agree with that statement (Diamant, 2021, n.p.).

Atheist Jews

In terms of religion, there are loads of Jews who carry out what appear to be religious practices and rituals, such as going to *shul* (synagogue), lighting candles on Shabbat (the sabbath), celebrating Jewish holidays, sending children to *cheder* (Hebrew/Jewish school), and so on, but we do this to connect with our heritage. It's the doing that matters rather than the being, so it doesn't feel hypocritical to recite a prayer that references God[2], even if you yourself don't believe in the existence of that God that God, or if you consider yourself to be praying to nature, or another entity. Treating biblical tales as stories with some basis in reality and that contain useful messages for how to live today is obviously different from taking them as the literal truth. But in both cases, people are reading them and analyzing them in part as a way of linking back to Jewish history and in order to help shape their identity today.

In the US, "Jewish adults…are twice as likely as the general public to say they do not believe in any kind of higher power or spiritual force in the universe (22% vs. 10%)" (Pew, 2021, n.p.). In Israel, the figure is similar,

2 It is a custom for some Jews to block out the "o" in that word as a sign of respect and to ensure that nothing related to God is desecrated or destroyed. I myself don't follow that practice in a religious sense, but I will do so in this book if I am quoting from another source that does so.

with around 23% of Jews saying they don't believe in a god or that they aren't sure (Pew, 2016, n.p.).

Humanist Jews

In the same general category as secular, atheist, or agnostic Jews, you also find humanist Jews, who are nontheistic but practice a form of Judaism that "celebrates Jewish life without religious prayer or appeals for divine intervention, instead putting faith in ourselves and our fellow humans as the best vehicles for improving the world" (Society for Humanistic Judaism, 2018, n.p.). Humanist Jewish groups "offer a connection to Jewish identity and community for people who are atheist and/or agnostic, "just Jewish," culturally Jewish, "Jew-ish," multicultural, "not religious," secular, humanistic, freethinker—and friends, family, and allies." (ibid.)

It is challenging to get a clear figure for the percentage of humanist Jews, in part because it's primarily in the US, though growing in the UK and elsewhere, but around 4% of Jews identify as humanist or reconstructionist (Pew, 2021, n.p.), and it seems that some people conflate these groups, although they are not strictly the same.

Reconstructionist Jews

Reconstructionist Judaism is more exploratory and less rigid than Orthodox forms of Judaism. "The starting point of Reconstructionism is our quest to understand the historical and spiritual experience of the Jewish people. We believe 'the past has a vote.' Therefore, we struggle to hear the voices of our ancestors and listen to their claim on us. What did this custom or that idea mean to them? How did they see the presence of God in it? How can we retain or regain its importance in our own lives? We believe 'the past does not have a veto.' Therefore, we struggle to hear our own voices as distinct from theirs. What might this custom or that idea mean to us today? What might we borrow from this custom to create a new tradition that is more significant for us today? When a particular Jewish value or custom is found wanting, it is our obligation as Jews to find a means to reconstruct it—to find new meanings in old forms or to develop more meaningful, innovative practices. A vital, contemporary Judaism must respond fully to the changes in modern Jewish history... Only a combination of searching, questioning, and self-understanding within the Jewish tradition will create a Judaism that speaks convincingly to the contemporary Jew" (Reconstructing Judaism, n.d., n.p.). That is to say, reconstructionism is about reconstructing Judaism, using Jewish history as a way of understanding but not defining the present. Reconstructionist Jews may or may not believe in a god, whereas humanist Jews are in general not very likely to.

Reconstructionism is primarily based in the United States, and there are thought to be around 40,000 people who identify as being part of the Reconstructionist movement (US Religion Census, 2010, n.p.).

Reform Jews and Liberal Jews

Reform Judaism "affirms the central tenets of Judaism—God, Torah, and Israel—while acknowledging the diversity of Reform Jewish beliefs and practices. We believe that Judaism must change and adapt to the needs of the day to survive, and we see the Torah as a living, God-inspired document that enables us to confront the challenges of our everyday lives... We believe that there is more than one authentic way to be Jewish, and we stand for a Judaism that is inclusive and open" (Reform Judaism, n.d., n.p.). Humanist and Reform services may be more likely to use English than Hebrew, or to employ both, while more traditional forms of Judaism tend to have larger portions of their services components of their services in Hebrew.

Around 37% of American Jews identify as Reform (Pew, 2021, n.p.), while in the UK, the corresponding figure was thought to be around 20% (Mashiah & Boyd, 2017, n.p.), but I must acknowledge that figures were arrived at differently, because instead of surveying people, some percentages were based on synagogue membership. For various reasons, people may belong to synagogues that in actuality do not represent their religious views, or they may belong to multiple synagogues, or they may identify as belonging to a particular subset but not belong to a synagogue; nonetheless, the data provided here is a useful ballpark estimate. In Israel, which many people do not realize is quite a divided society, as approximately half of the population is secular, and half is religious (depending on ethnicity and gender to some) extent, only around 3% of the population identifies as Reform (Pew, 2016, n.p.).

Also, it's worth pointing out that there are Reform Jews in the US and the UK, but they aren't exactly the same. Reconstructionist Jews in the US are like Reform Jews in the UK, while Reform Jews in the US are more like the group that's called Liberal in the UK. To add more confusion, in the UK, the Reform and Liberal movements are currently merging. The Liberal movement is about "questing and questioning" (Liberal Judaism, n.d., n.p.). They describe themselves thus: "We are a movement with a sense of purpose, engaged in community life, study, spirituality and social action. We believe in personal freedom and responsibility, and the shared and collective bonds that unite us as Jewish people and members of humanity. We actively choose to live out our Judaism as part of a community, and welcome those who grew up as Jewish and those who, later in life, have become accepted into Judaism. We are inclusive and egalitarian, giving equal status within Judaism to those traditionally excluded. We help all our members to embark on their personal Jewish journeys" (ibid.). Once the unification of the Reform and Liberal movements in the UK is finished (as of this writing, it will hopefully happen in early 2026), the new group will be called Progressive, and it is thought that this will cover 30% of the Jews in the UK (Sherwood, 2023, n.p.).

Conservative or Masorti Jews

Next up on our imperfectly sliding scale of secular Jews to observant ones comes Conservative or Masorti Judaism. The former term is more common in the US, and the latter in the UK, but both describe a form of religious belief that is heading towards the stronger or more traditional side. Conservative Judaism has a "traditional approach—which combines fidelity to inherited tradition and the courage to integrate necessary change—[and this] motivates Conservative Judaism today. Whether asserting the equality of women, reaffirming the centrality of Shabbat (the Sabbath), *kashrut* (the dietary laws), *tzedakah* (charity/justice), and prayer, or applying timeless wisdom to contemporary issues, Conservative Judaism insists on observance of tradition and respect for visionary change. The Conservative Jewish community places its trust in its rabbis [religious leaders] to be interpreters of *halakhah* and guides to Jewish life and learning" (Rabbinical Assembly, n.d., n.p.). Meanwhile, the term *Masorti* "is Hebrew for 'traditional'. We believe in traditional Judaism for modern Jews. Masorti Judaism celebrates the diversity of our contemporary Jewish community while making its own, distinctive contribution. We have a steadfast commitment to integrating traditional Judaism with modern values, and maintain traditional observance while being fully inclusive and intellectually open-minded" (Masorti, n.d., n.p.). As you can tell, there is clear overlap here.

In the US, Conservatives are around 17% of the Jewish population (Pew, 2021, n.p.); in the UK, Masorti Jews are around 3% (Mashiah & Boyd, 2017, n.p.). In Israel, around 23% identify as Masorti (Pew, 2016, n.p.). Again, though, these are not exact figures, because the meaning of these words is somewhat different in the three nations, and Jewish Israelis are more likely to understand themselves as one of the following terms: *hiloni* (secular, 40%), Masorti (traditional, 23%), *dati* (religious, 10%), or *haredi* (ultra-Orthodox, 8%), and this doesn't map precisely onto the way American or British Jews understand Jewish identity (Pew, 2016, n.p.). I once heard someone refer to himself as "dati light", by which I understood him to mean that he was modern Orthodox and somewhat flexible with his religiosity.

Orthodox Jews

Orthodox Jews are more conventionally observant in their beliefs and tend to follow the traditions and prescripts of religious Judaism. They may also be more likely to avoid mixing with the rest of society and assimilating into the larger world in which they live. The term Orthodox is used as something of an umbrella that covers a range of different ways of believing and living, but in general, Orthodox Jews follow the Torah strictly and keep to traditions, such as gender segregation during services, or only boys having a full-blown coming-of-age ceremony (while girls in some communities might have a smaller event instead of reading from the Torah).

There are Modern Orthodox Jews. "Modern Orthodoxy is a philosophy within Orthodoxy that synthesizes traditional Judaism with modern knowledge… Modern Orthodoxy views non-Torah fields, such as science, and even literature, as having inherent potential value…Modern Orthodoxy believes in Torah and secular education, for both men and women. It believes in earning a living (though that's not to say that nobody learns full-time; it's just not for everyone.) It doesn't believe in sequestering ourselves in a homogenous enclave. Generally speaking, Modern Orthodoxy is Zionistic" (Abramowitz, 2022, n.p.). It is not unusual to see cleanly shaven rather than bearded Modern Orthodox men, and you might meet Modern Orthodox people in school/university, or at parties.

Hasidic Jews are the ones people to tend to picture when asked what a Jewish person looks like, as they wear what might be considered to be old-fashioned clothes, often with big, sometimes fur hats. However, they are quite a small percentage of Jews overall. "Today the largest center in New York is home to around 190,000 Hasidim, about 490,000 live in Jerusalem, and close to 30,000 are in London. Altogether, the current Hasidic community is estimated at 700,000-750,000 people. Thanks to their distinctive dress visibility, and political influence, Hasidism is without a doubt the most visible and recognizable Jewish religious group, and perhaps one of the most recognizable religious groups in the world" (Wodziński, 2019, n.p.). In other words, the Hasidim, a term which means "the pious ones" (Wodziński, 2019, n.p.), are what people tend to believe all Jews are like, but in actual fact they are only about 5% of the total Jewish population. Hasidism is sometimes viewed as a mystical form of Judaism, and it stems from eastern Europe, so many Hasidic folks are Yiddish speakers. The original concept behind Hasidism was for people "to try and find God in the text as well as in their hearts…to experience connection with the divine" (Kutner, 2025, p. 117).

As you can tell, Orthodox is quite a broad category, running the gamut from the clean-shaven to the heavily bearded, among other things, and this reflects different beliefs and varying levels of strictness of interpretation of religious tracts. Nine percent of American Jews identify as Orthodox (Pew, 2016, n.p.), while 52% of British Jews consider themselves modern or "central" Orthodox (Mashiah & Boyd, 2017, n.p.). As noted above, the "dati" or Orthodox population of Israel is estimated to be 10% (Pew, 2016, n.p.).

Haredi or Ultra-Orthodox Jews

Finally, there are the Haredi Jews, who are also called the ultra-Orthodox. The word Haredi "stems from the Hebrew word *hared*, meaning to tremble" (Kolirin, 2021, n.p.), because the Haredi are very traditional people who are fearful before God, and also scared of their children becoming secular. "Something of a catch-all term, it usually refers to a broad range of groups who are socially conservative Orthodox Jews but of varying practices and traditions. Sometimes spelled Charedi or Chareidi, they are united, however, in their absolute adherence to the Torah in determining every aspect of their lives" (Kolirin, 2021, n.p.). They are currently the center of some conflict in Israel, because while nearly all Israelis are required to serve in the military, the Haredi have an exemption for political reasons. On the Haredi side, this is due to their grave concern that if their children were to serve in the military and were to mix with non-Haredi, they might become secular. Obviously, this doesn't go down well with the non-Haredi majority in Israel, who puts their own lives at risk to defend the country.

Haredi are 8% of the population in Israel (Pew, 2016, n.p.), but their number varies in the US, with "fully one-in-ten U.S. Jewish adults under the age of 30 [being] Haredim, or ultra-Orthodox (11%), compared with 1% of Jews 65 and older" (Pew, 2021, n.p.).

Other Types

As is presumably clear by now, there are many different types of Jews. I should also note that some synagogues identify as "independent" rather than following one movement, which means there can be some idiosyncratic or regional differences. The synagogue my family belongs to in Norwich, England, is one of those independent ones and at the moment, this means that three Saturdays of the month, Shabbat services are more or less Orthodox, although very few in our community identify as Orthodox, and on the fourth Saturday there is an egalitarian service that is more along the lines of Reform/Liberal/soon-to-be Progressive.

Obviously, there are also many people who consider themselves Jewish but wouldn't choose a movement to identify with, as they may feel culturally and not religiously Jewish. We will discuss this more later.

When I carried out a survey into Jewish people's experiences with the birth world, I asked people how they identified. I received so many interesting responses that didn't fit neatly into the categories I mentioned above that I thought it was worth including a few here, because they exemplify one of the more misunderstood aspects of Judaism, namely the erroneous idea that it's one overarching category. Here are five of the many responses that were sent to me:

We are *zachor* [remember/commemorate] but not *shamor* [guard/keep] Jews (i.e. we don't take on a lot of restrictions but do take on positive commandments, if that makes sense).

◇◇◇

I'm an Ashkenazi Jew who doesn't believe that God exists. My husband isn't Jewish and is an atheist. We celebrate major Jewish holidays. Both kids have gone to a Jewish daycare/pre-school and my kindergartener goes to Hebrew school. We also celebrate Christmas without any mentioning of God or Jesus. It's like a second Thanksgiving but with different food, presents, and a Christmas tree topped with a magen David.

◇◇◇

We light candles most Fridays and the kids attend a URJ [Union for Reform Judaism] summer camp.

◇◇◇

I am Conservative and active in our shul, but I am also an atheist. I don't keep Shabbat or kashrut, but I attend shul most weeks.

◇◇◇

I'm Israeli and 100% Jewish but don't classify myself as religious. I believe in God, do the holidays, light Shabbat candles, but don't keep Shabbat or kosher (apart for pork—I don't eat it though the rest of my family does). I don't call myself religious, because to me that means keeping Shabbat and kosher and other things... but then again maybe that's being Israeli versus Jewish from another country.

So there you have it—a spectrum that ranges from atheist and secular through to the very faithful, who take the Torah literally and shape their lives around their religious beliefs. Jews are evidently not one single group with a firmly shared set of beliefs, but rather vary according to background, custom, and practice.[3]

Ethnicity and Tradition

As for what being Jewish means, well, as you can tell, it's partially about carrying out age-old Jewish traditions, doing what your parents or grandparents did and what other Jewish people around the world are doing at the same time, and honoring that background. It's also partially about demarcating a sense of self. For instance, even though Christmas was historically a pagan celebration that then was adapted by Christians and connected to their belief in Jesus, many people around the world today celebrate Christmas despite not identifying as Christians. They feel that Christmas is a cultural event, possibly one that their parents or other ancestors would have celebrated in a religious sense, and they enjoy the togetherness and joy that the holiday brings for them. They also may feel that it gives their family something to hold on to and to identify with. (Incidentally, as a non-Christian, I don't celebrate Christmas, as it feels like a Christian holiday, though I know lots of people, including some Jews, who disagree with me.)

You can begin to understand how some Jews feel if you take Christmas as an analogy. Many Jews honor and celebrate Shabbat, Purim, Passover,

3 Some readers who are not themselves Jewish may have heard of a group called "Messianic Jews" and might be wondering why I've skipped over them. The truth is that despite the name, "Messianic Jews" are not considered to be Jewish. They are people who have accepted Christ (hence the "messianic" bit, since they see Christ as the messiah) and while some of them may have originally been Jewish or may choose to celebrate some Jewish holidays or may even call their leaders "rabbis", a core aspect of Judaism is that Jews do not accept Jesus Christ as a savior, messiah, or prophet. "Messianic Jews" are in fact Christians. In other words, the name is misleading, which is why "Messianic Jews" are not included in this book, which is about Jewish traditions and beliefs. I've seen "Messianic rabbis" quoted in newspaper articles that are about Jews, and this shows that the journalists have not done due diligence and have mistaken views of Judaism.

Rosh Hashanah, Hanukkah, and other Jewish holidays without necessarily finding them moving from a spiritual perspective. For them, it is more about identity and family. The same is true for many aspects of Judaism, not just the holidays. For instance, the majority of Jews feel a deep connection to Israel, even if they have never been there and have no intention of moving there or even visiting.

So, yes, being Jewish is about religion for some people, but not for all Jews. For other Jews, being Jewish is about their ethnic heritage; some people will identify as Jewish the way others might call themselves Chinese or Irish or anything else (and obviously, you also will find Chinese Jews, Irish Jews, and so on). Some people even refer to being Jewish as an "ethno-religion," in that it is both an ethnicity and a religion, and you can pick and choose which elements from each aspect you want to hold on to. It is about doing Judaism and being Jewish, in whatever way feels best for you, and the primary importance for many is placed on taking part in Jewish community and culture. As Noa Tishby puts it, "Judaism is different from Christianity and Islam because it's not just a religion, it's an ethno-religion. Meaning being Jewish is not solely about being observant or practicing daily rituals. It's about a shared story and history, a shared culture, and a shared ancestral homeland—in Hebrew, it's an *Am* and *Uma*, a peoplehood and a nation" (Acho & Tishby, 2024, p. 9).

Lest you start to think that the Jewish ethnicity is just one thing, or that all Jews share the same traditions and cultures, I need to further complicate matters by explaining that there are three main branches of Jews. These are the Ashkenazi, the Sephardi, and the Mizrahi. They are distinct groups based in large part on where they originate from, and this then influences everything from what they believe, how they practice, what foods they eat, and even how they pronounce Hebrew. When I say "where they originate from", I mean where their ancestors went after they left what is now Israel. I must acknowledge that some people do not like the terms Ashkenazi, Mizrahi, and Sephardi, and instead prefer to specify the country they or their ancestors are from, such as Belarusian Jew or Iranian Jew.

It's fair to say that all Jews come originally from Israel. "Around 1030 BCE, the country [what is now Israel] became a sovereign Jewish kingdom, referred to in the Hebrew Bible as the United Monarchy" (Acho and Tishby, 2024, p. 165). Though many Jews continued to live there through the decades and centuries after that time, given that that area was subsequently colonized by different groups of people and those people often forced Jews out, or made things so unpleasant, such as by trying to insist that Jews convert to other religions or by murdering Jews, that some Jews decided to leave, some Jewish people ended up in different parts of the world.

"The Ashkenazim (from the Hebrew term for Germany, *Ashkenaz*) trace their roots mainly to central and eastern Europe" (Pew Research Center, 2016, n.p., italics original). Meanwhile, people often conflate the Sephardi and the Mizrahi. "Mizrahi (from *Mizrah*, meaning eastern in Hebrew) often is used interchangeably with Sephardi (or *Sfaradit*, meaning Spanish in Hebrew)" (ibid., italics original). Sephardim and Mizrahim have similar religious traditions and practices, distinct from those of the Ashkenazim. Sephardim typically trace their roots to ancestors who lived in Spain until they were expelled during the Spanish Inquisition.

"The Sephardim then migrated eastward and lived largely among the Mizrahim in the Middle East and North Africa" (Pew Research Center, 2016; also see Danon, 2018 for more on this). In other words, you can think of the Ashkenazi as Jews who left Israel and ended up in eastern and central Europe, the Sephardi as those who came to live in Spain, Portugal, or Greece, and the Mizrahi as Jews who then lived in the Middle East or North Africa, though this delineation is not quite as straightforward as it may appear. Some people, of course, have a mix of Jewish ancestry, and some Jews also identify with the culture or ethnicity of other places where their family has lived or currently lives. Also, because of where the Ashkenazi lived, the Holocaust generally impacted Ashkenazi families more than other types of Jews, but certainly not exclusively.

It is also worth acknowledging that the three branches sometimes don't see eye-to-eye. People talk about Ashkenormativity, or the outsized influence of Ashkenazi practices and perspectives, on both Judaism itself as well as on how it is perceived. Many non-Jews aren't even aware that there have been and continue to be Jews in countries such as Spain or Iraq, as they link Jews with eastern Europe. I've also heard disparaging comments said by one group about another, and it still makes me chuckle ruefully to recall a display I saw at a Jewish museum in Italy. Most Italian Jews identify as Sephardic and Orthodox, and an exhibit at the museum showed some of the beautiful silver items this community had in their synagogues. There was a little note that, in my paraphrase, explained that because Ashkenazi Jews are poor and uncultured, they never had gorgeous decorative pieces in their synagogues that the wealthy, cultured, more advanced Sephardic Jews had. The fact that curators were willing to state this publicly shows that there can be stereotypes and animosity at times between these groups.

While those are the three main branches, there are also Jews elsewhere. There were many Jews in Middle Eastern countries, but they have been successively kicked out over the years, so few remain. There are Ethiopian, Indian, and Yemenite Jews, among others. India, for example, has been home to a Jewish population for ages, though people often only think of Hinduism, Islam, and Buddhism as being relevant to the country. "India is home to three historically distinct Jewish communities: the Bene Israel ("Sons of Israel"), the Cochin Jews, and the Baghdadi Jews. It is thought that the first Indian Jews were members of the biblical "Lost Tribes of Israel," having settled on the Malabar coast after the Assyrian conquest of the Kingdom of Israel in the ninth century B.C.E…They were allowed to practice Jewish life freely and openly, and they were quite successful in maintaining Jewish religious practices while also assimilating into the local culture" (World Jewish Congress, n.d., n.p.).

We also mustn't forget that people can combine different ethnic backgrounds and that groups can and do marry and reproduce, so this is all not quite as clear-cut as I may have made it sound in this section.

Someone in my survey wrote this about ethnic identity:

> I strongly relate to the notion of Jewishness as an ethnoreligious identity—we're an ethnic group with common ancestry, language, and traditions that surpass contemporary understandings of organized religion. But our religion, Judaism, is woven through and intrinsic to our culture through tradition and ritual—it therefore feels indivisible from secularized Jewish life to me.

Another said:

I feel strongly that I'm Jewish, though I can't explain why. My mother was Jewish (American) but my English father wasn't. My parents were not at all religious and so my brothers and I weren't brought up with any religion, although weirdly we were christened, maybe to please my English grandparents. My English grandmother had many Jewish friends and loved the culture and ironically it was she more than anyone who instilled in me a pride in being Jewish.

Coincidentally, my husband also had a Jewish mother and gentile father (both South African) but absolutely no religious upbringing. In fact, he only discovered his mother was Jewish and born in Palestine when he was in his 30s. She hid it from everyone. In recent years, my husband has discovered a whole lot of Jewish cousins in Israel and South Africa.

All three of our (now adult) boys identify as being Jewish despite not having had any religious upbringing either. We have all been to Israel together twice with some Israeli friends and we found it fascinating. I think we all felt drawn to the culture. It's a very strange feeling, almost like a genetic recognition. I had a kind of out-of-body experience at Yad Vashem. I only found out recently that a first cousin of my mother's and her daughter died in Auschwitz.

Race

Now we need to complicate things further by referring to the concept of race. First of all, race is widely understood to be a social construct. In other words, some people are described (or choose to self-describe) as white, black, brown, or another color, and this is based on the level of melanin in their skin (though you can have, for instance, an albino person with little melanin who identifies as black). It may also be based in part on how they are treated by society, in that one could say that someone is racialized because of the discrimination they may face. However, two people with an apparently similar color of skin may come from completely different cultures and backgrounds and have little in common. For example, someone from South Africa and someone from Nigeria might both be referred to as black, but have different languages and cultures and not think there was much that bound them other than them both being from a country in Africa. On the other hand, a black person from South Africa and a white person from South Africa could also have different languages, backgrounds, cultures, and experiences, and yet relate more because they are from the same country. It's really tricky if you try to put everyone with a supposedly similar skin color into one category and expect them to relate to one another or to get along.

Jewish people come in every skin tone. There are Jews on and from every continent (except Antarctica, unless they're there as research scientists). There are Arab Jews, Indian Jews, Ethiopian Jews, Spanish Jews, Greek Jews, and many, many more. And yet, one of the issues we face today is that in countries such as the US and the UK, Jews are perceived as being white. This is possibly because the majority of Jews that immigrated to those countries were from eastern Europe and so may appear to have paler skin.

Traditionally, Jews, even the Ashkenazi ones from eastern Europe or Germany, were viewed as something other than white or Caucasian, and were perceived as something in their own category. In my own family, US census records list my relatives' race as "Hebrew", which is not a racial category recognized today, although I have heard people describe their race as "Jewish". When large numbers of Jews were immigrating to the US, they faced massive amounts of discrimination, with certain jobs, schools, restaurants, apartments, and other places or institutions explicitly setting out signs or rules stating "no Jews allowed."

Over time, Jewish people began to be more accepted in the US and elsewhere, and this is naturally something to be celebrated; all groups should be accepted and treated equally. A negative aspect of this, however, is that Jews started to be viewed as part of the establishment and therefore as White and, thus, as "rich and powerful" (yes, many, perhaps most, White people are not rich or powerful or part of the establishment). Meanwhile, many non-White people still experience prejudice and discrimination because of their skin tone. Since many Jews in the US are perceived as being White or at least as having White privilege, they now are treated as part of the majority—or even as oppressors. And in these days, when there's a post-colonialist view of the world, which divides people up into oppressors and oppressed, the colonizers and the colonized, and often into Black and White (which is odd, since, as noted, race is a cultural/social construct), Jews are frequently considered by non-Jews to be colonizing oppressors who are on the wrong side of history. This leads to increased antisemitism, which we'll come back to below. There are clear advantages and disadvantages to being considered White, and Jews are in the unenviable position of being only recently defined as White, but nonetheless as being White oppressors who must be resisted.

Some Jews do define as white and/or acknowledge any privilege they get because of their skin tone, but this is not true of all Jews by any means. Research shows that only about 30% of Israelis have eastern European (Ashkenazi) origin, while the rest are from the Arab world, Africa, Latin America, and elsewhere (Mazzig, 2019, n.p.). In other words, if you still want to think about Jews as "white", then looking around Israel might change your mind, as the majority of people there would not be considered "white" by American/Western standards. Of course, judging people by the level of melanin in their skin isn't a particularly helpful way of going about things anyhow.

In sum, I'd suggest that Jews aren't White, even if some are perceived or treated that way. Furthermore, I'd argue that there is no need to identify people based on race anyway, and I hope that in the future, we won't describe ourselves in terms of race. Understanding Jews in terms of cultural and/or religious identity is much more appropriate, and we can probably say the same is true of any other group of people.

One person in my survey wrote this about racial identity:

> I'm racially Jewish on my dad's side. I identify as half-Israeli and, in the last couple of years, as Jewish. I'm not religious, although recently I've been learning about Judaism, though my Israeli family are secular!

Genes

Just to add another little complication to the subject, being Jewish is quite literally in our genes for many Jews. These days, more folks are trying to trace their ancestry or find relatives using biotechnology companies where you send off a bit of your spit and then get your genome analyzed based on your DNA. There are lots of interesting things to discuss regarding such tests, not least the ethics of it all (just think how many people are getting the shock of finding out that one or both of their parents aren't who they thought they were). What's relevant to us here is that our genes can reveal our Jewishness. Someone using Ancestry or 23andme or other sites like those might find that they're 33% Ashkenazi, 46% Sephardic, 11% Eastern European, and 10% East Asian, for example, and this might or might not align with what they knew about their family history. For some, this can cause great excitement, as they feel they are getting a chance to learn more about themselves and their family history or they can have old family stories confirmed as fact. For others, it's deeply disappointing and upsetting. There have been research projects and newspaper articles about all this and, in some cases, people feel that the "truth" they grew up with is truer or more accurate than the truth in their genes. Some people have even rejected the science of gene testing because they are so disgusted and disturbed by the results (Bahrampour, 2018, n.p.).

More recently, one of the big DNA testing websites has been hacked, with Ashkenazi Jewish people's data being stolen, along with Chinese people's data (McCallum & Tidy, 2023, n.p.). Unsurprisingly, this is actually making some people worried about whether to get their DNA analyzed and, if so, what they should do with the data and who might access it. If some nefarious types are searching for lists of Jewish people, what do they intend to do with that information?

At any rate, for many people, their Jewishness is encoded in their genes, and this can arouse a range of feelings, while also providing evidence, if it were needed, that Jews are in some ways different from other groups of people.

In regard to DNA testing, one person wrote this:

> I decided to test my genes because I was hoping there was something in there that I didn't know about. All I'd been told growing up was that I was Jewish, and this seemed kind of boring to me. Unfortunately, my test results showed that I was 100% Jewish. I was pretty low at first, but after some time, I came to be accepting of this. I ended up learning more about being Jewish and I felt pride in my background. And I realized that other people thought I was exotic for being Jewish, even though I'd thought it was boring!

Another person said:

> I felt Jewish and identified with Jewish people in some way, even though I'd never been told there was any Jewish in our family. So I did the DNA test and, sadly, it confirmed that I wasn't Jewish. That was deflating.

Other

We've now spoken about Jews as a religion, an ethnicity, an ethnoreligion, a race, and a genetic group. To this, we can add a few more terms. More religiously observant Jews might refer to Judaism as a covenant, meaning that Jews are bound to a God and need to obey this God's laws. "The Jewish people, then, are best described as the "People of the Covenant"—meaning that they are a people *because* of a covenant. What is special about this covenant is that it is not a covenant between two individuals, or even between an individual and God (as Abraham had made), but a covenant between an entire nation and God… even if we stop keeping our obligations under that covenant or decide not to believe in it, the covenant endures. A covenant, you see, is a two-way deal. It takes two to make it and two to break it. Just because the people have let go, doesn't mean God has. That's why it's called an "eternal covenant"—because even if the people may be fickle, God doesn't change His mind" (Freeman, 2001, n.p. italics original). The vast majority of Jews wouldn't call themselves a group because of a covenant, even if strictly speaking, this is probably how the Jewish people formed. Still, if someone wants to convert to Judaism in a religious sense, they will need to accept this covenant and the related "yoke" that it brings. When people talk about Jews as "the chosen people", this doesn't mean that Jews are better than any other group or that we perceive ourselves as such; on the contrary, it means that Jews are considered more burdened than others, because we are expected to follow stringent rules and to live our lives in particular ways due to this covenant.

In the UK for a time, the terms BME and BAME were in relatively wide usage, with the former standing for "Black and minority ethnic" and the latter for "Black, Asian and minority ethnic". These terms were "used to refer to people in the UK who do not consider themselves to be White" (Cambridge Dictionary, n.d., n.p.), and yes, this tricky definition means that we're back to race being a way of defining and differentiating groups. Some people placed Jews in the generic "minority ethnic" category; indeed, I knew of workplaces that insisted Jews didn't need their own employee affinity group because they belonged in the BAME group, although sometimes the BAME group requested that Jews not join. It was, as so much of this definitional sort of work can be, confusing and at times upsetting. The UK government then determined that BME and BAME were not appropriate terms; "[i]n March 2021, the Commission on Race and Ethnic Disparities recommended that the government stop using the term BAME" (Gov.UK, 2024, n.p.). The explanation given was that "[w]e do not use the terms BAME (Black, Asian and minority ethnic) and BME (Black and minority ethnic) because they emphasise certain ethnic minority groups (Asian and Black) and exclude others (Mixed, Other and White ethnic minority groups). The terms can also mask disparities between different ethnic groups and create misleading interpretations of data" (ibid.). This seems sensible, as the terminology was exclusive rather than inclusive.

However, some workplaces and people in general then ran with the broader term of "minoritized," by which they meant "anyone who feels like a minority or has been treated as a minority." This is also rather complex and subjective, and doesn't necessarily help the formation of affinity or support groups.

The final words we can look at in relation to our understanding of Jews are "nation" and "peoplehood." As Jews have lived in both Israel and the diaspora for centuries, they have many differences in regard to language, beliefs, clothes, customs, foods, rights, and more. Nonetheless, Jews still do have much in common, and one thing tends to be a shared belief in the sense that Jews are a people.

One aspect of this nationhood or peoplehood for many is the belief in the Jewish homeland, which is Israel. Today Zionism is treated by some as a bad word or a disturbing concept, when in fact it is very simple and straightforward. "Zionism is the Jewish people's right to have self-determination and self-governance on parts of their ancestral land. That's it. It's Israel's right to exist" (Acho & Tishby, 2024, p. 158). In the way that no one argues about, say, Swedish people living in Sweden or Thai people living in Thailand or, well, Arabs living in any of the 22 Arab countries, it shouldn't be controversial for there to be a Jewish country where Jews can live safely and freely. "Israel is, in fact, a refugee state that was literally decolonized from Britain…a majority of Israeli Jews are people of color, many of whom are from families that were ethnically cleansed from other parts of the Middle East…Jews originate from the Land of Israel, derive our religion and our practices from the land, and—despite centuries of exile and displacement—have always kept and unbroken presence there" (Acho & Tishby, 2024, p. 183). Also, Israel is meant to be a safe country for many peoples, and it is home not just to Jews, but also to Druze, Muslims, Christians, and others. Note that not all Jews need to live in the Jewish country for Jews to feel a connection to it or to think of themselves as one nation.

Perhaps another way of referring to Jews' nationhood is with the word community, because that suggests that Jewishness is an umbrella that encompasses many people.

So hopefully now we have a better understanding of what Jews are in a general sense—or, maybe, it's actually both a more nuanced and a more convoluted perspective.

Intersectionality

Of course, it must be said that intersectionality plays a role for Jews, as it does for all other people. In other words, someone can have both Sephardic and Ashkenazic background, or they can have come originally from the Ethiopian Jewish community but now live in a predominantly Mizrahi area and be influenced by the customs around them. Or they might be Jewish and also identify with the culture in the nation where they live. Or they might have been raised with one level of religiosity but then have married into another level and have to shift back and forth between the two sets of families.

Then, beyond Jewishness, there are all the other aspects of identity that play a role. For instance, all Jewish people also have a gender identity, a sexuality, a level of ability, a class, a level of education, a skin color, a form of brain functioning that might be defined as neurotypical or neurodivergent, and so on. However important someone's Jewishness is to them, that isn't all there is to them, and we would do well to remember that when we engage with others.

Legal Issues

Here in the UK, Jews are doubly protected. Religion or spiritual belief is one of the protected characteristics, and so is race. Race is understood somewhat more broadly as color, nationality, and ethnic or national origins. In the US, employees are protected from discrimination based on color/race or religion or national origin/ancestry; Jews also fall into all those categories (Office of Institutional Equity, n.d., n.p.). What is worth pointing out is that as far as I could tell, these characteristics are only protected in the workplace, and other rules apply outside employment situations. I want to note that lists such as these use separate categories, as if they are unrelated things, and that is indeed how many people understand them. Whereas, as shown in the previous sections in this chapter, the concept of Jewishness falls between the categories because it belongs in multiple ones. So if you feel discriminated against and want to raise a legal case about it, you unfortunately must check the laws in your country to ensure that what has happened to you "counts" as discrimination there. Speak to your union representative, a lawyer, or another expert (and I'm terribly sorry that such a situation has arisen).

Summary of Definitions

After all that, what does it mean to be Jewish? As should be clear by now, Jews come in all sorts of flavors, and this then means that how they understand their Jewishness varies. Jews are some combination of religion, ethnicity, nation, race, shared culture, minority ethnic group, and more. One study that focused on Israel found that "[o]verall, 22% of Jews say being Jewish is primarily about religion, while more than half (55%) say being Jewish is essentially about ancestry and/or culture" (Pew Research Center, 2016, n.p.). I would wager that the statistics are pretty similar for the US or the UK. That is to say that despite the fact that many non-Jews assume that being Jewish is primarily or solely about religion, a majority of Jews feel it is about their culture, ethnicity, and/or ancestry. Another useful quote reads, "Judaism is not only a faith but a tribe, a culture, and a life style" (Gersen, 2024, n.p.).

Maybe the following comment that tries to sum up the key aspects of Judaism will help: "It's a decentralized religion. Meaning you don't really need a single designated place, such as a synagogue, to practice it… It emphasizes community…It celebrates nature [lots of nature-based holidays, such as *Sukkot* or *Tu Bishvat*]… It evolves as we do…Meaning Judaism is rigid in some ways and flexible in others, which is yet another superpower and a source of Judaism's long-lasting resiliency…It's a big tent. As in, no matter who you're married to, how often (or not often at all) you go to synagogue, or which Jewish laws you observe, there's still a place for you under the big Jewish tent…" (Acho & Tishby, 2024, pp. 18-20).

How then can you become part of the Jewish community or come under the Jewish tent?

How Do You Become Jewish?

It may surprise you that for an ethnoreligious group, there are multiple ways to join. You can become Jewish through birth, although this is slightly complicated in some situations, or through confirmation, affirmation, or adoption.

Familial Descent

Historically, Jewishness has been defined matrilineally; this means it is passed down through the mother, so someone's mother has to be Jewish for the child to be considered Jewish. "The Code of Jewish Law clearly states that a child of a Jewish mother is Jewish, regardless of the father's lineage (or whatever else may show up in a DNA test), while the child of a non-Jewish mother is not Jewish. Matrilineal descent has been a fundamental principle of Torah since the Jewish people came into existence" (Freeman & Shurpin, 2007, n.p.). There's evidence for this in the Book of Ezra and Deuteronomy (Freeman & Shurpin, 2007, n.p.). I've heard some people comment that you usually know who the mother of a baby is, but you can't always be sure of the father, without DNA testing. Defining Jews matrilineally means you are absolutely certain of someone's Jewishness.

However, some groups of Jews now accept patrilineal descent, which means that if someone has a Jewish father, but a non-Jewish mother, they may still be considered Jewish. This is not without controversy, unfortunately. "The basic question of what makes someone a born Jew is…divisive. American Reform Judaism, since the nineteen-eighties, has recognized 'patrilineal Jews,' but the Orthodox and Conservative denominations do not. As a result, a large portion of people who consider themselves Jewish are not acknowledged as such by some of their fellow Jews" (Gersen, 2024, n.p.). In other words, someone might be raised Jewish, live as a Jew, be a member of a community that views them as a Jew, and feel themself to be Jewish, and yet not be accepted as Jewish by other denominations; one can only imagine how hurtful or frustrating that might be.

Conversion or (Re)Affirmation or Adoption

Another method of becoming Jewish is conversion. This means that someone who is not already Jewish chooses to become Jewish. For most people, the process involves learning Hebrew, attending synagogue services regularly, celebrating Jewish festivals, following the commandments and mitzvahs (technically, the plural is mitzvot), and generally living as a religious Jew because, despite our earlier discussion about ethnicity and religion, a conversion is usually a religious ceremony and it involves being recognized as a Jew from a religious perspective.

The process differs according to country, type of Jew, and level of Jewish observance. For example, among more liberal Jews, it may be enough for a non-Jew to be marrying a Jew for them to be accepted as Jewish. In such a case, there may be some flexibility about how much study the person is required to carry out and how many holidays and rituals they have to prove that they are observing. Among the more conservative, it may take several years of study, and then the person will go before the *beit din*, which is a Jewish religious court, and be officially converted by the rabbis on the court. Converts will also go into the *mikveh*, the special Jewish purifying pool, and they will emerge as Jews after their dip. There are different types of conversions, depending on the level of religiosity (i.e., an Orthodox conversion will be stricter than a liberal one). Men and boys converting will be expected to have a circumcision (don't worry; we'll be talking a lot more about circumcision in a couple of chapters). If parents convert, then their underage children are also converted. Chabad, which is an ultra-Orthodox organization and thus has more traditional perspectives, explains the process of conversion as follows:

"Conversion to Judaism has a few components, which are undertaken under the supervision of an established *beit din*:

1. **Accepting the yoke of the commandments.** When you convert, you must verbalize your commitment to live in accordance with all of the Torah's commandments as they are explained in Torah law. It is not enough to commit to some or even most of the precepts. A convert must commit to every single one of them. Also, this needs to be done out of a sincere desire to serve God as a Jew, not

because of any other motive, such as the desire to marry a Jewish man or woman.

2. **Immersion in the *mikveh***. A *mikveh* is a pool of natural water, usually rainwater. At your conversion, you will dunk into this spiritually cleansing bath. It is at this moment that you will accept the Torah upon yourself.
3. **Circumcision**. If you are a male, you will need to be circumcised. If you were circumcised as a baby, a symbolic drawing of blood is all that will be done at this point" (Posner & Shurpin, 2015, n.p.).

If someone converts in an Orthodox *beit din*, they can usually be accepted as a Jew by the other denominations, such as Masorti/Conservative. The opposite is, however, not true, so someone who converts as a Liberal/Reform Jew may not be accepted by Masorti/Conservative or Orthodox Jews.

For people who are Jews patrilineally, or who have lived as Jews for other reasons for a long time (perhaps through their marriage), they may choose to officially convert in order to have the paperwork. Understandably, some in this situation may find the term conversion irrelevant or even offensive. A well-known rabbi in the US, Angela Buchdal, instead prefers the term "reaffirmation." She herself was a Jew patrilineally and had lived as a Jew. Buchdal writes, "I decided go to a *beit din* and go to the *mikveh* and have what I called a reaffirmation ceremony. I didn't think of it as a conversion, because I had been a Jew my whole life. Instead, I wanted to affirm that I was choosing to be Jewish actively. At 21 years old, that was a really powerful ritual for me. Like most really good rituals, it transformed something in me. It really solidified, quelled and softened some of those deep questions of doubt and inauthenticity. In some ways, it wasn't just the ritual; it was all the work that got me to the ritual that helped me get there" (Posner, 2019, n.p.).

Perhaps it goes without saying that there are also people who live as Jews and who feel Jewish but for whatever reason choose not to have a formal conversion. They may not be seen as Jews by a particular group or synagogue, but then again, that might not matter to them.

Finally, Humanistic Judaism "uses the term "adopt" rather than "convert" because the person wishing to be Jewish is adopting both Judaism and our community, and the community adopts those desiring to be part of the Jewish people" (Society for Humanistic Judaism, 2024, n.p.). For Humanist Jews, they believe "that a Jew is a person—of any heritage—who declares [themselves] to be a Jew, and who identifies with the history, ethical values, culture, civilization, community, and fate of the Jewish people (ibid.).

In short, you can become Jewish through birth or by choice. A surprising number of people have chosen to do so in the wake of the October 7th attack in Israel (Gersen, 2024, n.p.), thereby throwing their metaphorical hats in with a group that has frequently been feared and even despised. I wonder if they are totally aware of what they've let themselves into (we'll get back to antisemitism shortly, sad to say).

The father in a family of converts told me about their conversion story:

> My wife and I, along with our five children, started our conversion process during the Covid-19 pandemic. When we finally went to the *beit din*, it was about 6 months after October 7th. We moved countries to convert, selling most of what we had to make it financially viable. With the timing of world events, it was not an easy journey. Our homecoming to the Jewish people was even more challenging when, having sacrificed so much, we were deceived into thinking our original conversion was with a legitimately Jewish group. It was in fact with a non-Jewish "messianic" group. By the time we realized that no one in the community was using their real names, were not really Jewish, and had fake rabbinic ordinations, our lives and identities were shattered. Having sacrificed so much, we had to decide whether to re-evaluate our dire circumstances, or give up entirely because the cost was incredibly high. The people we had trusted the most had broken us each individually in ways that would be hard to recover from.
>
> We were obviously clueless about Judaism, which is what caused us to get into this situation, but we'd soon discover we weren't the only ones with a similar story. We decided to take a trip to Israel after saving for years to be able to go there as a family. In the messianic group, we were forbidden from attending a genuine Jewish synagogue and this trip to Israel would be

our first experience of Jewish life, having being deprived of it for 3 years. Of course we were flooded with the authentic, genuine article within the first moment of stepping off of the El Al plane in Israel. We very quickly felt a strange sensation of being at home despite having travelled halfway across the planet to be in an entirely new place. In our family, there was a unanimous feeling of a very different and potential future for us all and we were completely overwhelmed with the dream of what could be. Somehow, some way we had to regather our energy and decide what to do, to find the ability to trust again, and look for a truly Jewish organization to start afresh. We knew we would have to rebuild our lives as converts to Judaism and leave our past behind.

When we returned, the full scale of the loss was realized. We had given up our entire lives for an invalid identity being mis-sold as Jewish. Incredibly, we managed to get in touch with a rabbi who understood our journey. We weren't the first nor would be the last to find ourselves in this situation. Through many tears, we worked through our issues and decided to begin the application process for a conversion for 7 people. We found a phenomenal group of rabbis who truly empathized with us and could see our Jewish potential. When we were then certain we wanted to proceed, they helped us to embrace a Jewish identity in full as part of an observant community. The process involved discovering the richness of Jewish family life. We embraced Shabbos each week, which enabled us to reconnect with each other and set aside the business of normal life. We all individually healed over time, from younger to older, and in our own way as we embraced one mitzvah to the next. When we emotionally approached the Jewish *beit din*, immersed ourselves with our 5 children and stood under the *chuppah* to be re-married as Jews, we felt like we had finally come back home, only this time we truly belonged.

To us, Judaism is a masterpiece. It has the most beautiful story, culture, language, tradition, heritage, people and food. Above that, though, at its core, conversion is about belonging. It's difficult to know how we ended up on this path. Everything in our lives was set up to affirm other types of beliefs but something ancient and deep within us drew us out of where we were to another place, like an ancient call we were always meant to answer. After our conversion, I remembered the moment we knew we wanted to be Jewish. I sat with my eldest son next to the Western Wall and he said to me, "Let's never leave, Dad. We belong here." From that moment on, no matter what, we knew what we'd been missing our whole lives.

Another conversion story was shared with me:

I am patrilineal through my biological father. I underwent a Reform conversion in 2019 and am now undergoing Orthodox conversion through the Spanish and Portuguese *beit din*. We live a traditional life.

CHAPTER 2

Antisemitism

I'm really sorry, but after all that interesting discussion about what Jews are and how to become one, now we have to talk about antisemitism. I know it's not the happiest of topics, but unfortunately, it's necessary. This book is a primarily positive one and I don't want to give too much space to antisemitism, antizionism, or anti-Israel sentiment, but we do need to understand what Jews are up against, both in the birthing world and the world at large. So what is it and why does it matter?

Defining Antisemitism

Racism refers to prejudice, discrimination, marginalization, and/or violence against an ethnic group or race. Given what we've already discussed about Jews being an ethnic group, that means Jews can be the victims of racism. However, we also use the term "antisemitism" when we want to be specific that this is racism against Jews.

The word "Semite" came from Shem, one of the sons of Noah in the Bible, so any of Shem's descendants was considered a Semite. In more recent times, "Semite" has been employed to describe people who spoke a Semitic language; technically, this would include Jews who speak Hebrew, people who speak Arabic, Ethiopians who use Amharic as their tongue, those employing Maltese, and more. Now "Semitic" is considered an old-fashioned, outdated, and inaccurate term, because other than the issue of language, not much connects those peoples; antisemitism was never meant to label, say, racism against Ethiopians, unless they were also Jewish.

The German scholar Moritz Steinschneider is thought to have coined the term "antisemitism" as a way of referring to prejudice against Jews. The word has stuck, but obviously is slightly problematic in that defining Jews as Semites isn't the full picture, plus, as already discussed, Semite itself is a broad and unhelpful term. Still, despite the vagueness of the word, "antisemitism" persists as the term of choice to specifically describe racism against Jews.

The International Holocaust Remembrance Alliance states that, "Antisemitism is a certain perception of Jews, which may be expressed as hatred toward Jews. Rhetorical and physical manifestations of antisemitism are directed toward Jewish or non-Jewish individuals and/or their property, toward Jewish community institutions and religious facilities" (International Holocaust Remembrance Alliance, n.d., n.p.). You might note that an interesting part of this definition is the reference to "non-Jewish individuals." That means that even non-Jews can experience antisemitism, if they are perceived to be Jewish, or are thought to be an ally to Jews, or are otherwise linked to Jews in some way.

A related "ism" is antizionism (also written as anti-Zionism), which is the belief that Jews should not have their own country, the idea that Israel should be destroyed or converted to non-Jewish land, and/or prejudice against or violence towards someone who is or is perceived to be a Zionist. Many Jews find antizionism puzzling or frightening, and see it as a double standard, where Jews are expected to live in a way that is different from how other groups get to live. As Noa Tishby points out, "there are twenty-three countries where Islam is the official state religion and thirteen where Christianity is the official state religion and only one Jewish state. Why target that state in particular? You see, when it comes to Israel, the Jews are in an impossible situation. We are damned if we do have a state, and we are certainly damned if we don't... The bottom line is that anti-Zionism is a movement to deny Israel's right to exist, and Israel is the only country in the world where that's up for debate" (Acho & Tishby, 2024, p. 199[4]).

A third category within the field of racism against Jews is anti-Israel sentiment, which tends to be when someone says something along the

---

4 Although Noa Tishby refers to 23 Muslim countries, other figures say it is closer to 30 countries that have Islam as the state religion, and there are actually over 50 countries that are Muslim-majority.

lines of, "I don't have anything against Jews, but I don't like Israel." It's perfectly possible, and sometimes sensible, to criticize a country's politics or leaders. You can also dislike, say, a country's weather or scenery or food, and so on. However, when people veer into saying that they are against Israel because of the Jews who live there or because Jews shouldn't have a country, then anti-Israel views have joined together with antizionist and antisemitic ones. Other problematic aspects of anti-Israel views include holding Jews outside Israel responsible for things that happen in Israel (naturally, not all Jews or Muslims or Druze or others inside Israel are fully responsible either); holding Jews to different expectations than other groups (back to that double standard again); comparing Israel or its leaders to Nazis; and more (American Jewish Committee, 2021, n.p.). Often, those who are anti-Israel are not simply taking issue with Israeli politicians but rather are against Israel existing at all.

It isn't always easy to tell these three categories apart, and realistically, they are very similar. As one explanation of antisemitism puts it, there are four layers to it: peoplehood, religion, racial/political, and anti-Israel. In more depth, they are, respectively, these ideas: "Jews are weird, dirty, scheming, and threatening—they need to go…Jews are God killers and baby killers and/or not Christian or Muslim—they need to convert or go…The Jewish *race* is inferior, revolting, and evil; they can't convert out of it—we can blame them for political gain…and they should go…Israel is all of the above. And it should go" (Acho & Tishby, 2024, p. 114, italics original).

Some Jews have internalized antisemitism and choose to convert away from Judaism, to hide their Jewishness, to change their names to something less Jewish-sounding, to get plastic surgery to look less Jewish, to denigrate Jews and Judaism, or to otherwise act or think negatively about being Jews. In a society that by and large is not very positive about Jews, it's understandable that some people might feel the pressure to, say, get nose jobs, straighten their hair, adapt their surnames, move to non-Jewish neighborhoods, or to disavow their background, because that feels safe to them. I've certainly known many people who have felt or acted like this, and I myself have sometimes been influenced by such ideas (Woodstein, 2015, n.p.). I know how tough it can be to feel pride in yourself when so many other voices are telling you to be ashamed.

Antisemitism isn't just limited to what you think about Jews. It also encompasses actions people carry out because they are prejudiced against Jews. This could include giving someone worse care or treatment, assuming they must think or feel a certain way, telling "jokes" or making comments about them based on their Jewishness, expecting them to explain their beliefs or background or to speak for their entire group, not hiring them, not promoting them at work (or even demoting them), excluding them; not paying them equally; turning them away from events or services, intimidating or harassing them; physically harming them, or even killing them. I'm sure you can think of other examples of racism in deeds and words.

If you're unsure whether you are being antisemitic in your actions, then analyze whether you are treating a Jewish person differently than you would a non-Jewish person or speaking to or about them differently. If you aren't certain whether your words are antisemitic, consider whether "your criticism 1. is an indictment of all Jews, 2. capitalizes on stereotyping tropes, or 3. lays blame for an entire issue solely on Israel" (Acho & Tishby, 2024, p. 200). If so, you might be acting or speaking antisemitically. In the birth world, this could make your patients or clients feel or actually be unsafe.

Zionism

I just want to say a few words about Zionism, which is an incredibly misunderstood concept.

In brief, Zionism is the belief that the Jewish people have the right to a Jewish homeland in Israel and that they have the right to self-determination. That's it. It's actually no different from any other group of people, in that we all should have the freedom to live safely and to be able to direct our own lives.

Zionism has nothing to do with a hatred towards other groups of people or a desire to displace them or any other negative thoughts. It is simply about Jews wanting to be safe in their ancestral motherland.

Sadly, many Jews working in the birth world—not to mention plenty of other fields and industries, including publishing—have been told that if they are Zionists, they are not welcome and will not be hired for jobs. Consider whether any other people would be told the same thing, i.e. "You come from X country and you believe your ethnic group deserves to live in your native land without being under threat of danger. Therefore we will not allow you into this space." It's pretty ridiculous when you think about it that way.

Unfortunately, Zionism is so misconstrued that many people use their erroneous beliefs about it as a basis for antisemitic words and deeds. This should not be the case. The majority of Jews are Zionists who feel that Israel, as the sole Jewish country in the world among dozens of Christian or Muslim countries, should be a safe space for Jews and anyone else who wants to live there. That's easy to understand and should be easy to accept and respect.

Stereotypes

You may well be wondering what people dislike about Jews and where these ideas came from. It would be an entirely different book if I were to go into that in the detail it deserves, so I'm just going to briefly mention a couple things, so we can better understand the experiences many Jews have of antisemitism. Remember that it's easy to "other" people, to think they are different and weird and disgusting just because they have different beliefs or traditions. This can lead to us stereotyping and scapegoating them, and, in the worst-case scenario, to also persecuting, torturing, and killing them. This is something we've seen throughout history, around the world. The more we learn about them—say, by reading a book about their birth practices—the more we can see that we're all humans who ultimately have a lot in common.

Noa Tishby sums it up well when she says that some of the key aspects of antisemitism are the following stereotypes or fallacious beliefs: "There are too many Jews and they're making me nervous…Jews are godless and bloodthirsty…Jews killed Christ...Jews are dirty interlopers…Jews are the devil…Jews are untrustworthy, disease-spreading demons…Jews are not

Christian...Jews are money hoarders...Jews are too powerful...Jews are disloyal...Jews are evil rogues and cheats...Jews are conniving conspirators for world domination...Jews are race polluters..." (Acho & Tishby, 2024, pp. 93-102).

One of the regularly recurring stereotypes is called the blood libel, and this is the specious idea that Jews employ Christian blood in religious rituals. As Jewish people have different celebrations from Christians—even though in many cases, Christian holidays are built on top of Jewish ones, with the aim being for Christianity to replace Judaism—Jews must have seemed scary and strange and threatening to Christians in early historical periods. If you don't know what the Jewish holiday of Passover means and how someone celebrates it or if you want to eradicate it, it's easy to imagine the worst. It's also useful to accuse people of devilish behavior when mysterious things happen, such as unexplained deaths or disappearances, because then you have a group to blame. I currently live in the very city in England where the blood libel got out of control nine hundred years ago and started a chain of events that caused Jews to be expelled from the country. In the 12th century, a boy called William of Norwich died violently during the Easter holiday. Since Passover takes place at the same time of year—indeed, Jesus's last supper was a Passover *seder*, or ritual meal—the Jews of Norwich were blamed. They were said to have tortured and murdered young William because they wanted his blood to make their Passover feast. This eventually led to Jews being persecuted, murdered, and eventually expelled from Norwich and other cities. The blood libel has been used in propaganda in many other times and places, including Nazi Germany. In fact, Jewish law doesn't allow people to ingest blood, whether animal or human.

Another common Jewish stereotype is the one about all Jews being rich and powerful. Some part of me wants to say, "If only! I'd love to be rich and powerful!" Some religious groups, including Christians and Muslims, have traditionally held that they could not loan money, especially with interest, whereas Jews have had no such prohibition. Meanwhile, Jews living in Christian- or Muslim-majority countries have often been severely restricted in terms of which jobs they were allowed to have. Thus, in something of a perfect storm, some Jews became money-lenders, providing a useful and important service…and then were looked down upon by non-Jews for it, and said to be greedy. In other words, they were doing the dirty work no one else wanted to do, because they couldn't do much else, and then were disparaged for it. Related to this, Jews have been said to have a secret conspiracy to try to rule the world. If so, we're not doing a very good job of it, as it's not primarily Jews who are key politicians, or the people running Hollywood/Bollywood or the media, or those who top the Fortune 500 CEO list. Sure, Jews have a higher than average share of Nobel Prizes— "One of the most remarkable Nobel statistics is that 22 per cent of winners have been Jewish, despite our people comprising less than 0.2 per cent of the world's population. In other words, Jewish Nobel laureates number at least 11,250 per cent above average" (Aziz, 2022, n.p.). But intellectual success doesn't translate into riches. Still, all this has been a handy way to blame the Jews (yes, once again), this time for economic crises. In actuality, Jews are not the posh upper-class folks that some believe. One statistic suggests that "Forty-five percent of children in Jewish homes are living in poor, or near poor, households" (Fingerman, 2019, n.p.). That figure might make people question where all those rich Jews are. Meanwhile, the fact that Jews are a tiny population with only one little country of their own ought to challenge the idea of their supposed omnipotence.

Speaking of that solitary Jewish country, another stereotype is that all Jews support Israel and are thereby disloyal to all other governments. First of all, Jews have a huge variety of opinions about Israel (and, frankly, about any other subject you care to name). There are even nonzionist or antizionist Jews, who don't want a Jewish state (see Gersen, 2024, n.p., to read about a recent Jewish convert who is against Israel, which sort of boggled my mind), even though Israel's existence tends to be a key part of Jewish belief for many Jews. Furthermore, even among the vast majority of Jews who consider themselves Zionist, many disagree with the actions that particular Israeli governments or politicians have taken. Beyond that, there are other odd assumptions baked into this stereotype. For example, for those Jews outside Israel, should they have to care about what happens in Israel? Should they be held responsible for it? (No and no.) And can

Jews care about Israel and also about a second or third or even more countries? (Yup.)

If you replace "Jews" with any other group, you'll see how bizarre this gets. What if someone moved to the United States from China or Australia? Would you say that that Chinese-American or Australian-American person can no longer care about their native country? Or that they couldn't possibly care about both that country and the US? Would you call them disloyal if they still showed an interest in the country they grew up in, where they presumably still have friends and family and maybe even visit? (The answer to all of those questions: nope!) And what about someone who was born in the US but then moves to another country? Is that allowed? And are they able to keep up with politics in the US as well as engaging in what's happening in their new land? (Yes, obviously.) Can someone of particular ancestry care about a country, regardless of whether they have visited there, as well as the country where they live? (Of course.) So why are people being so suspicious of Jews in a way they wouldn't be about another group? (Let's say it all together: double standards!)

I'm just going to touch on another stereotype and that's white privilege. I mentioned it earlier in this book, when discussing whether Jews are a race. First of all, it's completely unhelpful and impractical to divide up the world by something as random and as unimportant as skin tone (Your pigment determines your intelligence and morality? *Really??* So what happens to people's brains if they get a sun tan or vitiligo?). Even if we were going to do that, where do Jews fit in? As already noted, Jews come in a whole spectrum of tones, so you couldn't even categorize them based on that. Jews in the US were historically considered "not fully Black...They were Black-adjacent or maybe White-*ish*" (Acho & Tishby, 2024, p. 44, italics original). This made people who considered themselves truly white, whatever that is, look down on Jews as being "less than" (and hey, sadly this was true for Italian and Irish people too). Now, however, this haphazard pendulum has swung, and today Jews are considered "too White," and therefore to possess "White privilege." The idea is that because Jews are more accepted in Western society today—in part because universities and country clubs and workplaces can't officially discriminate any more, even if they do so informally—they must be part of the establishment. Since obviously anyone part of the establishment is an oppressor (yes, you can roll your eyes here), Jews must be White oppressors, eager to colonize and control all other groups. Over time, as you can see, Jews have sometimes been not White enough, while now they're too White; this alone should make us realize that the whole concept of race being a good way to determine someone's value is utter nonsense.

Another big stereotype to mention is the concept that Jews are obsessed with the Holocaust and use it as an explanation or defense for everything we do. Now it's absolutely true that the Holocaust looms large for Jews, especially for Ashkenazi Jews. Sephardic and Mizrahi Jews also suffered, but it was the Ashkenazi who were targeted to a greater extent given their location in Europe. The Holocaust was a unique event. However, genocide, sadly, is not unique in human history or in contemporary times. Due to the uniqueness of the Holocaust, which Jews also call the *Shoah*, it should be commemorated, as should other genocides. This means we should have museums and educational programs dedicated to helping people understand what lead to the Holocaust, what happened during it, and how we can learn from it (Horn, 2023, n.p.). But the Holocaust is not all there is to Jewish identity. It has shaped the way many Jewish people and families feel about themselves, their history, and their place in the world, but Jews are more than the Holocaust. We must tell Holocaust stories, and we certainly do…but we also tell other stories about being Jewish. We don't focus on it like a laser, and we don't use it to explain away choices we make, other than our need for a safe place, namely Israel.

When someone says that Jews have made up the Holocaust to give themselves power, this is antisemitic and patently false. Also, the Holocaust is sometimes held against Jews, with some noting that "[i]f you believe that Israel derives moral legitimacy and political power from Western guilt over the Holocaust, then it can lead to a perverse logic by which people try to bring down the Holocaust a peg or two in the hierarchy of competitive victimhood by claiming that Israel, the Jewish State, borne out of the ashes of Auschwitz, is now behaving no better than the Nazis did. One genocide cancels out another, supposedly" (Rich, 2024, n.p.).

To close, let's mention a slightly less negative stereotype about Jews, the one about Jewish mothers (when I saw less negative, I just mean in comparison to ideas such as that Jews kill people and use their blood in *matzoh*). The main part of this book is about parenting, so I won't get into the whole Jewish mother thing too much here, but suffice it to say there's a conception that Jewish moms are needy, oppressive, and pushy. There are parents like that in all groups of people, and the majority of Jewish mothers do not tick the "demanding and overbearing" box. What is probably true is that family really matters to many Jews, which means they prioritize togetherness. This could seem stifling to some people, sure, whereas others might find it very comforting, safe, and warm.

Before October 7, 2023

Antisemitism has been rife throughout history. This book is not the place for a detailed exploration of it (see Nirenberg, 2013 or Baddiel, 2021 if you want more on that), so I'll just focus briefly on the period before the attack in Israel on October 7, 2023. Let's just say that things weren't great for Jews even then.

Indeed, in the US, antisemitic incidents were at an all-time high. The Anti-Defamation League writes, "Antisemitic incidents surged to historic levels in 2022, with a total of 3,697 incidents reported across the United States, an increase of 36 percent compared to 2021—also a record-setting year—according to new data released today by ADL…The ADL Audit of Antisemitic Incidents found, on average, 10 incidents for each day in 2022—the highest level of antisemitic activity since ADL started keeping records in 1979—following an upward trend line of hate and vitriol directed against the American Jewish community over the last five years. This is the third time in the past five years that the year-end total has been the highest number ever recorded" (ADL, 2023, n.p.).

The statistics are similar here in the UK in 2021, with nearly 2,300 antisemitic attacks per year (1 incident per 117 people) (Farley, 2022, n.p.). However, as sad as this figure is, it's likely to be a low one, because one survey that took place before the attack in Israel by Hamas found that "96% [of Jews surveyed] say…they had encountered antisemitism in their daily life" (BBC, 2024). Furthermore, the survey showed that, "A total of 84% considered antisemitism to be a "very big" or "fairly big problem" in their country, while fewer than one in five (18%) thought governments were handling it effectively" (Rankin, 2024, n.p.).

Just to clarify, this means that 84% of Jews felt antisemitism was a pretty concerning issue and that 96% had experienced antisemitism. That gap in statistics makes me wonder what was going on with the 12% who experienced antisemitism but didn't feel it was a big problem in their country. Perhaps they all experienced those incidents while on vacation in other countries? Or maybe it was internalized antisemitism, and they felt they deserved what happened to them? Regardless, those are appalling figures. And the fact that they didn't believe their government was handling it well suggests that the number of incidents may have been underreported since Jewish people wouldn't have had confidence that the police or other authority figures would be capable of dealing with the situation.

After October 7, 2023

Disturbingly, those figures seem low compared to what happened after October 7, 2023. Regardless of what one thinks about the Israeli response to Hamas's attacks (and remember, you can criticize the Israeli government and its choices without necessarily being antisemitic), surely most right-minded people would think that any attack that involves torturing, raping, kidnapping, and killing people of all ages and backgrounds is unjustifiable and wrong. Nonetheless, in large part because of a lack of knowledge about the history of the region, and also partially due to the misapprehension already discussed about Jews being "White oppressors" and "colonizers," many people quickly turned on Israel and Jews. This led to a rapid and severe increase to antisemitic attacks.

Some Jewish organizations "have reported a 400% increase in antisemitic attacks since October 2023" (Rankin, 2024, n.p.), although the figure of 400%, as shocking as it is, is probably low because "[s]urvey data demonstrate that the number of antisemitic incidents being recorded by the police and community monitoring agencies vastly underestimates the amount of antisemitism taking place" (Boyd, 2024, n.p.). Furthermore, "[w]hile 90% of respondents said they had encountered antisemitism on the internet, the FRA [the European Union Agency for Fundamental Rights] said "antisemitic harassment and violence mostly take place in streets, parks, or shops." More than half of those surveyed expressed concern for their own safety or that of their family, while 76% said they hid their Jewish identity at least occasionally" (BBC, 2024, n.p.).

Just to make that absolutely clear, over 75% of Jews are trying to conceal their identity. This is easier for some than others, because a religious Jew with, say, *payot* (sidelocks) or a *shtreimel* (fur hat) can't just hide those things away. People can and do hide their *yarmulke* (skullcap) under a baseball hat, or they can tuck their *magen David* (star of David) necklace under their shirt, or they can stop attending synagogue services or they can choose to go in the back door to Jewish schools, buildings, or other facilities. Sure, they can do those things. However, should people have to live like that?

For young people and families, this may be particularly worrying. Research found that antisemitic "incidents in and around British schools have more than tripled since 2022," with security having to step up a gear at Jewish schools (McSorley & Dunkley, 2024, n.p.). A different survey, one based in the Netherlands, found that "42% of secondary school teachers witnessed antisemitic incidents in the classroom in the past year. These mostly involved swearing and abusive language that was not directed at specific individuals" (Anne Frank House, 2023, n.p.). In America post October 7th, there was an "135% increase [in antisemitic harassment, vandalism, and assault] from the prior year" (ADL, 2024, n.p.). The Anti-Defamation League, an anti-hate organization, notes that "K-12 Jewish students are facing a dramatic increase of antisemitism and marginalization" (Community Service Trust, 2024, n.p.). All this may make children afraid to go to school. I won't even go into the massive and worrying antisemitism seen on college and university campuses in the US and the UK (e.g., Hillel, n.d., n.p.).

In terms of healthcare, which is a key part of this book, antisemitism has increased in that realm too, both for medical professionals and their patients. In the US, for example, "Jewish students and professors on medical school campuses say they were taken aback by the outpouring of anti-Israel schadenfreude. Incidents have included direct harassment, such as when a student at Georgetown University Medical School direct-messaged "Free Palestine" to Jewish peers during a Zoom class lecture, as well as official statements from student organizations…Instead of the support they expected from peers, Jewish practitioners in hospitals, clinics and health care facilities have found themselves marginalized for perceived Zionist sympathies, attacked on social media and shunned in professional forums" (Danailova, 2024, n.p.). Healthcare professionals report feeling shunned or harassed, and say that antisemitic and anti-Israel comments have been normalized and accepted. Meanwhile, Jewish people who need care are frightened to go to appointments or to visit the hospital. A particularly egregious case was reported by a man who said, his "'visibly Jewish' nephew 'was kicked out of his bay, by one of the nurses who was covered in Pro-Palestine badges and stickers,' and due to that 'had to lie on the floor with a canula in'" (Luck, 2024, n.p.).

In the workplace, generally, since the war in Israel and Gaza began, one research study in the UK reports that "64% of Jewish employees surveyed experienced antisemitism from co-workers or clients in some form. Whilst many incidents were infrequent, about 1 in 9 respondents faced antisemitic harassment regularly (frequently/very frequently). This indicates a widespread issue affecting Jewish professionals across industries" (Board of Deputies, 2025, n.p.). All this research suggests that both Jewish employees as well as Jewish patients and clients are experiencing antisemitism at what seem to be unprecedented rates.

Many Jewish people do not feel safe now. "An evident rise in antisemitism since October 7 has had a significant impact on Jewish people's feelings of safety and security in the UK and across Europe. The degree to which the Hamas attacks on October 7 were marked by open celebration and affirmation of violence reveals a level of antisemitic hate that exists within parts of Western Europe that poses a severe threat to Jews living on the continent. A culture of 'ambient antisemitism' has emerged in the post-October 7 period, marked by incidents such as defacing or tearing down posters of Israeli hostages, that, whether strictly antisemitic or not, create a broader milieu that feels threatening and hostile to many Jewish people" (Boyd, 2024, n.p.).

As these statistics and facts reveal, antisemitism has been on the rise since October 7, and it is affecting how people live, how they feel, and the care they receive.

One person wrote to me:

> All of us have felt deeply affected by the 7th of October and are fiercely pro-Israel (albeit not pro-Netanyahu). One of my sons is thinking of applying for an Israeli passport. I've never before felt so affected by anything as I have by what happened on 7th October and so upset, bewildered, and furious about the world's reaction. The only thing that comes close is Brexit, but even my disgust at that pales in comparison.

What to Do About Antisemitism

So far, so negative. But let's turn to the positive and think about how we can change things. There's a chapter later in the book dedicated to improving the situation for Jews specifically in the birth world, so here I'll just mention a couple of things we can do generally about antisemitism.

Education

First of all, every single one us, no matter our background, can do better. We can all educate ourselves more about other groups of people. Let's read more books or articles, attend more lectures or webinars, watch more films, and so on. The more we learn about a particular group and their habits and customs, the more we'll understand them and their needs. We'll also realize that we're not quite so different from them as we might have assumed. Knowledge reduces discrimination, so it's a win-win, because we can feel smarter and also get closer to our fellow humans.

To Hide or Not to Hide

Everyone will have their own sense of whether to hide their Jewishness, and that will be dependent on individual circumstances and perspectives. I've known people who have begun wearing a yarmulke or an Israeli lapel pin post-October 7 as a way of highlighting their Jewish identity and showing pride and strength. On the other hand, I've also known people who've quietly taken down the mezuzah on their doorpost, or moved it indoors, or who have stopped wearing their *chai* necklace because they worry about people attacking them. Whatever you choose to do or need to do, there's no judgement here.

If you're somewhere and you feel unsafe, please leave, and if you can't leave, do what you can to reduce how much danger you're in. If that feels ethically wrong to you, remember the important Jewish idea of *pikuach nefesh*, which states that saving a life overrides other commandments and all other considerations. Keeping you safe and alive is more important in the moment than ensuring everyone can see the magen David necklace you're wearing.

Allyship

If you're not Jewish, can you be an ally to Jews, beyond educating yourself further? If it's safe for you, *pikuach nefesh* applies to non-Jews too. Maybe you could speak up when you hear someone make a wisecrack about Jews, or you could suggest your workplace have a training session on antisemitism, or you could just check in with your Jewish friends to see how they're doing. You could do anything you can think of that could help educate people and support Jews. Even if it seems small to you, it could really make a difference to someone else.

Report Antisemitism

If you are the victim of antisemitism—and remember that this applies to both Jews and non-Jews—or if you have witnessed something antisemitic, please report it. As you've seen from the statistics mentioned earlier, rates of antisemitic harassment and violence are high and still climbing, and yet those figures are considered gross underestimates, because many people are scared to tell HR or to call the police or to contact the media. Sometimes we don't report antisemitism because we're worried about reprisals, or about not being believed, or about nothing being done, or we might think it wasn't important enough to complain about. Sometimes we might even believe we deserved what happened to us. But we have to report these things, not just so we have accurate data, although that's important, but also because if governments and organizations see how much of a problem antisemitism truly is, they might be moved to do something. As it is, they can dismiss antisemitic attacks and say they don't affect that many people, but if human resources managers and police officers and others are forced to face the facts, they might realize how essential it is to put different policies or punishments in place.

That is to say, if you find out your Jewish colleague is paid less, tell your manager or your contact in the personnel department, and if you are spat at in the street, inform the police. If you find graffiti on your synagogue, or someone bullies your child, or your friend is refused service or care, report it. Report it. I will return to antisemitism later in the book, when we explore the situation for Jews who work in the birth world.

I will admit that this chapter has been heavy-going, but it was vital for us to have this discussion. Now, however, I'd like to move on to cheerier topics, the ones you've arguably been waiting for: Jewish birth practices.

CHAPTER 3

Jewish Pregnancy

While not all Jews want to have children, and this should certainly be respected, it is also thought to be a particularly Jewish expectation or hope to do so. “In the Bible, God creates the world for habitation and blesses Adam and Even with the words ‘be fertile and increase’ (Genesis 1:28). The biblical phrase contains both the blessing of fruitfulness and a commandment to reproduce” (Klein, 1998/2000, p. 3). This commandment, which is often translated as “be fruitful and multiply,” is something that many religious Jews feel is a *mitzvah* that must be carried out for the good of the world. Furthermore, for some Jews, religiously observant or not, the Holocaust weighs heavily on us, and there is a sense that we must try to repopulate the Jewish world, which was devastated in World War II, with children, so our lineage doesn’t die out and also to show the Nazis that they didn’t win. “Jews have always had a strong sense of being a people. Because children ensure the continuity of the people, childbearing has always played a central role in Jewish communal life” (Klein, 1998/2000, p. xxxii).

As Melanie Klein, who wrote a book exploring the folklore and customs of Jews over time and in different countries noted, “the Bible, the Talmud, the later Codes of Jewish Law, and the huge body of rabbinic commentaries and responses set down Jewish laws and recorded traditions concerning conception, pregnancy, birth, and the postnatal period” (Klein, 1998/2000, p. xviii). In what follows, I will explore some of these religious-based laws and traditions, but I will also look at more modern and secular practices because, as already emphasized, Jews come in a lot of different flavors.

Marriage

Obviously, not all children throughout history have come from marriages or will be produced within marriages, and that is absolutely fine to my mind. For observant Jews, however, it is generally considered important to be married in order to have children and indeed that is one of the main points of marriage. "So important was the fulfillment of this commandment [i.e., Genesis 1:28] that the Rabbis ruled…that even the study of Tora may be suspended in order to rejoice with, and bring joy to, a bride and groom" (Kolatch, 1995, pp. 27-8). In other words, getting married was seen as an occasion that surpassed almost everything else, including the all-important Torah study.

Marriage was traditionally also viewed as essential because it was seen "as an institution basic to healthy living, an antidote to loneliness" (Kolatch, 1995, p. 28). Research has shown that people who are married tend to live longer and to be happier and more cared for[5], and Judaism has been aware of this concept for a long time, hence the emphasis on getting married. Weddings involve the signing of the *ketubah*, or marriage contract. For the observant, sex and childbearing will usually only take place within a marriage.

Jewish Sex

Okay, this isn't a book about sex exactly, but I am sure you'll forgive a detour into it. Of course not all Jewish children result from sex (which I can speak to personally, since I'm part of a two-mother family), but arguably the vast majority do. Unlike in some other groups, for Jews, sex is not seen as shameful or wrong. Rather, it is thought to be an obligation

---

5 Actually, I need to be honest and to clarify this by admitting that the research tends to suggest that men in particular are happier and healthier when married, whereas marriage isn't always the best option for women. Our social narrative in the West tends to override this fact in order to push the idea that marriage is the right choice for everyone, and yes, of course, patriarchy plays a major role here. See Dolan, 2019, for more on this, and also to read about why having children isn't always the best decision. Since this book is about pregnancy and childbirth, however, I'm going to swiftly move on and assume that you're reading this because you want to have children, or you want to support those who have chosen to do so.

(in part, so you can "be fruitful") and also a pleasurable gift, even a divine one. Depending on your level of religiosity, however, some types of sex may be frowned upon.

Dr. Ruth Westheimer, who was sent on a Kindertransport out of Germany as a child and lost her entire family in the Holocaust, later became a sex therapist with a doctorate in education. She was instrumental in helping people, both Jewish and not, find joy and satisfaction in sex, and she strongly believed that whatever two consenting people wanted to do together should be accepted. In an interview, she said, "In the Jewish tradition, sex has never been a sin. Sex has always been an obligation from a husband to a wife" (Lovy, 2024, n.p.).

When asked about the Bible's view of sex, she explained that "sex is an important part of life. You and I would not be in this world without sex. However, you are absolutely right. For example, the Book of Ruth talks about how she kind of seduced Boaz. On Friday night, the (Jewish) husband says a prayer, "A Woman of Valor." (Proverbs 31:10-31). Towards the end is one sentence that I believe is the most sexually arousing in the world. The husband says to the wife, "There are many wonderful women out there who do wonderful things, but you are the very best." And in my experience as a sex therapist, there is nothing better for a woman to hear than that. Really, that book is the best sex manual of all time" (Lovy, 2020, n.p.). Westheimer went on to elucidate how Judaism doesn't go in for guilt around sex, and she noted instead that it's a Jewish attitude to encourage and celebrate sex. "Never, in the Jewish tradition, is there anything prohibiting sex in any position. They wanted people to have sex. They wanted people to be married. But never is sex associated with guilt. On the contrary, it is an obligation on a husband to satisfy his wife, which is fascinating if you look at other religions that have many more problems… The most important sentence in [the Torah], in my opinion, is that God did not want man to be alone. Period. I think this is true even today, when so many people, young people and older people, have trouble committing to a relationship because they always think there's something better out there. The Bible, and certainly the Jewish tradition, wanted people to be in a relationship" (Lovy, 2020, n.p.).

Rabbi Shmuley Boteach, the author of the famous (possibly infamous) book *Kosher Sex* (which is well worth reading for the more religiously inclined, and anyone else interested in Jewish ideas around sex), writes, "In fact, of all the blessings and universal gifts and wisdom the Bible and the Jewish religion has to offer the world, its view of sex is by far the most profound" (2023, p. xvi). Boteach goes on to say that Jewish writings and thought offer a few key ideas about sex, including the understanding "that sex is not for procreation," which he says is supported by evidence, such as pregnant women wanting sex, postmenopausal women enjoying sex, and the way male-female couples have evolved to have sex face-to-face, which facilitates intimacy (2023, p. xvii). Sex is not purely for recreation either, he argues; rather, it is about connection, which is highly regarded by Jews. So sex is to be encouraged and enjoyed. For observant Jews, this should happen within a Jewish-shaped framework, but the idea of Jews delighting in sex, as Ruth Westheimer described it, is one that should inspire everyone.

For observant Jews, "[s]ex should only be experienced in a time of joy. Sex for selfish personal satisfaction, without regard for the partner's pleasure, is wrong and evil. A man may never force his wife to have sex. A couple may not have sexual relations while drunk or quarreling. Sex may never be used as a weapon against a spouse, either by depriving the spouse of sex or by compelling it. It is a serious offense to use sex (or lack thereof) to punish or manipulate a spouse" (Jewish Virtual Library, n.d., n.p.). Also, it may seem surprisingly feminist that for Jews, "[s]ex is the woman's right, not the man's. A man has a duty to give his wife sex regularly and to ensure that sex is pleasurable for her. He is also obligated to watch for signs that his wife wants sex, and to offer it to her without her asking for it. The woman's right to sexual intercourse is referred to as *onah*, and is one of a wife's three basic rights (the others are food and clothing), which a husband may not reduce.

"The Talmud specifies both the quantity and quality of sex that a man must give his wife. It specifies the frequency of sexual obligation based on the husband's occupation, although this obligation can be modified in the *ketubah* (marriage contract). A man may not take a vow to abstain from sex for an extended period of time, and may not take a journey for an extended period of time, because that would deprive his wife of sexual relations. In addition, a husband's consistent refusal to engage in sexual relations is grounds for compelling a man to divorce his wife, even if the couple has already fulfilled the halakhic obligation to procreate" (Jewish Virtual Library, n.d., n.p.).

Dr. Ruth wasn't necessarily traditionally religious, and she was much more open in regard to different aspects of sexuality than the more conservative branches of Judaism, as we'll see below. But her overall take on the Torah as positive towards sex is very useful to keep in mind. Rabbi Boteach also emphasizes this when he notes that "the ancient rabbis were giving explicit sexual advice… [for how people] could enjoy pleasurable yet holy intimate relations" (2023, p. 10).

Purity Laws

For more religious Jews, family purity laws, or *taharat ha-mishpachah*, shape some aspects of their lives, including in regard to sex. As Rob Kutner ironically points out, "the all-male rabbis sometimes bordered on obsession with legislating women's bodies and choices (a shocking departure from the modern world). There's an entire book of the Talmud, for instance, devoted to laws around menstruation and ritual purity" (2025, p. 67). This is also referred to as *niddah*, or separation, because custom dictates that men and women should be separate during a woman's period. What follows is quite a long quote, but it is a useful explanation for those who are not aware of *niddah*:

> According to the Torah, a man is forbidden from having sexual intercourse with a *niddah*, that is, a menstruating woman. This is part of the extensive laws of ritual purity described in the Torah. At one time, a large portion of Jewish law revolved around questions of ritual purity and impurity. The law of *niddah* is the only law of ritual purity that continues to be observed today. All of the other laws applied only when the Temple was in existence, but are not applicable today. The time of separation begins at the first sign of blood and

ends in the evening of the woman's seventh "clean day." This separation lasts a minimum of 12 days. The Torah prohibits only sexual intercourse, but the rabbis broadened this prohibition, maintaining that a man may not even touch his wife or sleep in the same bed as her during this time.

Weddings must be scheduled carefully, so that the woman is not in a state of *niddah* on her wedding night. At the end of the period of *niddah*, as soon as possible after nightfall after the seventh clean day, the woman must immerse herself in a kosher mikveh, a ritual pool. The *mikveh* was traditionally used to cleanse a person of various forms of ritual impurity. Today, it is used primarily for this purpose and as part of the ritual of conversion, though in some communities, observant men periodically immerse themselves for reasons of ritual purity. It is important to note that the *mikveh* provides only ritual purification, not physical cleanliness. In fact, immersion in the *mikveh* is not valid unless the woman is thoroughly bathed before immersion. The *mikveh* is such an important part of traditional Jewish ritual life that traditionally a new community would build a *mikveh* before they would build a synagogue (JewFaq, n.d., n.p.).

This might seem quite strict to those unfamiliar with such rules, but according to some people, it actually can heighten the bond and sexual attraction between couples. What's happening there is that if someone is made off-limits, you might desire them more. You want to make the most of the times when you can enjoy each other sexually. You have half the month to "get in the mood" and to feel that anticipatory excitement. Plus, from a "be fruitful and multiply" point-of-view, restricting sex to the days in someone's menstrual cycle when they're most likely to get pregnant is beneficial and can give them a needed break at other times of the month, as trying to get pregnant can be quite stressful for some people, which makes sex distinctly less enjoyable and more of a practical necessity (although arguably there are many people with irregular periods who could struggle to get pregnant if they follow these laws, and they might then require fertility treatment).

From a non-traditional perspective, *niddah* can sound misogynist, as it implies that a woman is "unclean" when she has her period. Without women and their periods, humans wouldn't survive, so menstruation is necessary and doesn't make someone dirty or impure. This attitude seems to slightly conflict with the position mentioned above that women in traditional Jewish marriages are more in control of their sex lives than the men. Some women might not like to be limited in regard to what days they're allowed to have sex. I remember a woman telling me she felt incredibly sexy and aroused when she was menstruating and that it was her favorite time to have sex, so she definitely wasn't going to follow family purity laws.

Taharat ha-mishpachah are important for observant Jews, and provide a clear structure for when they can have sex within a marriage, and when they need to be separate. This can ultimately improve their likelihood for getting pregnant as well as increase their desire for their partner. Some less observant Jews might find it beneficial or enjoyable to try out some days of separation now and again.

Premarital Sex

Dr. Ruth Westheimer was, as you saw, very encouraging about sex as an important part of people's lives, and she felt there was a Jewish basis to this. In terms of the Torah, attitudes towards premarital sex, on the other hand, are less clear. It is considered unacceptable to more traditional Jews, who feel that couples need to be legally committed first (Silberberg, 2008), but isn't technically forbidden by the Torah. "Many people are surprised to learn that the Torah does not prohibit premarital sex. I challenge you to find any passage in the Jewish scriptures that forbids a man from having consensual sexual relations with any woman he could legally marry. It's just not there!... This is not to suggest that Judaism approves of pre-marital sex or promiscuity. Quite the contrary: traditional Judaism strongly condemns the irresponsibility of sex outside of marriage. It is considered to be improper and immoral, even though it is not technically a sin. In fact, to prevent such relations, Jewish law prohibits an unmarried, unrelated man and woman from being alone long enough to have sexual relations. But these laws come from the Talmud and the Shulchan Aruch, not from the Torah" (Jewish Virtual Library, n.d., n.p.). This is to say that the Torah itself has little to say about premarital sex, but later books and schools of thought have decided that it isn't acceptable.

People who are less traditional in their beliefs may not have an issue with premarital sex, and indeed might consider it essential so they can confirm whether they have the right chemistry with someone before they permanently partner them, whether through marriage or living together. Religious Jews might argue, "Judaism does not ignore the physical component of sexuality. The need for physical compatibility between husband and wife is recognized in Jewish law. A Jewish couple must meet at least once before the marriage, and if either prospective spouse finds the other physically repulsive, the marriage is forbidden" (Jewish Virtual Library, n.d., n.p.). But meeting someone and sleeping with them are two quite different things, so people need to go with their own beliefs and their own conscience when it comes to premarital sex.

Masturbation

Masturbation is another tricky subject. Like many other religious or ethnic groups, there are slightly different approaches to this subject for men versus for women. In Judaism, male masturbation is viewed as being unacceptable because it means that a man is wasting his seed. This idea stems from the story of Onan in Genesis (38:8-10), who didn't actually masturbate, despite giving his name, involuntarily, to the act. Instead, he used coitus interruptus (i.e., pulling out) as a form of birth control, and he was killed for this sin. For this reason, "Jewish law takes a very broad view of the acts prohibited by this passage, and forbids any act of *ha-sh'cha'tat zerah* (destruction of the seed), that is, ejaculation outside of the vagina. In fact, the prohibition is so strict that one passage in the Talmud states, "in the case of a man, the hand that reaches below the navel should be chopped off." (Niddah 13a) (JewFaq, n.d., n.p.). So people extrapolated from a story about pulling out, and thought that any form of seed spilling outside its apparently intended home shouldn't be allowed.

There isn't a single Torah-based prohibition on female masturbation, in part because women can't spill seed or waste their eggs the way Onan wasted his sperm, and partially, I'd guess, because women often aren't seen as being sexual creatures in the same way that men are assumed to be. However, "Judaism generally frowns upon female masturbation as 'impure thoughts'" (JewFaq, n.d., n.p.).

I've written elsewhere about masturbation, and how research shows it is one of the first sexual activities that people engage in when they are becoming sexual. It continues to be important for many, even though many religions and cultures have tried to call it problematic or to stop people from doing it (see Epstein, 2013, pp. 194-199). Non-religious Jews are therefore likely to engage in masturbation and to dismiss ideas about spilling the seed or impurity. I would imagine some religious Jews likewise masturbate, even though they might feel guilty or ashamed about it because of the prohibitions around it and would therefore not admit to it.

Birth Control

There will be a bit more about contraception later, in the section on breastfeeding, but here it's important to note that observant Jews tend to be against the use of contraceptives. "Jewish tradition has stressed that children are a fulfillment of marriage and has recommended contraception and abortion only when human life is at risk" (Klein, 1998, xxxiii).

Birth control is permissible for religious Jews in some cases, with the most important reason being if pregnancy or giving birth would put a woman's health (physical or mental) at risk. I'll return to this idea below, when we look at abortion, but it's considered more important to protect an already existent life, namely the woman's, than to try to create a new life, even though it's also a commandment to reproduce. "When a woman knows that pregnancy is likely to be life-threatening, she may take contraceptive precautions or, failing this, seek an abortion. This is the case among Jews, for Jews have always valued the preservation of existing life more than potential life Some Jews have considered contraception and abortion in other circumstances, too, such as during periods of anti-Semitic persecutions or during war or famine" (Klein, 1998/2000, p. 45). This is a sad statement, frankly, the idea that it's better not to give birth to more Jews.

The Talmud also states that a woman who is underage, already pregnant, or breastfeeding can use contraception (BBC, 2009, n.p.), although this is slightly confusing because someone pregnant can't get pregnant again, and also because women who are exclusively breastfeeding often have a natural form of contraception as their periods may not have returned. "Other Talmudic passages permit women to drink potions that make them infertile, and this doctrine is now used to permit the use of the birth control pill" (BBC, 2009, n.p.). Do note that it's thought that a woman should be the one to use birth control, such as a pill or diaphragm, in order to avoid the possibility of a man wasting seed (as in a condom), and also because it's a requirement for men to reproduce. "Although doctors perform [vasectomies] for men who want this form of contraception, Orthodox rabbis consider it a serious offense, and many Jews who no longer adhere to tradition still recoil at the thought" (Klein, 1998/2000, p. 50).

Apparently, "early rabbis explained that...once a couple had produced a family of reasonable size (2 sons, or a son and a daughter, depending on which rabbi you follow) they were free to avoid having further children" (BBC, 2009). However, more traditional Jews today believe that two children would not be enough to create "a family of reasonable size," so for them, using contraception after two children would not be acceptable, unless it were to help with spacing the timing of the children out or to protect the woman's health. Religiously observant Jews will, as necessary, consult their rabbi to get advice about what to do when they are considering birth control.

It goes without saying that less religious Jews are less liable to follow such restrictions on contraception and will rely on their own judgement and the advice of their doctor. "Many Orthodox Jews maintain the traditional view that only women may use contraception, and only for medical reasons. Outside Orthodox communities, however, most young Jewish couples, like non-Jews, use contraceptives to plan the size and spacing of their families. Their choice of method is likely to depend on medical considerations and not on Jewish tradition" (Klein, 1998/2000, p. 54).

Just to note, though, that "Jews, like non-Jews, have always considered the prevention of conception preferable to abortion" (Klein, 1998/2000, p. 45). This means there is some flexibility around this.

LGBTQ+ Relationships and Sex

I would imagine that based on the foregoing sections, you probably have a pretty good guess about the views of Judaism and lesbian, gay, and other kinds of queer sex. Nevertheless, it does vary. Some point to Leviticus 18:22 or Leviticus 20:13, and say they absolutely forbid male homosexuality, while others argue that there are other interpretations to these verses, or that they should be understood in the context of their time.

Some observant Jews may consider it to be the case that if God chose to create lesbian, gay, bisexual, trans, and other queer people, then they themselves are not wrong per se. However, as the expectation for romantic relationships is to produce children, traditional Jews believe that LGBTQ+ folks should not live a queer life. In other words, you may feel attracted to someone of the same sex, but you should not act on this attraction. You can't be blamed for your orientation, but you do have to take responsibility for your actions. Men having sex with men would very blatantly be wasting their seed, à la Onan, and any type of LGBTQ+ sexual interaction could fall under the "impure thoughts" category we read about before. For more traditional believers, even remaining celibate while still having a same-sex relationship wouldn't be good enough, because you wouldn't be fulfilling the commandment to have children, and they believe in following the letter of the law, not merely the spirit. "There are occasional [Orthodox] congregations that take a welcoming stance, and individual rabbis who may prove supportive, but they will not condone or perform a same-sex marriage or bless children of same-sex couples. The experience for transgender people can be especially complicated since many Orthodox traditions are built upon strict gender divides" (HRC, n.d., n.p.).

It is worth mentioning that some Orthodox Jews have more flexible perspectives regarding this, such as Rabbi Shmuley Boteach, who argues that the Torah encourages people not to be alone (in other words, a same-sex relationship would be better than a single life), and who writes, "All I ask from my religious brethren is this: Even as you oppose gay relationships because of your beliefs, please be tortured by your opposition. Understand that when our most deeply held beliefs conflict with our basic humanity, we should feel the tragedy of the conflict, not find convenient scapegoats..." (Boteach, 2023, p. xvi). Views on LGBTQ+ Jews are changing rapidly, and more synagogues, even Orthodox ones, are starting to accept and welcome a greater variety of people, but of course there are still some who adhere to more traditional lines of thought.

Less religious Jews are not as likely to share Orthodox views, although some certainly might for other cultural reasons. The Human Rights Campaign has some useful information about different religious denominations and their stances. Reform Judaism is particularly inclusive regarding LGBTQ+ folks, and has been for a surprisingly long time. "The Union for Reform Judaism passed a resolution in 1977 stating that "homosexual persons are entitled to equal protection under the law" and affirming their opposition to "discriminating against homosexuals in areas of opportunity, including employment and housing." In the decades following the adoption of these two resolutions, the Union for Reform Judaism and the Central Conference of American Rabbis have passed over a dozen resolutions on this subject, covering a range of issues from same-sex marriage to the inclusion of LGBTQ+ Jews in Jewish life. In addition, the Commission on Social Action of Reform Judaism, a joint instrumentality of the Union for Reform Judaism and the Central Conference of American Rabbis, passed a resolution in 2003 on the inclusion and acceptance of the transgender and bisexual communities and an additional resolution in 2014 on the rights of transgender and gender non-conforming individuals (HRC, n.d., n.p.).

Conservative Judaism in the US is slightly more varied in its approach. "Some [Conservative synagogues and institutions] are welcoming and affirming, ordaining LGBTQ+ rabbis and celebrating same-sex marriages. Others are not. As a denomination, however, Conservative Judaism has taken a firm and public stance for inclusion" (HRC, n.d., n.p.).

The Reconstructionist Jewish movement, which is thought to be the smallest one in the US, is also the most inclusive. "Of the four leading

Jewish denominations, the Reconstructionist Movement is considered the most consistently welcoming and affirming. The Reconstructionist Rabbinical College was the first Jewish seminary to accept openly LGBTQ+ students, and the Reconstructionist Movement is committed to creating communities that welcome all people, including LGBTQ+ individuals and their families. The Movement celebrates same-sex marriages, allows LGBTQ+ ordination, and includes the representation of LGBTQ+ people in its religious school curricula" (HRC, n.d., n.p.).

You might think this is irrelevant, but there are many LGBTQ+ Jews; research suggests that around 4% of Jews in the US (Pew, 2021) and 4.5% of Jews in the UK (Jewish News, 2023) identify as LGBTQ+. Many of us LGBTQ+ folks have children, with estimates ranging, depending on gender and identity, from 8% to 26% (William, 2024), and thus there are plenty of LGBTQ+ Jews who have kids (Hi, I'm one of them!). Some of these children will have been created through sexual relationships (such as previous opposite-sex relationships), but many will have been "made" through IVF or will have been adopted. LGBTQ+ Jews also need support through pregnancy, birth, and the postpartum period, and many will also want to find synagogues or communities where we feel welcome and accepted.

To sum up, we can say that Judaism is pretty sex-positive, as far as religions go. Dr. Ruth can be quoted one more time on the subject. When asked whether sex should be religious, her perspective was, "I'm a sex therapist and I'm saying sex should be sex. Period. If you want to make it spiritual, make it spiritual. If you want to just make it bodily, make it bodily. The important thing is to be sexually literate, to know when there is a problem to go for help and to make sure to keep sex alive even in older age. Now, I'm not saying that everybody can have a baby, like Sarah, at the age of 90. Not likely. The Bible teaches us about relationships and about companionship" (Lovy, 2020, n.p.). In other words, Jews should have sex if they want to and if it matters to them; for the traditional-minded, it might take on more religious overtones, but that doesn't have to be the case for everyone. Those of us who are more liberal in our outlooks and lifestyles may dismiss certain or even all aspects of the religious views on sex, but it can still feel meaningful to recognize that for Jews, sex generally isn't considered to be anything to be ashamed of.

Choosing to Have Children

Sure, many people have a biological urge to reproduce, and some just do it because it feels like "the done thing" or because they buy into the idea that people aren't happy and satisfied without kids (see Dolan, 2019), and still others have children on accident. But for Jews, there are additional religious and secular reasons why they might want and choose to produce children.

I briefly mentioned above, before discussing sex, the importance, especially to religiously observant Jews, of having children. For this reason, it may not seem right to refer to reproduction as a "choice." Nonetheless, even someone devoutly religious has to choose to get married and to follow the commandments in order to reproduce. Also, those who are not observant in their religious beliefs may consider it important to have children as a way of helping to repopulate the world in the wake of the Holocaust, and other genocides or forced conversions that Jews have suffered. In a general sense, then, what makes Jewish people want children?

Religious Reasons

Blessings as part of the wedding ceremony "express the…hope that a marriage will be blessed with children" (Klein, 1998/2000, p. 8), and this stems from commandments in the Torah and commentary in other religious texts, such as the Talmud. "Procreation is considered a blessing in the Bible and it is a commandment (Gen. 1:28; 9:7…) applicable to all Jewish men, although not to Jewish women (Yev. 65b-66a[6]). The world was created to be inhabited (Isa. 45:18) and God's blessings bestowed on Israel always included fecundity (Lev. 26:9; Deut. 28:11), and the absence of barrenness (Ex. 23:26; Deut. 7:14). Children are seen as the greatest blessing: "a heritage

6 *Yevamot* is from the Talmud, which is a book of commentary and religious law. It explores the Torah and *halakhah*, religious laws, in depth.

of the Lord" (Ps. 127:3–5), Procreation is one of the main purposes of marriage" (Encyclopaedia Judaica, 2008, n.p.). Indeed, "The Hebrew Bible refers to God speaking of Himself as a mother "bearing the Israelites in His bosom." No less than in the surrounding religions, Judaism celebrated fertility and considered a woman "complete" once she had given birth to male offspring" (Schipper, 2024, p. 58).

If someone chooses to live their life observantly, then all the quotes in the Torah together with the commentary and laws in the Talmud will shape their views. They are likely to see reproduction as being a key part of marriage and life (even if today many Jews are less likely to see "male offspring" as being of overriding importance as they once were). "In the Jewish community, we joyfully welcome babies, celebrate pregnancy, and give playful nudges to young people who have yet to bear children" (Mason-Barkin, 2016, n.p.). Having and raising children, for many people, is life's raison de être, and as the Bible states, "[t]hese commandments that I give you today are to be on your hearts. Impress them on your children" (Deuteronomy 6:6-7), which suggests that having children and raising them Jewishly is what should be "on [Jewish] hearts," particularly as "Judaism considers the intimate act of conceiving a child and bringing that child into the world as a process involving God" (Klein, 1998/2000, p. xviii).

Secular Reasons

Even those who are no longer observant or who were raised secularly may be influenced by the emphasis on babies and children in Jewish religious texts, as this in turn has affected Jewish cultural beliefs. Jews tend to prioritize and cherish family (we'll come back to that later, when we discuss Jewish parenting). But another key aspect that may impact our thought processes around reproducing, and incline us towards choosing to do so, is the fact that we're such a tiny population in the context of the greater world. We're also a group that has particularly suffered from forced conversions, hate crimes, and genocide, which has further diminished our numbers. Some Jews actively choose to have children as a way of counteracting all this, and also as a way of trying to augment our numbers, even if they do not intend to raise children in accordance with the commandments.

One professor of Jewish history notes, "In truth, except for rare instances, small numbers have always plagued the Jewish people. The precariousness of minority existence with its attendant attrition exacted a steady toll. While no loss comes close to the staggering number of six million Jews killed by the Nazis and their accomplices, our numerical recovery since 1945 has been grievously slow. Professor Della Pergola of the Hebrew University estimates that the world Jewish population in 2002 approached thirteen million or nearly two million more than the eleven million alive in 1945, yet still four million short of the seventeen million prior to the Holocaust. Impeding that recovery is no longer persecution but the consequences of living securely in an open society" (Schorsch, 2003, n.p.). Some Holocaust survivors, and their descendants, have spoken about wanting to help Jewish numbers recover.

In the wake of October 7th, 2023, some people have found themselves wondering if it's time to use birth control and not produce more Jews (so future generations don't keep suffering), or whether, on the contrary, we need to make more Jews and be proud of our Jewishness. One mother notes, "I am a proud Jewish mama, raising proud Jewish children. And I'm doing it in a world that is increasingly hostile to our presence, let alone our ability to thrive, within it. I'm as committed to Jewish joy being the benchmark of our family as I was on October 6, 2023—but like so many, my eyes are open to the reality that joy is no longer simple. I'm literally embodying Jewish hope in the form of the next generation, and for the piece of it in my arms, and the piece of it in my belly, I have to make sure it's a beautiful one" (Vinokor-Meinrath, 2024, n.p.). While such events may make us more likely to "monitor…the world for who is a friend, who is silent, and who actively wishes harm on my growing Jewish family", and we're aware that we need to protect our young, many also feel the time is right to choose having children and to learn how to "nurture Jewish joy in a world of Jewish vulnerability?" (ibid.).

It's not an easy decision to make, especially for those who don't feel the pressure or encouragement of the commandments. A parent wrote this on choosing to have children:

I wanted to have three children because I thought it was important, especially with a husband whose parents were Holocaust survivors.

Whether someone is religiously observant or not, their Jewishness is likely to impact their decision about whether to have children in some way. "Jewish tradition teaches that people's behavior affects the society in which they live, the world at large, and even the coming of the Messiah. Thus, the arrival of a newborn is important not just for the baby's family, but also for Jews as a people. That's why there is social pressure in many Jewish communities to have children—pressure from prospective grandparents, from those who already have children, from the family, and from Jewish leaders. Rabbis teach that having children is an act of faith. Ultimately, the reward for having children, like the reward from the fulfilment of other religious commandments, is great, stretching beyond the limits of one's life on earth and benefiting the Jewish people as a whole" (Klein, 1998, 261).

The Impact of Having Children

Once you do choose to have children, your life changes forever. Sure, there are lots of practical considerations, such as the lack of sleep (the fact that the simile "sleeping like a baby" is used to mean "sleeping well" implies to me that whoever employs it has a sarcastic sense of humor); a need to structure your life around children's schedules, in terms of nursery opening hours, school semesters, playdates, parties, and extracurricular hobbies; and that teeny-tiny minor detail that little people are extremely needy and have to take priority. On top of that, for many of us, having children forces us to look at ourselves in a new way. You never recognize your own flaws or have to face your own insecurities, deficiencies, or shortfalls quite as much as you do once you have children. Your desire to do the best you can for your children makes you aware like nothing else of all the gaps you have in your patience, skills, and knowledge.

You may also have to consider your own childhood afresh, because you will want to make decisions on whether to do things the way your parents or guardians did, or whether you might want to do things differently. Sometimes this can be incredibly painful or clarifying to think about. I've spoken to people who have changed their relationships with their parents as a result of having children themselves, sometimes even cutting off contact, because they realized that they couldn't accept their parents' behavior any more. On the other hand, it might give you renewed satisfaction and gratitude for your parents or guardians and the childhood you had.

Besides the practical, the personal, and the philosophical impacts, people sometimes find that they experience a spiritual effect from having children. Looking at your baby or child can make you appreciate the world anew or can challenge your sense of your place in it. For observant Jews, "[h]owever much is explained by microscopic cameras and genetic codes, the birth of a child makes one realize the existence in our universe of a power, or even a world, beyond our understanding. Judaism calls this power "God." Childbirth is the prerequisite for perpetuating God's world" (Klein, 1998/2000, p. xv). It's worth pausing over this, because it seems so central. Whether you are observant or not, having a child can make you feel the power of the universe.

As Michele Klein notes, "childbearing is often a time when people become particularly sensitized to the spiritual dimension of their experiences" (Klein, 1998/2000, p. 253). I would add that this is true of cultural dimensions too. Becoming a parent is an intense and meaningful experience that can shake people to their very cores and change their personalities and their lives in manifold ways. For some Jewish people, it can strengthen their spirituality or even pull them to a more observant way of life, and, regardless of someone's level of religiosity, it can encourage them to reevaluate many aspects of their lives and their beliefs.

Infertility

As in all communities, infertility can be an issue for some Jewish people. It may be considered to be particularly distressing to deal with, however, because of the emphasis in the Torah on having children, as already mentioned above. Interestingly, though, the Torah does seem to be especially attentive to the topic of infertility, sometimes in ways that can be construed as misogynist. Intriguingly, "three of Judaism's four matriarchs—Sarah, Rebecca, and Rachel—were each infertile" (Zoll, 2011, n.p.). This suggests that Judaism was attuned to infertility in ways that do not chime with other cultures.

Religious Beliefs Around Infertility

The key biblical texts were written a long time ago. What's odd is that although infertility has most likely always been a fact of life—from an evolutionary perspective, most people need to reproduce in order for life to carry on, but not all do, and indeed it would be useful to have some childless people to help take care of the children, provide food, and otherwise support communities—it was probably not so prevalent that long ago. For one thing, people had children earlier in their lives, and it gets harder to become pregnant, or to make someone pregnant, at older ages, and people didn't live as long as they do today. Infertility is increasing rapidly today. Rates vary in different countries, but it is thought that "the total fertility rate worldwide has dropped by nearly 1 percent per year from 1960 to 2018," a figure that is "faster than the rate of global warming" (Swan & Colino, 2021, n.p.). One reason for the rapid decrease to fertility rates is "the presence of hormone-altering chemicals (a.k.a., endocrine-disrupting chemicals, or EDCs) in our world. These hormone-hijacking chemicals, which include phthalates, bisphenol A, and flame retardants, among others, have become ubiquitous in modern life. They're in water bottles and food packaging, electronic devices, personal-care products, cleaning supplies, and many other items we use regularly. And they began being produced in increasing numbers after 1950, when sperm counts and fertility began their decline" (ibid.).

As you might imagine, EDCs did not exist five thousand or more years ago. Of course there are other reasons for infertility, such as fibroids or endometriosis, and sometimes infertility is unable to be explained, and all such issues existed back in the times of the early Jews. "Even in Talmudic times, sages recognized that infertility could have physiological causes and was not always a moral punishment or the result of evil forces. They pointed to a husband's impotence as one cause of infertility. The sages also recognize that developmental factors in a woman could account for her barrenness, for example, if she had never menstruated. These wise men recommended various foods to increase sexual potency and desire, such as garlic, fish, and eggs" (Klein, 1998/2000, p. 31).

Despite this, I still find it somewhat surprising that fertility, or the lack thereof, is such a focus. "Infertility is a major motif of biblical literature. The list of woman who endure hardship conceiving is long and distinguished: Sarah, Rebecca, the nameless mother of Samson and Hannah, the mother of Samuel the prophet. The Bible is full of pathos. Reality seems to mock the ideal. The very first commandment of Scripture to Adam and Eve and repeated to Noah after the flood in almost identical language, is to fill the earth with progeny (1:28; 9:1). Adam names his spouse Havvah, "the mother of all the living" (3:20), despite the ordeal that awaits them outside of Eden. And yet, in the narratives that follow there is a pervasive angst about barrenness. Not infant mortality, surely more common and acute, but the inability to bear children is the focal point, time and again" (Schorsch, 2003, n.p.).

As noted, having children is hugely important to many Jews, but there are different thoughts about why infertility appears to be such a prominent theme. Some argue that a person might be infertile due to immorality and "**that infertility is valued as a historical, cultural lesson within Judaism**...[and that] **the Torah never says that their infertility is the result of something they did or God's punishment**" (Zoll, 2011, n.p., bold original). It could even be said that for those who believe in divinity, someone is infertile because of God's choice, so that they learn a particular lesson and can contribute to their community in a different way. Naturally, even if you did believe that, it doesn't take the pain of infertility away. You might feel you have an important role to play and still grieve your lack of children.

This sorrow is not helped by some of the approaches to infertility in Jewish texts. "The Jewish picture of the childless couple is painful and sad. It depicts their suffering, their physical and spiritual destitution, the stigma, and the threat of marital breakdown that they face. It also stresses the harm to the Jewish people as a whole when an individual does not fulfill his procreative duty" (Klein, 1998/2000, p. 17). Indeed, "[t]he Mishnah and Talmud permit a man to divorce his wife if he remains childless after ten years, so each can remarry and try again" (Klein, 1998/2000, p. 19). Do note, however, that it is the man's choice to divorce, not the woman's, even if there seems to be some recognition that they might have better luck with other partners, as it is known that sometimes the combination of the two people involved simply doesn't work.

Klein argues that because of how much infertility is discussed in Jewish writing, "[t]he pain and suffering of infertility can be shared. Jewish literature is replete with tales of pain and suffering; this is part of our heritage" (Klein, 1998/2000, p. 44). I understand the concept of sharing the burden in theory, but I also can't help but wonder if the laser-like focus on reproduction and the extreme attention paid to infertility, particularly in women, might actually have increased the anguish for some childless people who longed to become parents.

Fertility Treatment

In biblical times, people were reliant on a belief in divine intervention, or on superstitious or homeopathic-style treatments, such as poultices. Today, in the modern era, we have medical approaches available for handling infertility, so it makes sense to look briefly at religious views on fertility treatment. Despite the belief that Jews should reproduce, there is some uncertainty about whether fertility treatment is fully kosher, so to speak. "Of the three monotheistic religions, Judaism through rabbinic law presents the longest list of concerns over technologically assisted reproduction. The implications for observant Jews are somewhat underappreciated in scholarly accounts of the booming fertility industry in Israel, however … The rabbis negotiate *halacha* (rabbinic law) to make "kosher" an array of reproductive technologies, including surrogacy and gamete donation…" (Ivry, 2013, n.p.). In other words, for those who strictly follow religious Judaism, there is uncertainty about how permissive their rules are regarding IVF and other assisted forms of reproduction. This isn't a surprise, since the Torah was produced a long time ago, way before there were fertility clinics.

One issue is around insemination. Many people assume that a woman ovulates around two weeks after the end of her period, but this isn't the case for all people, since there is a wide range of normal when it comes to menstrual cycles (and everything else in life). However, for those who follow Jewish tradition, there are regulations about when a married, heterosexual couple can or cannot have sex, as noted earlier when discussing purity laws. Sex is not allowed during a woman's period or for a certain number of days after. Where this becomes a problem is when a woman ovulates at some point outside the prescribed period of time when sexual intercourse is permissible, which would mean that they miss the window for insemination. "The term *halachic* infertility (*akarut hilchatit*) was coined in the medical community to describe woman's inability to conceive due to mismatch between the time of ovulation and the time, according to contemporary rabbinic law, when a married couple may renew sexual relations after a minimum of 11 or 12 days of abstinence (depending on the Sephardi or Ashkenazi tradition) following the onset of the wife's menstrual flow" (Ivry, 2013, n.p.).

There are other concerns, too. For instance, religious Jewish men are not supposed to masturbate, lest they waste their seed, but many rabbis feel that this can be overlooked in service of fertility treatment. "Interpretations vary among Orthodox, Conservative, and Progressive rabbis, but it is only rabbis who have authority to advise infertile couples on which procedures concur with Jewish law, and their appraisals tend towards leniency in the interests of domestic happiness. Prohibitions against "wasting seed", and against marriage to a man with "wounded testes or severed membrum", may be waived to allow semen collection for analysis and treatment for male infertility. All types of assisted conception are approved, including in vitro and micro-assisted fertilization, provided the gametes are from married couples. In short cycles, artificial insemination can be permitted in the post-menstrual week of *niddah* when coitus is forbidden" (Hirsh, 1998, n.p.).

Some communities have concerns about gamete donation, i.e., the use of a donor egg or donor sperm. This may especially be the case when it comes to having a donor egg, since being Jewish is traditionally passed down through the mother, and if a non-Jewish donor provides the egg, there may be uncertainty about the Jewishness of the resulting child. "Donor gametes are largely unacceptable to Orthodox rabbis, since egg donation confuses the definition of the mother, and because sperm donation creates subterfuge in a child's genealogy and a risk of consanguinity" (Hirsh, 1998, n.p.). Jews who are secular, Reconstructionist, Reform, Conservative, or otherwise not Orthodox may not have these concerns, though they may still insist on converting the resulting child just to be sure.

Also, for traditional Jews, "[o]bjections to treating unmarried couples, single or lesbian women, and to posthumous conception, arise because such households are not traditional families" (Hirsh, 1998, n.p.). Again, however, this is less of an issue for Jews who are not as traditionally religious, but some same-sex Jewish couples may find that their synagogues or other Jewish communities do not fully accept them or their children. Some may be asked to prove their child's Jewishness. This is a larger topic and unfortunately I don't have the space to discuss it here, though it is of importance.

Although some people raise potential issues with undergoing fertility treatment as a Jew, I quite like this analysis from a rabbi: "Difficulty in childbearing is a trope in Torah that ties together three of our matriarchs: Sarah, Rebecca and Rachel. Each of these women eventually becomes a mother through divine intervention. In the Torah, God responds to their cries by granting them the experience of motherhood. In other words, God makes miracles for these women, enabling them to become not only the mother of a family, but the mother of a people. Today, God responds differently to the cries of couples with the availability of medical intervention, and organizations like Hasidah that help make these interventions possible. God responds through each one of us, as we expose the pain of this experience and bring it out into the open. God responds when we understand infertility not as a taboo topic, but as a painful experience. God responds through each one of us when we are more careful with our language: holding our tongues and not making assumptions when we meet a couple that does not have children. God responds through us: with awareness, with gentle words and open hearts" (Mason-Barkin, 2016, n.p.). That is, one way of viewing medical advances in the field of fertility is to think that it is God who developed them and God who wants people to take advantage of them.

This long quote provides an overview of observant perspectives: "The Jewish views on IVF and modern reproductive technology issues are therefore readily deducible. According to the Talmud, the soul does not enter the embryo until 40 days after conception. Furthermore, we all have an obligation to have offspring and to 'be fruitful and multiply.' IVF is absolutely obligatory when it is medically indicated in order for a couple to have children. It is not just allowable, but it is obligatory. Preimplantation genetic diagnosis (PGD) represents no moral or ethical risk, because the soul has not yet entered the embryo. Selective reduction of a multiple pregnancy is acceptable if its goal is to enhance the possibility of life. Embryo research to promote life is, therefore, acceptable. Not only is therapeutic cloning acceptable but it is an obligation to do any research which can enhance and promote life-saving treatment, such as stem cell and cellular replacement therapy. In orthodox Judaism, which is otherwise a 'right to life' and anti-abortion religion, the early embryo does not yet have a soul and so is not yet a person. Nonetheless it cannot be just discarded for no reason, because it is a step toward the commandment 'be fruitful and multiply.' But it would not be considered murder to utilize an early embryo for research that might eventually save lives" (Silber, 2010, n.p.). However, people may have different views on this, and religious Jews will likely want to consult their rabbis as well as doctors in order to feel they are making a decision that suits their life and beliefs.

In short, "the first biblical commandment 'be fruitful and multiply' sanctions most treatments for infertility" (Hirsh, 1998, n.p.). Nonetheless, be aware when going into fertility treatment that it is an intense experience with many mental and physical effects on the individual experiencing it and on the couple and the wider family.

One Jewish mother wrote this about her experience with infertility:

I had secondary infertility between my first two children. They are 3 years apart. It was hard in the Hasidic community where most women have a child every 18 months. I spoke often to my mentor and Rebbetzin. I davened [prayed] daily for another baby and it tested my trust in HaShem. But I learned to accept His timing rather than my own.

Another said:

Before we even decided to have kids, I told my husband that I was not at all interested in pursuing any fertility treatments. If we had trouble conceiving, then that was that. I feel like a lot of people never consider that they could have trouble, or they don't consider how far they will go to have biological children of their own. It wasn't important to me to have biological children, and I wasn't interested in making efforts to help that happen if it wasn't going to happen naturally.

A third mother wrote:

I experienced infertility with my first two children due to PCOS. We follow the rules of *Taharas HaMishpachah*, so we consulted with a rabbi regarding some of the testing and best times to start treatments relative to my menstrual cycle. I also said lots of psalms. One year, I ate an *etrog* on *Hoshanah Rabbah* as there's a custom that this increases fertility.

For more on the *halachic* view of fertility treatment, the women's wellness and *halacha* center in the US Nishmat Yoatzot Halacha and the British Jewish charity Chana both offers a lot of information, including a useful video by the latter called, "Judaism, *Halacha*, Assisted Reproductive Technology:

Everything You Wanted to Know about Fertility but Were Afraid to Ask" (Chana, 2018b). The rabbi who speaks in this video, Shmuel Simons, mentions that the main *halachic* challenge, in his view, is how the male partner is to provide the semen. He acknowledges that not all methods of fertility treatment are permitted according to Jewish law, but that even for the most religiously observant, there are ways of getting support and treatment.

Being Pregnant

Interestingly, long ago, some groups of people weren't sure what caused pregnancy or how to identify pregnancy, but this knowledge has actually been codified in Jewish writing. "The Talmud gives criteria for the early identification of pregnancy: menses cease and convert to breast milk, and a woman experiences heaviness of head and limbs. Knowledge of the time of conception was sometimes important to determine an expected child's paternity, to determine inheritance rights" (Klein, 1998/2000, p. 85). This isn't strictly correct (the blood you'd have in a period doesn't convert to milk to feed the baby), but it's interesting to know that enough attention was paid to how women felt in order to recognize the changes within them that came from pregnancy.

Once you are lucky enough to get pregnant (or to be partnered to a pregnant person, whichever the case may be), you have to get through the pregnancy. For some people, this is easier than for others. In addition, there are some Jewish beliefs or customs that accompany a pregnancy.

Some Jews, like many other people, believe that how you behave, what you ingest, and what you are thinking about both specifically during conception and during a pregnancy can impact the baby. The effects are thought to be physical (the actual formation of the baby) or spiritual or personality-based (what the baby ends up being like). Jewish people "have sometimes exploited these beliefs to encourage morality" (Klein, 1998/2000, p. 73). In other words, you'd be told to behave yourself so you'd end up having a healthy, dutiful, and well-mannered child who lived in accordance with Jewish customs. The influence of the mother on the baby wasn't one-sided, however. Some people thought and some still think that the reverse is true too. "Some have also believed that the fetus is capable of self-expression and can influence the mother's behavior" (Klein, 1998/2000, p. 89). Research shows that some cells from the fetus remain in the mother's body for years after birth, so it isn't actually farfetched to think that the influence is bidirectional.

One way of behaving morally could involve restraining from sex, but this was considered an individual choice, dependent on how the pregnant woman felt. "In all their statements about sexual relations during pregnancy, rabbis have advised expectant parents according to their ideas of what is respectable and moral. The overall intention has always been to encourage couples to be considerate of each other's needs and comfort" (Klein, 1998/2000, p. 95). If there are no health concerns that would preclude a couple from indulging in sex, then it's a personal decision about how they feel and what they want.

In the West today, we have a tendency to believe that people shouldn't openly discuss their pregnancy until at least the first 12 weeks have passed. This is because there is an awareness that miscarriage is more common in the first three months and people, for some reason, feel they cannot say they are pregnant until the "danger has passed," and they are "sure" the pregnancy will be sustained, even though, sadly, of course miscarriage and stillbirth can happen at any point in the pregnancy. I suspect many people think they will be ashamed and embarrassed if they miscarry and perhaps even that they won't need or be deserving of support and help if that happens. I sincerely wish this weren't the case. We should all feel able to discuss anything that matters to us, and we should actively work to change the conversation around difficult topics such as miscarriage.

For some Jews, there is another layer here in not discussing pregnancy. "Ashkenazi Jews in the *shtetl* believed that proud talk when a pregnancy was barely established would invite catastrophe. Like other Jews, they feared the Evil Eye, expecting it to do harm when their affairs were prospering" (Klein, 1998/2000, p. 86). Some Ashkenazi Jews still feel this way today. "In contrast, Sephardic Jews have often celebrated a first pregnancy" (Klein, 1998/2000, p. 86). Additionally, some people note that the "Talmud states that at 40 days after conception, the embryo finally forms into a fetus. Whether or not the fetus receives its soul at this point was debated in the Talmud and the Mishnah" (Kraft, n.d., n.p.), but the idea of 40 days has meant that some Jewish people have waited until that time has passed before telling others. In other words, some might share the good news and celebrate immediately, some might wait 40 days, some might wait closer to 84 days (the 3 months of the first trimester), and some might not celebrate the pregnancy until even later.

While it hasn't been traditional for some Jewish people to celebrate being pregnant—not least because of the aforementioned fears about the evil eye—this has been changing in recent times. But now, "increasing numbers of Western Jewish women are celebrating events in the life cycle that are unique to women. Some Jewish women have sought to create a new ceremony, in the style of a Jewish ritual, to express their feelings of spirituality and Jewish identity at this milestone in their lives" (Klein, 1998/2000, p. 88).

Since this is so new, people can decide for themselves how to honor and celebrate their gravid state. "Going to the *mikveh*, chanting psalms, reading poems, lighting candles, and gathering friends together to share stories of birth and motherhood are some of the ways that women have sought to amplify the spiritual experience of pregnancy" (Kraft, n.d., n.p.). Other people pray, give to charity, ask the legendary midwives from the Passover story, Shifrah and Puah, for guidance and help, or study the stories of the Jewish matriarchs. Still others find further, less religious ways forward, such as parties or blessingways, which I'll come back to below. "These ceremonies reflect the fact that, for most Jewish women outside the Orthodox tradition, childbearing is no longer a foregone conclusion, but is now a particular stage in life, reached after conscious decision making. In such a ceremony, a woman acknowledges her responsibility for creating a new life, prepares herself to accept her new role, and commits herself to fulfilling it within the framework of Judaism, just as she may have done at her wedding or at her Bat Mitzvah when she was 12 years old. Although these new ceremonies may have some common aims, they differ greatly in their performance and are not a formalized part of Jewish ritual. As each woman chooses the ideas, blessings, and rituals of her celebration, she endows the occasion with her own personal spiritual significance" (Klein, 1998/2000, p. 88).

There are many different ways to experience and honor being pregnant, and it's exciting that Jewish people and families are coming up with new approaches that are significant and meaningful to them.

Prayers

As mentioned earlier, the rabbis traditionally were men. Pregnancy and labor seem to have escaped their attention, which means that there aren't many prayers or traditions set out long ago to help ease us through this period. However, a doctor and her rabbi husband have written some suggestions. For example, when a couple learns they are pregnant, Falk and Judson recommend that they say, "Blessed by the presence whose sanctity fills our lives, we give thanks for life, health, and this sacred moment" (2004, p. 3). There is a Hebrew version of this in their book as well). You can find more specific prayers for different stages and aspects of pregnancy and birth in Falk and Judson, or online.

Fasting and Cravings

The Talmud suggests that the pregnant or lactating woman's needs rank higher than the commandment to fast or to eat kosher food. "The Rabbis presumed it was medically unsafe for the woman if she did not satisfy her cravings" (Falk & Judson, 2004, p. 9). While it may not always technically be medically unsafe, you could certainly bring the ire of a hungry pregnant woman upon you if you don't let her eat what and when she needs to!

Genetic Issues

There are certain diseases, disorders, or other medical concerns that are more common among particular groups of people. Sometimes this is due to economic disparity and access to healthcare, sometimes it may be about the location or area of origin, and sometimes it clearly comes down to genes. For instance, sickle cell anemia is more common among

Black people. As Jews are a tiny portion of the world's population and have often either lived in primarily Jewish places and/or have not intermarried with non-Jews, we are prone to certain genetic illnesses that some other groups don't get, or don't get to the same extent. "Many years ago, Jewish communities were small and isolated, with members tending to marry within their communities. A small number of people over many, many generations can pass on a DNA abnormality within an ethnic community, even when that community is no longer small and isolated. For this reason, most ethnic groups have genetic disorders which are more common in that population than in the rest of the world" (Jnetics, n.d., n.p.).

Many people have heard tell of Tay-Sachs as a "Jewish disease," but aren't familiar with the larger list of syndromes that are more common among either all Jews, or certain groups of Jews. For example, there's Usher syndrome, Tyrosinemia, Walker-Warburg syndrome, Wolman disease/ Cholesteryl Ester Storage disease (which is more common for Iranian Jews), Zellweger syndrome spectrum, Fragile X, Acute Infantile Liver Failure (particularly for the Yemenite Jewish population), Bloom syndrome, Costeff Optic Atrophy syndrome (common among Iraqi Jews), Cystinosis (which affects the Moroccan Jewish population), Fanconi Anaemia (more common among Indian Jews), and many more (see a long list on Jnetics, n.d., n.p.). Also, "1 in 40 people of Ashkenazi Jewish origin, and 1 in 140 people of Sephardi Jewish origin have a BRCA gene mutation, compared to 1 in 250 people in the general population" (ibid.). For those unfamiliar with the BRCA mutation, it means an increased chance of getting breast cancer. The UK is currently carrying out a study in which Ashkenazi Jewish women can get checked for this mutation. If you are in the UK and are ethnically an Ashkenazi Jews (not a converted Jew) who is female or who was born female, it would be well worth it for you to get tested, since information is power. This study suggests that knowledge about Jewish inclination towards certain genetic issues is growing to a certain extent (see the Jewish BRCA website, n.d., n.p.).

An interesting point here is that "unlike Ashkenazi disorders which are relevant to all types of Ashkenazi Jews irrespective of country of origin, Sephardi, and Mizrahi JGDs [Jewish genetic disorders] are often linked to country of origin. For example, Iranian Jews are at risk of carrying different JGDs than Iraqi or Yemenite Jews. There are some JGDs that are relevant to more than one Sephardi sub-group, and some that are relevant to both Ashkenazi and Sephardi Jews" (Jnetics, n.d., n.p.). In other words, if you are Jewish, look into your ancestry to see which genetic disorders might impact you.

While some observant Jews may worry that it is not acceptable to get genetic testing, "[g]enetic screening, gene therapy and other applications of genetic engineering are permissible in Judaism when used for the treatment, cure, or prevention of disease. Such genetic manipulation is not considered to be a violation of God's natural law, but a legitimate implementation of the biblical mandate to heal" (Rosner, 1998, n.p.). In other words, it is not only permissible but perhaps should even be strongly encouraged.

Some people choose to get genetic testing before marriage, so they know if they and their future spouse are likely to have genes that combine in potentially problematic ways or how large the chance is that they might pass on the genes that cause Jewish-specific syndromes. They can then get advice, which is called genetic counseling, about how to proceed in terms of reproduction. Others may want to get tested after marriage but before getting pregnant, and others may wish to test their baby while it is in utero or soon after birth. This potentially raises some ethical and practical questions, as "today both prenatal diagnosis of various disorders and genetic counseling for carriers of inherited syndromes have created new issues for Jewish medical ethics" (Klein, 1998/2000, p. 45). If a test confirms a congenital abnormality in a fetus, especially one that will likely cause suffering and an early death, the parents may wish to consider abortion. "For example, the Tay-Sachs syndrome, which is caused by a genetic enzyme attacking the brain and nerves and results in the death of the child usually with 5 years of birth; Gaucher disease, which is caused by an enzyme deficiency that results in organ damage, bone weakening, and even death; Niemann-Pick disease, yet another enzyme deficiency, which causes metabolic disorder and degeneration resulting in death in early childhood; and mucolipidosis 4, which is a disorder of the central nervous system that causes partial or complete blindness and mental retardation. When a test confirms such a fetal abnormality or another severe disorder, abortion is often possible" (Klein, 1998/2000, p. 102). Of course, if a baby already born is confirmed to have a syndrome or disease, abortion is not an option, and instead you must be sure to find supportive and well-educated healthcare professionals, because you will need information and care.

However, it's essential, where possible, to go to a doctor or clinician who actually knows something about Jewish people. My experience here in the UK was problematic in several ways, and I know from other people that there is a similar situation in the US. First of all, the forms you need to fill in during pregnancy leave little space for Jewish identity. You get the following options: White British, White Irish, Black, or Asian. None of those are applicable to Jews. Sometimes you get lucky and there's an "Other" category, but then you have to explain what you mean by "Other", or there might not even be a text box for you to fill in. If you can't easily be categorized, then people feel like they don't understand who or what you are, and they don't know how to help you.

The second problem I and others I know have also experienced is that the midwives and doctors seem to have little idea what Jewish even meant, much less that there are specific genetic disorders that should be looked into or tested for. That's one reason why I went into great detail earlier in this book about what Jews are, as this isn't well understood. The health of the pregnant person and the child they are carrying is of critical importance, but it's hard to see to these things when the healthcare professionals haven't been taught that Jews are an ethnicity with specific medical concerns.

I think this is good advice: "Before taking any test, we suggest you and your partner discuss what you will do with the information each test will provide. If a screening test indicates that there may be a problem, will you do a follow-up test? Will you terminate the pregnancy? Are you unsure about what you will do, but feel that you would like to know, at least to prepare yourself?" (Falk & Judson, 2004, p. 21). In other words, do you want to take tests and why, and what would you do with the information gained? In their book, Falk and Judson also offer prayers that can be said before such testing.

One parent wrote:

> We did do the Ashkenazi genetic panel for various diseases including Tay Sachs and Cystic Fibrosis (all negative).

This is my own story about genetic testing:

> When I was pregnant and went for my first appointment with the midwife, she asked about my ethnic background. She needed to know in order to ensure that I got the appropriate prenatal checks. I told her that I was Ashkenazi. "Ashke-what?" was her response. "Ashkenazi is a Jewish ethnic category," I told her, trying to explain in simple terms. "Ashkenazi people are Eastern European Jews."
>
> She told me she had never heard of this and in fact didn't think there were any such people in the city where I live. The obvious rejoinder would have been to point out that a) I was sitting right there in front of her, living proof that such people exist in Norwich, and b) there is a synagogue in the city filled with others like me, but I politely restrained myself. Instead, I offered her some more information about what Ashkenazi is. I also pointed out that she needed to know because of the possibility of Tay-Sachs disease (I only mentioned one genetic disorder rather than confuse the poor woman further). Her eyes appeared to glaze over. She hadn't heard of this genetic illness before.
>
> "So you're Eastern European then?" the midwife finally said, her pen poised over the form, anxious to just tick a box and move on. Not exactly, I told her. "Middle Eastern?" she tried next, squinting to find the right square. Still not quite correct. Her last suggestion was, "African?"
>
> I said, "Originally, we're all African." This was perhaps not the best thing to say, because it just bewildered the health professional even more. She studied me, as if wondering whether I was, in fact, African. Finally, the midwife ticked "other" and moved the conversation on.

At a later appointment with a different midwife, I brought up the issue of ethnicity, and asked if I (and potentially the fetus) would be tested for any genetic illnesses related to being Ashkenazi. I was told to "ask the sonographer" to look at the ultrasound. I'm not a medical doctor, but I was pretty sure that an ultrasound wouldn't reveal Tay-Sachs. When I tentatively suggested that, the midwife shrugged and repeated the advice about talking to the sonographer.

I never did get any Ashkenazi-relevant testing. Luckily, my children don't have any genetic disorders. But I was left wondering about other expectant parents who might find themselves in my situation. If trained midwives, doctors, and others in the medical profession aren't familiar with different ethnicities/races/cultures, how can they ensure that people get the healthcare they need?

(Note: a slightly different version this story was originally published in *Kveller* (Woodstein, 2014).)

It's worth mentioning here that more observant Jews, such as the Haredi, tend to live in their own communities and to be treated by Jewish healthcare professionals, or at least those who are very knowledgeable about Jews. For these reasons, they are more likely to get tested, including before marriage. However, as many Jews around the world are assimilated into their wider communities, and are served by non-Jewish healthcare professionals, it is important both that Jews know to ask for genetic testing, and for non-Jews to know to offer this to their Jewish patients.

Sex Testing

Besides screening for genetic illnesses, you can also test for sex now during pregnancy, including in conjunction with genetic testing, such as through what is called non-invasive prenatal testing (NIPT). Unlike some other groups of people, Jews are not known for carrying out abortion or infanticide due to disappointment over a baby's sex. However, it must be noted that "[a] preference for sons over daughters is evident throughout Jewish history… [and boys have been more celebrated than girls and]. Such a double standard is typical of a patriarchal society with male-dominated attitudes and values" (Klein, 1998/2000, p. 9). In other words, some observant people will still feel this way.

In short, some Jewish people will be interested in pre-birth knowledge about a baby's sex, but this is not by any means widespread or hugely important before the baby is born. That is not to say that many parents, Jewish and otherwise, won't have preferences or desires related to sex and gender, but rather that this is not the most essential bit of information about a baby.

Hyperemesis Gravidarum

Morning sickness is common across pregnancies. Falk and Judson even offer a prayer that can be said as someone experiences it (Falk & Judson, 2004, p. 7). Hyperemesis gravidarum, also known as extreme pregnancy sickness, is much less common. Yet I thought I'd include a little section here on this illness because even though it is not a common sickness—about 1% of pregnant people suffer from it—there is some intriguing research that implies that Jews may be more likely to get hyperemesis gravidarum (HG) (see Bashiri et al., 1995). And, when you think about it, that makes sense. HG is known to have genetic links, in that if your mother had HG while pregnant with you, or if your older sister experienced HG in her pregnancies, then there is a higher likelihood that you would have it as well. Certain communities thus will have higher percentages of people who experience HG. And since, as already established, Judaism can be traced through genes, it could just as easily be Jews with higher numbers of HG than some other groups. However, it must be noted that there are multiple factors at play here, and there is very little research carried out into HG in general.

So what is HG? Basically, it's very serious pregnancy sickness. No, it's not morning sickness. It's all-day and sometimes all-night sickness, and it can involve nausea and vomiting, along with other symptoms, such as excess saliva, fatigue, depression, and more. Some people end up hospitalized and, in rare cases, HG can lead to death. It can be extremely upsetting to get so ill when you've been longing desperately to be pregnant. And, yes, I know from personal experience, having had HG in both of my pregnancies. I personally never would have gotten through those pregnancies without the support, care, and love my wife provided.

If you do experience hyperemesis during pregnancy, what can be done to help you? There are several HG charities (such as Pregnancy Sickness Support, or the specifically Jewish HG Help, both in the UK, or the HER Foundation in the US) that can provide information and personalized support, including in some cases a peer supporter who has been through HG and is willing to be there for you. In terms of medical help, you will need to see a doctor and/or midwife for medication; there is also a chance that you will require hospitalization.

HG Help also advises that those suffering get help from their family, friends, and wider community. They write from a religious point of view, which means they tend to assume that the ill pregnant person is a woman married to a man, and that the woman takes care of the family. So with that in mind, here is their advice:

> Consider who would be most helpful to you if you are unable to run the home as you usually do? Think about who would give you the most chance of reducing your potential feelings of guilt while as much as possible honoring your particular style of keeping your home and family functioning. You need someone who takes on the role of a Mother's Help. This person could be a family member, a friend or hired help. Additionally, you might need more than one person as there is cleaning, laundry and cooking to be done. You may need assistance with the morning and evening routines for children, babysitting, help with homework, and possibly rota. If husbands can help with rota, great, but this is not always possible. It is especially crucial to plan in advance particularly as many women prefer privacy early on in a pregnancy (HG Help, 2021., n.p.).

The head of HG Help notes, "There are practical things they can think about like planning extra support with childcare or getting people to cook for them outside the home to limit the exposure to food smells, which can be really difficult for women who are suffering" (Doherty, 2021, n.p.). That group also offers support to other religious Jews in London, including babysitting services and financial aid. There may be something like this available to you, depending on your location and community.

Hyperemesis is a terrible thing to experience. It can be especially difficult if you already have one or more older children. So do look for and accept help where you can.

Miscarriage and Abortion

Yes, this is a terribly sad section to include in a chapter on pregnancy, but unfortunately, it is part of life. It's thought that around 25% of all pregnancies miscarry. In addition, some people choose to, or need to, abort their fetus, for medical or personal reasons. It is important to understand what Jewish thought says about this.

Some may be surprised to hear that Judaism prioritizes the pregnant body over the fetus. Since some other religious or ethnic groups appear to prioritize the fetus and insist that a sick or disabled baby be carried to term, regardless of the impact on the mother, or without any attention paid to whether that baby has a chance at life after birth, it's easy to assume that the same is true of Jewish people. However, it's the opposite. Rather, it's the case that both the fetus and the person carrying it are important, but the pregnant person takes priority. To clarify, Judaism definitely recognizes the baby as a being: "Once a woman is pregnant, Judaism considers her fetus part of her body, just as her limbs are part of her body … Some [Jews] have thought that an unborn baby is capable of emotions and intellectual activity and that elements of its adult personality are evident even before birth" (Klein, 1998, pp. 88-89). This means that it is important both to protect the baby, because it is a person in some ways, but also that the baby is seen as part of the woman carrying it, and so her needs should take precedence, not least because she is already a living human being.

Also, there is no firm agreement about when the fetus's personhood becomes a reality that should be recognized. "When does the soul enter the baby's body? Just as opinions have varied about the nature of the source of the soul, so Jews have also differed in their thoughts about the timing of ensoulment. Some, such as the compiled of the Mishnah, believed that the soul entered at the time of conception. Others, such as the author of the Zohar, believed that the soul—the *nefesh* (the source of human vitality)—entered the body at the moment of birth, and the two other components, *ruah* and *neshamah*, the anima and the spirit, took form later in life, when the intellect had matured" (Klein, 1998/2000, p. 69). There's a lot of time and also a real difference in personhood and ability to survive between conception and birth, which allows for further discussion and some leeway about potential abortion.

In some circumstances, the fetus should be removed from the body carrying it. The Mishnah states that if it is endangering the life of the person carrying it, then it absolutely should go (Klein, 1998/2000, p. 55). In other words, the impact on the mother's health is what's deemed the deciding factor. If someone is pregnant with multiples, making the pregnancy even riskier, then a reduction to the number is acceptable, although there is some suggestion that the choice of fetus or fetuses to remove should be done based on which ones are least likely to be viable (Falk & Judson, 2004, p. 39). In addition, if the woman was impregnated through rape, then an abortion is acceptable: "a woman may destroy seed implanted within her illegally, against her will, especially if the rapist were not Jewish. The destruction of seed had to be done by a woman, however, because of the prohibition incumbent on men not to destroy male seed" (Klein, 1998/2000, p. 57).

The idea of abortion gets more complicated when it comes to the child's health. Rabbis "have been sympathetic and willing to take into consideration the risk to a mother's mental health, her severe anguish over the birth of a child with a genetic syndrome or disability, and her request for compassion. In contrast, rabbis have not been willing to consider aborting a fetus whose potential was unknown. However, now that diagnostic testing of the unborn fetus can produce reliable information concerning some severe disabilities, some rabbis have reviewed their attitudes to therapeutic abortion in these special cases. Although rabbis are concerned to safeguard the standards of Jewish medical ethics, their views many not concern non-Orthodox Jewish parents who discover that their fetus is multiply handicapped. Their decision regarding abortion is their own personal choice" (Klein, 1998/2000, p. 61).

This is to say that in less obvious cases, individual women need to make their own choices, and may wish to consult rabbis along with the necessary medical professionals choices. In my research survey, I asked people what they would like healthcare professionals to know about Jews or how they could better support Jewish families. One person said, "Abortion is part of Jewish law." This probably surprises readers, but it's important to remember when supporting Jewish families.

Miscarriage is a different circumstance, as this is a body's spontaneous abortion, not one chosen by the pregnant person for medical or personal reasons. Medical professionals know full well that there are many reasons for miscarriage—such as infection, abnormal fetal development, health conditions in the mother or baby—and they are overwhelmingly not the fault of the person carrying the baby (and even in cases where the mother was using drugs or alcohol, and this contributed to it, we must be understanding of what led her to the place where that was the choice she made or was forced into making, which means it is unfair to blame her here either). Unfortunately, some Jewish people may believe that miscarriage is something a person has earned or deserves. "The Bible portrays full-term pregnancy as God's reward to the righteous and pregnancy loss (like barrenness) as a divine punishment" (Klein, 1998/2000, p. 105). For those who take the Torah literally, they may think that they have done something to cause their miscarriage, despite the fact that the Torah and the Talmud "also blame pregnancy failure on physical and emotional trauma," which shows more awareness of factors outside of the person carrying the baby(ibid.). To avoid miscarriage, "Jews have encouraged a lifestyle of righteous behavior and prayer at all times in life, including during pregnancy. Thus, piety, donations to charity, and repentance have been especially important to Jews who interpret miscarriage as a punishment for sins. However, when a righteous woman repeatedly miscarries, and neither her own prayers nor anyone else's seem to help, she may look for other methods of avoiding such misfortune" (Klein, 1998/2000, p. 107). While praying, using amulets, giving to charity, and other such actions are generally harmless, it can seem unfair and inaccurate to tell a woman who has suffered repeated miscarriages that she just needs to repent through making charitable donations. Believing you are the reason behind your miscarriage certainly adds pain to an already horrible situation, and blaming a person who has lost a baby is not medically or emotionally justifiable.

Some people wish to mourn a miscarriage or an abortion—remember that even if a fetus was aborted, that doesn't mean that the loss of the potential baby isn't palpable—but there is no single ritual in Judaism to do this. In some ways, this means that people can make their own choices, but on the other hand, this puts the onus on the person or people who lost the baby to come up with an approach at a time when they have many other things to cope with and manage. "Much of the social behavior surrounding pregnancy loss is a matter of custom, not law; some customs may ease the pain, the shock, the frustration, and the feelings of guilt and helplessness, whereas others may not. Judaism allows a certain freedom of behavior for bereaved parents in the special case of pregnancy loss. Thus, there is no prescribed ritual mourning for pregnancy loss, and customs regarding the circumcising, naming, and burial of a miscarried or stillborn child, which all affect the mourning process, have varied from place to place" (Klein, 1998/2000, p. 115). Some wish to recite prayers or poems, such as this one:

Healing After a Miscarriage
by Merle Feld

Nothing helps. I taste ashes
in my mouth. My eyes are flat,
dead. I want no platitudes,
no stupid shallow comfort.
I hate all pregnant women,
all new mothers, all soft babies.
The space I'd made inside myself
where I'd moved over
to give my beloved room to grow-
now there's a tight angry
bitter knot of hatred there instead.
What is my supplication?
Stupid people and new mothers,
leave me alone.
Deliver me, Lord,
of this bitter afterbirth.
Open my heart
to my husband-lover-friend
that we may comfort each other.
Open my womb that it may yet bear living fruit (Feld, n.d., n.p.).

Note how this poem acknowledges the utter pain of loss while ending with a reference back to the Jewish theme of being fruitful and multiplying, which suggests that this mother would like to go on to try again.

Other people may take comfort in different ways, such as having a naming ceremony and a burial, or by taking photos of their deceased infant. I'll return to rituals after miscarriage or stillbirth below.

Antenatal Classes

Beyond throwing parties and buying necessary supplies, another aspect of pregnancy for lots of people is attending antenatal classes. For many pregnant individuals or couples, this is a great way to learn what to expect during pregnancy, labor, and the early days and weeks with a baby. In addition, it's a form of networking, as you get to know other pregnant people in your region who are due around the same time.

It is less usual, outside of observant communities, to find Jewish-specific antenatal classes. Within the observant communities, there may be antenatal classes tailored to their beliefs and what they are comfortable talking about. One Haredi woman wrote in her memoir, "In my final month of pregnancy, I visited a lady in the community who invited expectant mothers into her living room and explained how to breathe during labor, but beyond that there was nothing else to prepare me. Women weren't meant to share details of their births, so other than a general gist, I had no clue what awaited me" (Fletcher, 2025, p. 138).

If you live in an area heavily populated with Jews, you may be in luck and might find a Jewish class that is more detailed, or you could start your own. You may also find one online. What's different about a Jewish antenatal class? "Jewish prenatal classes, where they exist, combine an exploration of the Jewish values of parenting with breathing and relaxation exercises, and only sometimes the spirituality of birthing." (Klein, 1998/2000, p. 153).

Also, as Klein points out, there are differing rabbinic views of whether to use anesthesia (and, it could be added, differing perspectives on this among healthcare professionals and pregnant people too). A Jewish antenatal class may explore this.

"The prenatal class can devote some time to considering the rabbinic interpretations of Genesis 3:16, although the traditional assumptions about the pain of birth that were handed down from generation to generation are outdated. Anesthesia effectively reduces the suffering of labor and delivery, and women who opt for natural childbirth can try to overcome their pain with relaxation and breathing exercises" (Klein, 1998/2000, p. 153). Some people, in other words, may find it beneficial to attend a class that explores pregnancy, birth, and parenting from a Jewish perspective, so they can discuss these fascinating and complex biblical matters along with meeting new people and getting information about the practicalities of labor and having a baby.

Incidentally, some people prefer reading over attending in-person or online courses, or they might like to do both. There have been a couple of other Jewish-focused birth books before this current one (e.g., Falk & Judson, 2004; Klein, 1998), but both are dated and Klein focuses on traditions from the past more than practical information for current times. However, Klein and Falk and Judson both offer some interesting facts and ideas, so do partake of those older books along with this one and try attending antenatal classes.

What to Say

In English, we often say "congratulations" or "good luck" when we learn someone is pregnant, and there are similar phrases in many other languages. For Jews, especially those who, even if they have modern outlooks or are not religious at all, are still somewhat steeped in superstitious ideas. Different phrases might be more appropriate.

Many non-Jews will be familiar with phrases such as *mazel tov* (good luck, also written *mazal tov*) or *siman tov* (good sign) or *l'chaim* (to life), such as at weddings or bar or bat mitzvahs. However, when you have learned someone is pregnant, those are not the expressions to employ. Instead, you should say *b'shaah tovah*, where you "wish that the baby comes at a good and auspicious time" (My Jewish Learning, n.d., n.p.). This neatly sidesteps the potential of bringing the evil eye down on someone or somehow causing a miscarriage. "A pregnancy is a state of unknown, and thus to "congratulate" is too worrisome for Jews. What if something goes wrong? What if the pregnancy ends in miscarriage, and we have congratulated prematurely? What if—and here Jewish worry is in a league of its own—our premature *mazal tov* somehow even induces a miscarriage? Instead, we pray that no matter what happens, may the child and the mother be healthy, "in a good hour" (Fischel, 2020, n.p.). That is, "pregnancy is considered a liminal state, a state of potentiality", and we hope people get through it safely (Falk & Judson, 2004, p. 2).

Also, *b'shaah tovah* nicely puts the focus on the person who will be going through labor. It's all too easy for people to get so excited about the baby that they forget that someone is experiencing pregnancy and will be expected to get the baby out of her. So this phrase both avoids superstition and allows us to hope that things go well during labor and birth, and that it happens in a timely fashion.

Baby Showers and Gender Reveals

Similarly, to the cautiousness around what to say to a pregnant woman, some Jewish people believe that it is tempting fate to prepare a room for the baby, or even to buy clothes or other supplies for the baby. "The purpose of this practice [not buying things for the baby or getting a room ready] is to protect you emotionally, just in case, God forbid, something goes wrong with the delivery and you don't return home with a baby. Seeing a room full of baby things could only add to what would already be an incredibly difficult experience" (Falk & Judson, 2004, p. 45).

And yet, if the pregnancy progresses, as a baby's due date gets closer, many people in the West like to have a baby shower. Traditionally, this has been less common among Jews, as implied in the earlier section, *Being Pregnant*, which explored how some Ashkenazi Jews wouldn't even announce a pregnancy until absolutely necessary.

There is nothing in Jewish law or writings that explicitly prohibits buying baby clothes, preparing a baby's room, or having a baby shower during the antenatal period. It's purely superstition based on the worry that celebrating the birth before it happens could bring down bad luck on the mother, the baby, or the family as a whole. "This superstition stems from the notion of the evil eye, or *ayin hara*. In the Mishnah, a person with *ayin hara* is someone who cannot be happy for another's good fortune, and in fact is distressed and angry when good things happen to his or her friends. This person's gaze is considered dangerous, because he or she would prefer that others not enjoy good things, and might somehow cause misfortune to others via a malicious gaze. As a result, many Jewish communities have developed a tradition of not calling attention to good things, so as not to provoke *ayin hara*" (My Jewish Learning, n.d., n.p.). To add to this, this taboo is "based on a superstition that held that celebrating the child before he or she is born could endanger his or her safe and healthy arrival. In addition, this taboo developed in a time of high infant mortality. Many people feel that facing an abundance of baby-related items in the home compounds the devastating loss felt by a couple who experiences a miscarriage or stillbirth. While the risk is significantly lower today, we must acknowledge that a tragic outcome is still a possibility" (Zulpan, 2015, n.p.). As noted above, if an abortion, miscarriage, or stillbirth does occur, there are ways to honor and mourn the loss; also it's useful to remind people that buying a Babygro or a car seat doesn't cause a miscarriage.

"According to *halacha* (Jewish law), there is nothing wrong with having a baby shower" (My Jewish Learning, n.d., n.p.). So Jews who wish to do this should feel enabled to go ahead and have a shower. They can even incorporate Jewish elements as they like, such as prayers or Jewish foods. On the other hand, people could organize a more Jewish-style event by having blessings for the pregnant person. One suggestion even describes how people could sit in groups of six (to make the points of a star of David) and sing a *niggun*, offer blessings, and dance (Falk & Judson, 2004, pp. 45-46).

While gender reveal events are a modern custom—due to the self-evident reason that it has only been possible in very recent times to find out the sex before birth, with the use of ultrasound scans or blood tests—they tend to be quite limited in terms of which groups of people enjoy having them. There are a couple of key points here. One is the fact that just because someone has, say, XX chromosomes, they might not identify as female, so a gender reveal could turn out to be erroneous. Another is that for many, perhaps even most families, the most important part of a pregnancy is the safe delivery of the baby and the health of the mother. What sort of baby a family has matters less to many people. Also, "the Rabbis say that one should not pray for the gender of the fetus," as it is determined at conception, and so people should instead pray every day that "the fetus remains healthy and develops normally" (Falk & Judson, 2004, p. 5). Still, for Jews who wish to partake of this newly created tradition around gender reveals, there is nothing in *halakhah* that says they cannot. As there are no typical Jewish customs around stating a fetus's sex antenatally, a Jewish individual or family will have to create their own, which may be nerve-wracking or liberating, depending on your point of view.

A parent wrote this on their approach:

I didn't publicize my pregnancy until 5 months due to modesty and Jewish custom. We also did not find out the baby's sex.

Specifically regarding the baby shower, another parent said:

My family was very upset that I had a baby shower before the baby was born but I didn't share their superstitious feelings.

Superstitions

As the foregoing sections have shown, some Jews, like people in many other ethnic groups, have superstitions. There are a variety of superstitious beliefs, such as the fear that buying items for the baby before birth tempts fate, the decision not to refer to the baby by a name until after they are born and formally named, and the idea that red can be protective (which I'll return to in the section on postpartum practices).

There is also the concept of the evil eye, or *ayin hara*, where it is thought that a person who is jealous or who has nasty intentions can cause bad things to happen just by giving a particular sort of glance. You can try to ward this off by saying *kinehora*, by spitting three times, and/or by wearing or employing amulets, particularly the *hamsa*, which is a hand shape with an eye in it (you may see it in other cultures too, particularly Muslim ones). The *hamsa* is also called "the hand of Miriam" in reference to Moses's sister.

One parent noted:

> First and foremost, we are superstitious, which is common in many Jewish families. So, you don't tell anyone you're pregnant until at least 12 weeks, you don't tell the name, and no baby showers, or setting up the nursery until the baby is born.

Another said:

> I discovered that I am superstitious. I left all the baby items in their boxes until we needed them. My husband was strongly committed to circumcision. We named our children after important relatives, most of whom had already passed, and did not use the identical name for the one we wanted to honor who was alive.

A third described this feeling:

> I find it VERY weird and off-putting when people name their baby and refer to their baby by name before it is born.

A final parent wrote this about their choices:

> We didn't announce our pregnancies till they were becoming physically obvious to everyone, avoided talking about them as much as necessary, didn't hold a baby shower, didn't ask to find out the sex of our child, and I avoided gazing at things which were ugly, disturbing, or which showed the face of someone evil (like, not looking at photos of Hitler, for example) for the length of our pregnancy.

This rather long chapter explored a range of topics relevant to a Jewish pregnancy—including ideas about sex, reasons to have children, how to handle infertility, choices around abortion, genetic conditions, baby showers, the phrase *b'shaah tovah*, and more. Of course we should remember that how people feel about any of these will vary depending on their background and level of observance. Pregnancy can feel like it goes on and on, especially if the mother is ill or uncomfortable, but it has a clear ending point, so now we'll look at Jewish approaches to labor.

CHAPTER 4

Jewish Birth

After all those months of pregnancy, it's finally time for labor and birth. For many people, especially those pregnant for the first time, labor can seem like a very scary and unknown event, perhaps like a mountain that they have to climb even though they've had no preparation for the trek ahead. It's true that giving birth can be a risky and painful experience. But with good antenatal education and lots of support, giving birth can be a beautiful and meaningful event in someone's life.

For some Jewish people, it's important that birth, just like any other ritual or event in a Jewish life, be infused with Jewish traditions and spirituality. Indeed, in some ways, Jewish approaches to birth are slightly different from other types. "Throughout the ages, Jews have developed many different birth traditions, such as biblically prescribed postnatal rituals, customs associated with Eve, Rachel, Hannah, or famous rabbis, or practices handed down from generation to generation within a particular community. In addition, Jewish people have injected their own special flavor into contemporary theories about myths to explain the mysteries of childbirth" (Klein, 1998/2000, p. xxix). Interestingly, over time, "Jewish childbirth practices have been remarkably uniform in the different communities where Jews have flourished, largely because of the centrality of Torah and *halakhah* (Jewish law) in their lives" (Klein, 1998/2000, p. xxxi).

In this chapter, we'll explore Jewish beliefs and traditions when it comes to welcoming a baby into the world.

Jewish Birth Preferences and Rituals

In general, all pregnant people will want to think about their preferences for their birth (and, eventually, for their postpartum period). In Appendix 1, I have included the birth preferences document I use with my clients. It's not specific to any ethnic or religious group and can easily be adapted.

However, there are some things that Jewish people in particular may want to consider when it comes to their birth, and such things should be added to the document. Some are about rituals or behaviors that are specific to the antenatal, labor, or postnatal time. Others are more general preferences that can cover any and all of those periods. For example, some individuals and families may wish to be visited by a rabbi or other chaplain while in the hospital. Some may want to bring in their own food, especially if the hospital or birthing center doesn't offer kosher meals. And some may have Jewish ritual items with them (such as a *tallit, or prayer shawl)* that they may wish to employ but also might not want other people to touch. These are all issues that should be covered in the birth preferences document. I've included a Jewish-specific document in Appendix 2.

Mikveh

Some Jewish women choose to enter the *mikveh* (also spelled *mikvah*), or ritual bath, in the month before giving birth. There are various reasons for this, such as to have a connection to God, a sense of purification, to immerse both literally and metaphorically in cleansing water, or a chance to pray, whether for an easy birth or the baby's health or to be a good parent or anything else. Going into the *mikveh* is not a requirement, but rather a choice. In addition, "Jewish custom also holds that pregnant women have a special ability to bless others, so pregnant women in the *mikvah* may pray for others who wish to become pregnant. One custom for women who wish to become pregnant is to immerse themselves in the *mikvah* after a pregnant woman" (Falk & Judson, 2004, p. 56).

A *mikveh* is for one person only (usually) and the water in it must be collected naturally, not by human hands. In other words, a spring or rain water can be used to fill the *mikveh*, although tap water can be used to top it up.

"This woman's immersion evokes the idea of bringing *tahara*, purity and God's presence, into the birth process. The living waters of the *mikveh* parallel the waters of the womb. By immersing, the woman unites the spiritual aspects of the *mikveh* waters, that symbolize being enwrapped by Torah and the *Shekhina* [the divine feminine], with the physical nature of the womb and birthing process. *Tevilla* [immersion] is therefore a very female way to bring *Hashem* into the process of preparing for labor" (Blady, n.d., n.p.). Some *mikveh* even allow for partners to go in with the pregnant person (Gechter, 2013, n.p.).

Rabbi Miriam Berger, Founder Director of Wellspring (a center of well-being with the ritual of *mikveh* at its heart), and Emerita Rabbi of Finchley Reform Synagogue, in the UK, wrote the following about the *mikveh*:

> Biology tells us that we are born in water. It's from the amniotic fluid that we emerge into the world. Judaism also tells us that we are born in water, but in our tradition, it happens again and again, individually and collectively. Each new chapter starts by us emerging into our new role through water. Our shared narrative is one by which we are birthed as a people through the parted sea. We go from being a group of slaves in Egypt or *Mitzrayim*, literally the "narrow place," through the waters of the Sea of Reeds, to our early years seeking nationhood as the Children of Israel in the wilderness.
>
> In addition, Judaism traditionally gave us many more metaphorical birthing moments in water. We are encouraged to make these transitions from one state of being to the next. The tradition of using a *mikveh*, the Jewish ritual bath, recreates those images of birth or the parted seas to transform us. From being single to married. From the grief of a period showing there is no pregnancy this month, to the hope and potential of the next cycle. The *chevra kaddisha* [Jewish burial society] prepare our body for *ha'olam habah*, the "world to come", again using the flow of water.
>
> The tradition of a *mikveh* in your final month of pregnancy is something I think is truly beautiful. It takes the focus from the baby to the parents, to enable them to consider this momentous transition for them, giving them time to consider not just the new life being born to them, but the new life

they are going to experience in themselves. From putting your own needs first to putting your child first. How does one prepare for a depth of love never experienced before, a sense of responsibility never faced before, and our own happiness completely enmeshed with the happiness of a tiny new soul?

There is more than a need to welcome the baby into the world, there is a need to accept/embrace/face up to the new life the parent is being born into at that very same moment.

We often see our greatest responsibility as that of keeping our children safe and well. Yet that seems to be the animalistic instinct in most of us too. We are protective; we worry about real and perceived dangers way more than we need to. My son is almost 14 (years not months) and I still like to pop my head around the door to check he's breathing when he's sleeping—having neuroses is the hardwired bit. But how do we ensure we are passing on our values to our children? What is truly important to each of us, and when or how will our children work that out? With sleep routines, feeding choices and the bombardment of health and safety messaging, how do we make time to make the real-life choices which may mean our children turn into the *mensches* we would like them to become?

I offer courses through Wellspring to help people get ready for parenthood and of course as a rabbi, I have counselled many individuals. As one tool out of many, I recommend immersing in the *mikveh*, which gives you the space to prepare for what is to come.

Other Pre-Birth Rituals and Customs

Besides the *mikveh*, there are other things that some observant Jews choose to do. This might include baking *challah* bread, putting up a *mezuzah* (a miniature scroll with verses from the Torah), and donating money or items to charity. "Because "charity saves from death" (Proverbs 6:2), pregnant Jewish women have given to charity" (Klein, 1998/2000, p. 147). Others suggest that pregnant women should "be exposed to spiritual and holy sights and sounds," and sew a sash to cover a Torah scroll, while avoiding zoos (so as not to see non-kosher animals) or cemeteries, and not partaking in gossip (Zaklikowski & Zaklikowski, n.d., n.p.). All such rituals or customs are believed to keep the pregnant person's actions moral and pure and their thoughts focused on scripture and holy matters.

Where to Give Birth

Just as with any other group, Jewish people have to choose whether to give birth at home, at a birthing center, at a hospital, or at any other location. People will have their own personal feelings about this choice and they may also receive information or advice that leads them to feel that a particular location is the appropriate one.

For observant Jews who keep the sabbath and do not usually drive on Shabbat, it is permissible to break this if the pregnant woman begins labor and needs to get to the hospital or birthing center (or if a midwife, doula, or doctor needs to get to the person in labor to check on and support them).

The Influence of Shabbat and Other Festivals

The section above mentioned Shabbat and how observant Jews will not drive or carry out other forms of work on Shabbat or some other major festivals. It is important to remember that this may affect other aspects of the birth experience. For instance, they might not be willing to fill in paperwork, as this will be seen as a type of work, or they might not want electricity on, and they might even not want the medical professionals—whether observant or not themselves—to partake of such forms of work. In addition, some people may be cautious about pressing buttons, such as for the elevator or to call for help from a nurse, on Shabbat, and may want someone non-observant to do this for them. The individual or family giving birth should explain their preferences regarding this in advance, in a birth preferences document and also orally, so those supporting them are aware. Of course, as already noted, if it is necessary or an emergency, then saving a life takes priority over the rules around Shabbat or other holidays.

Food will be discussed shortly, but Shabbat and religious festivals also influence what foods someone may or may not want to ingest.

Hospital Bag

If you are giving birth in a hospital, of course you will need all the usual items, such as changes of clothing, diapers/nappies, clothes for the baby, preferred music or photos, snacks and drinks, and so on (see Appendix 3). If you are religiously modest, you will also want appropriate hair coverings and other such clothes.

"First on the Jewish packing list are objects that will make your delivery room feel spiritually like your own space" (Falk & Judson, 2004, p. 49). One suggestion is to bring four objects and to place one object in each of the four corners. It could be that the items represent "your past, your present, your future, and your hope for the baby" or "peace and strength," or your spirituality more generally (Falk & Judson, 2004, p. 50).

An important thing not to forget for the observant would be prayer books. One recommendation states that people should bring "a *siddur* or the Book of Psalms" (Falk & Judson, 2004, p. 51) and another says to "[k]eep a holy book, such as a prayer book, *Pentateuch*, or *Noam Elimelech* under your pillow in the hospital. Keep the book wrapped in two towels or other double cover. This book will serve as a tangible reminder of God's mercy and strength, and love of the Jewish people, as expressed through the gift of the Holy Torah. You can maintain your calm and sense of faith as the book reminds you that God loves you and that everything will turn out for the best" (Weisberg, 2024, n.p.).

Another possible item would be a *mezuzah*. If you are giving birth at home, you may well already have a *mezuzah* up on the doorposts of most rooms (not the bathrooms, though), but if you aren't usually that observant, some people like to put a *mezuzah* up now. If you are going to give birth in a hospital, and it is a non-Jewish one that has flexibility, you could choose to bring a *mezuzah* to put up on the doorpost of your hospital room, or else you could just keep it next to you. "Make sure that you have kosher *mezuzot,* especially at the entrance to your bedroom. The *mezuzot* are scrolls with verses from the book of Deuteronomy, and the Torah teaches us to keep them on the entrance of every Jewish home. The rabbis further teach us to post them at the entrance to every room within our homes, and to make certain to keep them in good condition in order that, in the merit of keeping a *mezuza*, God will guard us from harm" (Weisberg, 2024, n.p.).

"As a Jewish focal point, you may want to bring a *shviti.* A *shviti* is a traditional Jewish art form used for meditation," and it has a verse from the Book of Psalms in it (Falk & Judson, 2004, p. 51). Someone could focus on this while breathing through their contractions.

Finally, "it is customary to hang a *Shir LaMaalot* (Psalm 121) in the room of the new mother and the newborn immediately upon the expectant mother's arrival at the hospital" (Chabad, 2004, n.p.). This is Psalm 121, in a slightly modernized adaptation:

> A song of ascents. I lift my eyes to the mountains. From where will my help come?
> My help will come from Adonai, Maker of heaven and earth.
> Adonai will not let your foot falter; your guardian does not slumber.
> Indeed, the Guardian of Israel neither slumbers nor sleeps.
> Adonai is your guardian; Adonai is your protective shade at your right hand.
> The sun will not harm you by day, nor the moon by night.
> Adonai will guard you from all evil; Adonai will guard your soul.
> Adonai will guard your going and your coming from now and for all time.

One parent said this about their customs:

> We hang a *shir lamaalos* card on the door at the birthing center and on the baby's car seat so he or she is surrounded by Torah and blessings.

People Present

As with where to give birth, people will also already have opinions about who should be with them when they give birth. If they or the baby need help, doctors are more likely to be involved, as would be the case in places where birth is more medicalized. Jewish people, like any group, will make choices about whether to have doctors, midwives (independent or those linked to a particular hospital or birthing center), and/or doulas. If you're in the UK, you can find a Jewish doula, midwife, or other birthworker through an organization I'm part of, Shifrah. There may be similar organizations in other countries, such as the US.

For more observant Jewish women, their husband might not be with them while they give birth. For some, this is due to reasons of modesty. It could also be that for some, they choose to only have their husbands present when the women are covered up. For many people, it is because they follow the guidelines for *niddah* (which is a concept referred to earlier and discussed later). If you comply with ideas of *niddah*, then there is no physical touch between spouses when a woman is bleeding; this includes both menstruation and birth. So a husband might be present, but would not touch the wife. For this reason, it's usually helpful for the birthing woman to have relatives and/or friends and/or someone like a doula with her, because those people can touch her, offering massage, comfort, and other physical contact. "Labor assistants serve as a bridge between husband and wife, especially when the couple is Orthodox and the laws of *Taharas Hamishpacha* (Family Purity) are being observed. According to Jewish Law, whenever a woman's womb is open, she and her husband do not have marital relations nor any physical contact. After her bleeding has ceased and after the proper preparations, she has immersed in a kosher *mikveh* (ritual bath), the couple is reunited in physical, marital harmony. These laws set the rhythms of a Jewish marriage. Labor support is important to every birthing woman, but it is vital for the those adhering to the laws of *Taharas Hamishpacha* who are without the physical support of their spouse" (Ertel, n.d., n.p.).

On the other hand, rabbis and other scholars have explored this topic in more depth, and have suggested that that in this particular situation, *niddah* should be overruled by the concept of *pikuach nefesh. Pikuach nefesh* is the principle that states that saving someone's life should come above all else. In other words, if someone had to break another Jewish law in order to save a life, that is acceptable. Childbirth is considered risky, and therefore some argue that a husband should be able to give his wife physical comfort, if she requests it (Linzer, 2018, n.p.). As it's clear that views on this vary, if you're observant or if you're working with an observant family, it would be useful to discuss this in advance of the birth. One memoir by a Haredi woman talks about how she had a "religious doula" with her, to help her "navigate the culture clash, as was customary" (Fletcher 2025, p. 138). The doula said to her, "With every pain you should feel Hashem's [G-d's] light shine upon you (ibid.)"

As noted, some people have relatives and/or friends with them as well. Some like to have these people pray with or for them during the birth. This might even include a rabbi or other Jewish religious leader; some hospitals have one in-house, particularly in areas with larger Jewish populations.

Finally, if someone needs an interpreter while in a medical setting (for example, if Hebrew or Yiddish is their native language, but they are in another country with a different language), and they are more modest, they may prefer the interpreter to be behind a door (such as a closet door) or outside the curtain, if there is a curtain around their bed.

Whoever is with you, make sure you consider in advance what you want them to do to support you. You may wish to assign them roles (for example, think about who gives the best massages, or who you trust to ensure you are well fed and hydrated) or you can just think through what you might need and then see how it goes on the day.

One mother wrote this about her birth:

> I gave birth at home with the support of midwives, two close friends, and my partner. As a Liberal Jew, I do not follow the laws of *niddah* or modesty, and so my partner played an active role during my labor. He supported me through both emotional encouragement and physical touch. He assisted me into more comfortable positions, used massage for pain relief, and ensured I was fed and hydrated. It felt so important to me to have him there during this significant moment of both our lives and to witness the birth of our baby.

Another said:

I chose to go to a midwife so I would have less interventions and not need unnecessary ultrasounds. I believe a trusting, positive outlook is the safest thing for a mother to have for the baby to develop, whereas the ob-gyn industry operates on fear, what-ifs, and legal outlooks.

Prayers

Some have suggested that observant Jews might wish to have a spiritual birth plan, in which they decide in advance which prayers or blessings to say at which times. Marion Haberman, for example, recommends picking prayers for the following periods in a pregnancy and birth: "Before Labor Begins—in your Ninth Month; As Labor Begins; On Your Way to the Hospital; When Baby Arrives into the World; [and] Upon Returning Home" (Haberman, 2018, n.p.).

Shir Lamaalot (Psalm 121) was already mentioned above as being a psalm particularly relevant to childbirth, but other people may choose to read or recite from the Torah. Others may simply choose their own words to recite, in their hearts or aloud, to God.

After the birth, many observant Jews will recite *Birkat Hagomel*, which is a prayer of thanksgiving that is traditionally said after an illness or after having undergone something dangerous. Childbirth is inherently risky, even if it is an everyday occurrence, so it's understandable that this particular prayer would be recited after someone has gotten through it safely. However, this prayer isn't only for the very religious; "its recitation has become increasingly common in nonorthodox circles, perhaps because it responds very directly to a need of mothers to publicly give thanks for having survived childbirth physically and spiritually" (Falk & Judson, 2004, pp. 98-99). *Birkat Hagomel* is as follows:

בָּרוּךְ אַתָּה ה׳ אֱלֹהֵינוּ מֶלֶךְ הָעוֹלָם הַגּוֹמֵל לְחַיָּבִים טוֹבוֹת שֶׁגְּמָלַנִי כָּל טוֹב

Baruch ata Adonai, Eloheinu melech ha-olam, ha-gomel l'chayavim tovot she-g'malani kol tov.

Blessed are You, Adonai our God, ruler of the world, who rewards the undeserving with goodness, and who has rewarded me with goodness.

I will return to post-birth prayers below.

Music

Many laboring people like to set up a playlist in advance, which in the end may or may not suit their mood on the day. While every Jewish person giving birth will have their own preferred music, some like hymns, and others prefer *nigunim* (plural for *nigun*, which is an Ashkenazi religious song, without words but with a tune).

Some Jewish communities even have traditional birthing songs. For example, Yemenite Jewish women had many songs, which they used to "regain their voice, which had been silenced and policed by the patriarchal society that surrounded them, through the songs and poems they composed and sang … [They] sang songs for many different kinds of circumstances and events. Through song, they expressed themselves, their private world and yearnings in the diverse contexts of their daily lives. They did this both in the company of women—among their close family or in social gatherings during life cycle ceremonies—and alone, for example, before dawn while they would grind flour" (Malul, n.d., n.p.).

The Yemenite women had songs for labor, birth, the month-long postpartum confinement they observed, and the "day of completion" ceremony when the confinement ended, although they would make up new songs or vary old ones, so there was not simply just one set of songs that was always used. The current Jewish population of Yemen is thought to be, at most, five people (Ben Ari, 2024, n.p.), but it is certainly possible that descendants of Yemenite Jews elsewhere might still use the tradition of birthing and postpartum songs.

Similarly, there have been Jewish birthing songs among the Jewish communities in Morocco and the Sahara more generally. These were sung in Judeo-Arabic and they included songs for blessing the mother-to-be, trying to have a son rather than a daughter, breaking the water, and more (Paloma-Elbaz, 2015, n.p.). As few Jews live in the Maghreb now, these songs are in the process of being forgotten since they unfortunately aren't used as much.

Some Jewish women, therefore, will want traditional birthing songs, while others will want hymns or *nigunim*, and some will want music totally unrelated to Judaism.

Labor

Naturally, the experience of labor, making choices about issues such as cesarean versus vaginal delivery, whether it's acceptable to induce a birth or break the waters, whether to use pain relief, and so on will, in many cases, be similar for Jewish individuals and families as for non-Jews. Still, some beliefs and decisions will be influenced by Jewish tradition.

Many Jewish women will be aware of the line from Genesis 3:16 that seems to doom them to pain during labor and birth. "'In pain shall you bear children' (Genesis 3:16) is God's punishment to Eve for her sin in the Garden of Eden. Jews have interpreted this verse, like other biblical verses, to extract lessons for human behavior; in this case, the verse has been used to rationalize the pain of childbirth" (Klein, 1998/2000, p. 137). It could be that knowledge of this line from the Torah makes people afraid of giving birth, which could in fact increase the perception of pain, or else it could be that this empowers people, since they know to expect pain and can therefore prepare for it. Some people suggest the former. "Although, in the past, women pregnant for the first time knew about the pain of childbirth from observing their mothers or sisters, women today are less likely to have observed travail or delivery. Nonetheless, in modern times, 'in pain shall you bear children' is one of the best-known biblical phrases among Jewish women, and many fear childbirth. Although childbirth is now relatively safe, their fear is based on helplessness, on the feeling that the events of birthing are beyond their own control" (Klein, 1998/2000, p. 141). If someone is feeling frightened, they might find approaches such as hypnobirthing, using affirmations, or prayers to be calming.

Other people will connect in labor and birth to their ancestors, in particular the matriarchs (Sarah, Rebecca, Rachel, and Leah), and to Jewish experiences throughout time. Jewish women have given birth, sometimes in difficult or even dire circumstances, and that can give those preparing for or in labor a sense of strength. They are reminded that they are not alone. Furthermore, "[m]any readers of the Torah have noted that the labor and delivery process seems uncannily similar to the miracle of the Red Sea, which opened to allow the Israelites to pass and then closed upon the Egyptians. Just as a fetus moves through a narrow passage to life, so the Israelites who were in *Mitzrayim*, the biblical name for Egypt but also meaning "the narrow place," left from the narrow place to new life … the Red Sea imagery is almost unmistakable as a birth canal: A path is cleared through water (amniotic fluid), and the walls of the sea (the cervix) open to allow the Israelites (the baby) to be birthed into freedom….We encourage you to hold on to this image of God parting the waters as a focus for your birthing experience. You are the conduits for a miraculous experience" (Falk & Judson, 2004, pp. 67-68).

A mother expressed this on giving birth:

> Birth is a process of redemption; the birth canal is like the splitting of the sea.

Sadly, though, as with the emphasis on fear for some people, Jewish cultural and religious traditions may not always be helpful. One mother shared her experiences of induction not being accepted in her Jewish community:

> I was late with my first child, and my doctor wanted to induce me, but I didn't want to be induced or to have an epidural … because my Jewish social circles led me to believe there was something wrong with that. I ended up with a C-section, which I accepted even though I wished it could have been avoided. I delayed pregnancy with my second child by over three years due to the C-section. With my second child, I was induced for valid medical reasons. The induction was a terrific experience and everything went smoothly. The nurse was Jewish and Orthodox, and I liked her, and it was a much better experience than the first birth. Not that the first was bad, just the second was easier.
>
> I wish that I had had my priorities straight about having three kids being more important than these extra things like not having an epidural or not inducing. The research turns out to say that epidural and induction are probably beneficial to birth outcomes, such as lower chances of C-section. I wish the Jewish community didn't have such unscientific social pressures to avoid epidurals and induction, and to have doulas, and to double-guess doctors' clinical judgement.

In short, if you are Jewish and pregnant, or supporting someone who is Jewish and pregnant, it is useful to try to separate beliefs from medical fact, as a way of ensuring that decisions are made for compelling reasons rather than out of custom or folk belief, while also respecting culture and traditions where possible.

Pain Relief

Other books on birth will give more details regarding pain relief, but here I want to mention a few things specific to Jews. As noted, the Torah says that childbirth is painful, and this has meant that some Jewish women feel they shouldn't have pain relief because that is against what God has planned for them.

Some also believe that they can do something in advance to lessen the pain they will experience. That's one reason for some of the pre-birth rituals I've already referred to. Another folk custom that is meant to reduce pain is for the pregnant woman to bite of the end of the *etrog* (a citrus fruit that is important for the holiday of Sukkot) (Falk & Judson, 2004, p. 70). Other "[m]ethods for easing delivery, like remedies for barrenness and preventing miscarriage, depend on the perceived causes of the problem. Believing that the pain of childbirth has divine causes, Jews have prayed, repented, and made donations to charity in the hope of obtaining God's favor toward a laboring woman. At the same time, they have tried medical remedies to relieve pain and hasten delivery. When neither spiritual nor physical methods have produces results, Jews have sometimes resorted to magic" (Klein, 1998, pp. 141-142). I'm not sure if this exactly counts as magic, though I suppose for some it is a form of magical thinking, but "Jews used objects pertaining to Jewish ritual, in the hope that magical beneficial effects would ease childbirth" (Klein, 1998/2000, p. 148). Examples include the Torah, "the Torah cover, phylacteries, or even the key to the synagogue" (Klein, 1998/2000, p. 148). I have certainly seen it suggested that in order to lessen or relieve pain during birth, people should wrap a Torah and put it under their pillow or close to them in some other way, as if its mere presence might be enough. Obviously, of course, many people will also pray for a relatively pain-free birth or use a sort of incantation or intention (Falk & Judson, 2004, p. 74).

Positive intentions and affirmations are used by laboring folks, Jewish and non-Jewish alike.

For others, medical pain relief may be desired. In a few specific cases, different types of pain relief may not be options, specifically for reasons related to Jewishness, which might be surprising. The following story exemplifies this:

> I am a carrier for Factor XI deficiency, which has a much higher carrier rate among Ashkenazi Jews. Even though neither I nor anyone in my family has bleeding problems, the doctors made me go to a hematology consultation, during which it was decided that I couldn't have an epidural because of a theoretical risk of bleeding into the spine. I wasn't planning on an epidural, but this wasn't actually conveyed to me, so when I thought I did want one, I was shocked and angry to find out it wasn't available to me. The only reason we knew I was a carrier was because I was tested, since my father-in-law does have Factor XI deficiency, and he does have bleeding problems. We wanted to know if that was a concern for our children and if it would affect circumcision (being a carrier can make one have bleeding problems, but it is a lot less likely than if someone is homozygous for the deficiency). This means that literally tens of thousands of Jewish women have had epidurals without anyone knowing they were carriers, and I felt like this was more about legal liability than reasonable care.

In other words, this woman was denied an epidural because of being a carrier for a genetic issue (*hemophilia C*) that hadn't actually impacted her life thus far. I don't know whether she was given information about safe alternatives, or whether she was allowed to speak up to say she'd accept the risk that an epidural might bring, but those are conversations that definitely need to be had before labor starts. Also, this emphasizes the importance of having a partner, relative, doula, or other person with you who can advocate for you during labor, such as by discussing whether you will accept the risk of an epidural.

Pregnant Jews should be encouraged to think about the benefits and risks of various types of pain relief and to begin to set out preferences in advance. "There is no Jewish position on using drugs such as an epidural during labor. There is nothing written in Jewish traditional about natural childbirth, nor is there any standard belief about the value of pain" (Falk & Judson, 2004, p. 54). Remember that it is your body and your choice.

Praying During Labor

A form of pain relief that is frequently mentioned is prayer. I referred to it above in regard to pre-birth preparations, so I just want to emphasize it again here. "Prayer and atonement are two duties in the daily life of a Jew. Those who are accustomed to pray, repent, and give to charity in their daily lives also do so during childbirth" (Klein, 1998/2000, p. 142). Reciting biblical verses or traditional prayers is not the same as incantations, which would be considered magic and not allowed (Klein, 1998/2000, p. 149).

In an ultra-Orthodox community, a woman in labor will pray and if she cannot, her mother will continue for her, as "a woman in pain, even in danger, who pleads for another who suffers, rather than pleading for herself, is considered truly righteous; the hope is that God will grant mercy to both women" (Klein, 1998/2000, p. 153).

Although prayer can be viewed as pain relief, it is also simply part of Jewish life, so a Jewish woman praying during labor may not necessarily be doing so as a way of decreasing discomfort. She could instead feel as though she is fulfilling her role as a Jew. "Religious rituals enable Jews to share with others both joyous and frightening experiences, so no one should have to face these alone. Prayer can also redeem a person's isolation, if someone else is praying for or with that person or if others in the same predicament have uttered the same prayer before" (Klein, 1998/2000, p. 255).

Problems During Labor

When conflicts arise between a woman's health and the baby's, the mother will nearly always be prioritized. I explored this above in reference to miscarriage and abortion, but wanted to return to it here because problems can occur during labor, and the medical professionals together with the birthing person, and, if appropriate, their partner and/or relatives may need to make difficult choices. "The question of priorities regarding human lives at risk is not a recent problem of medical ethics, but one the sages discussed in Talmudic times. In the special case of birth, when labor was unduly difficult and human life was at risk, there was no doubt in their minds about whether the mother's or the baby's life had priority, because the *Mishnah* [also known as the oral Torah] stated the law on this matter … It is left to the midwife's or the physician's discretion to remove the baby to save the mother's life" (Klein, 1998, pp. 159-160).

As an interesting side note, "the *Mishnah*, written almost two thousand years ago considers caesarean section, not only on dead women, but also on live women" (Klein, 1998/2000, p. 160). It is intriguing to know how long ago people were carrying out and writing about c-sections. For those who are more observant, a baby born via c-section traditionally "does not enjoy the inheritance rights of a first-born child: only the baby born normally [i.e. vaginally], subsequently, enjoys these rights" (Klein, 1998/2000, p. 161). As inheritance rights are often a thing of the past now, this is not a guiding principle anymore.

Sadly, problems during birth, including stillbirth, can happen to anyone, and it isn't always clear why. In cases of stillbirth, parents can choose how to mourn or honor their lost little one. I will return to this later, in the chapter on the Jewish postpartum period.

Midwives

Depending on where someone lives, having a midwife (as opposed to or in addition to an obstetrician or other doctor) during birth may be the cultural norm. For obvious reasons—including cultural or physical safety, or more knowledge about Jewish customs—some Jewish women would prefer to be served by Jewish midwives. "Jewish midwives have traditionally offered emotional support, physical help, expertise, and even spiritual guidance to their clients. Since Talmudic times, Jews valued midwives' skills highly and were reluctant to trust a non-Jew with the dangerous task of bringing their newborn infants into the world. Jewish communities, therefore, often secured their own midwifery service, so even the poorest women could give birth with professional assistance" (Klein, 1998/2000,

p. 121). Midwives have been respected in Jewish culture; a "Jewish midwife is a "wise woman" in the Mishnah (second century), implying greater knowledge and skill than other women" (Klein, 1998/2000, p. 123).

In the aftermath of the massacre in Israel on October 7, 2023, I found a safe space in a community with a number of Jewish midwives and doulas, including Betsy Dwek. Betsy is an observant Jewish woman and midwife whose love of Torah and midwifery greatly inform her practice. She has an interest in the potential for profoundly spiritual experiences during pregnancy and childbirth for mothers, families, and the people who support them. She lives and works in North London and can be found at www.betsydwekmidwife.co.uk. Betsy generously wrote about the Jewish view of midwives:

> What is the definition of a midwife in Hebrew? The most common modern translation, simply put, is *meyalledet* מְיַלֶּדֶת, which is similar to the Old English meaning "with woman," one who helps the birthing woman. Yet deeper inspection of the etymology connected to the words for midwife used biblically and within rabbinic scripture reveals a connection to wisdom: another word for midwife is *hakhama* חֲכָמָה, wise woman, like the French *sage-femme*. The same root for birth, יָלַד, is used for one who has the ability to watch the unfolding consequences of actions, as displayed in this idiomatic story in the collection of the Ethical Teachings of the Fathers in the Talmud: *"Which is the correct path to which a man should cleave? ... Rabbi Shimon said, foresight (literally, the person who sees the baby being born, the person who has the ability to perceive the developing events)"* (*Pirkei Avot* 2:9; my own translation).
>
> It is not a coincidence then that midwives were historically and are still currently held in such high regard within the Jewish community. The first recorded account of midwives physically and emotionally helping women during birth is found in the Hebrew Bible in the cases of Tamar and her twins, with legal ramifications since the midwife signaled who the first-born was, and even naming the infants, highlighting their personalities, and Rachel and her difficult and tragic labor with Binyamin, where the midwife helps ease her passage into death as she brings about life. Even God is literally called a midwife when speaking of taking the Israelites out

of another nation, Egypt (Ecclesiates Rabbah 3:8:2). This lays the strong foundation for midwifery to be a holy calling, with spiritual, legal, practical and psychological dimensions.

There is another archetypal story that deserves a thorough reading in the book of Exodus chronicling the deeds of two midwives named Shifra and Puah. Pharaoh orders a genocidal decree to the "Hebrew midwives" to kill all male Israelites at the time of birth. In fear of God and not the ruling power of the land, Shifra and Puah disobey the command, and are thus honored by God "building them houses," exegetically understood as expanding their families and making them honored and distinguished. Yet we've skipped over something important here. The statement "Hebrew midwives" is vague. It could mean either midwives who were Hebrew themselves, making little sense that Pharaoh would ask someone to murder their own people, or Egyptian midwives to the Hebrews, in which case this shows their defiance as containing even greater moral courage. Midwives exemplified by this case are depicted as politically non-compliant, at great risk and cost to themselves, defenders and protectors of the intrinsic value of human life. This is what God rewards by granting them the very essence of what they serve to uphold: family and righteous living.

Nowadays it is very common to find many Jewish women in the service of midwifery, supporting women and their families during their various child-birth journeys. In fact, there is great emphasis placed on women being cared for by other women during this transformative period, and the community as a whole is expected to provide food, emotional support, and spiritual significance to this potentially volatile immediate postnatal period. Yet this does not replace the innate value of midwives, whose role is to guide and witness a woman as she undergoes immense metamorphosis, as the nameless midwives of Genesis exhibit in their capacity to care for women during labor and birth. We are shown how to act through the behavior of Shifra and Puah and their remarkable "inaction" leading to the saving of lives. Much of what we celebrate in midwives" skills is their ability to be with-woman and hold the space for the woman herself to act. How beautiful it is to discover that these multitudes are contained within the very essence of Jewish writings, philosophy, and practice.

Placenta

The third stage of labor is birthing the placenta and physically separating the baby from the home it has been nourished in for all those months. Many people choose to have their partner or another special person, such as a friend, relative, or doula, cut the cord, while others rely on the attending healthcare professional to do this. Traditionally, "[t]he obstetrician or midwife cuts the umbilical cord with a sharp tool, cleans the baby, and disposes of the placenta. In the past, the midwife also salted and swaddled the infant. From biblical times until the early twentieth century, salting and swaddling were common practices in many Jewish communities. Women thought that the salting of newborns was vital for the baby's skin, to thicken and harden it and thereby protect the inner organs, and to prevent rashes. Salt may help the navel to heal, but since biblical times it has been a well-known protection against the Evil Eye" (Klein, 1998/2000, p. 191). Salt is not generally employed today, but perhaps still is in some more observant or more superstitious families.

As for what people do with the placenta, "the Talmud says that after delivery, the placenta should be preserved in a bowl with oil, straw, or sand, depending on the wealth of its bearer. The custom reflects a belief in the symbiotic connection between the placenta and the child" (Falk & Judson, 2004, p. 80). Further writings say the placenta should be buried and the parents should "pledg[e] to the earth that the body of the new person will be returned when he/she dies(ibid.)." Today, some people do choose to take it home, bury it, or turn it into pills (the efficacy of placenta pills for humans has not been proven, despite it being known that some other mammals choose to eat the afterbirth). In the past, "[s]pecial customs surrounded the disposal of the afterbirth. Through the ages, people believed the placenta to be an extension of the baby and feared that if a stranger somehow acquired it, this person gain control over the baby. Thus, the Talmud recommends that it should be hidden, a practice that remained prevalent among some Jews at the beginning of the twentieth century, when birth usually took place at home" (Klein, 1998/2000, p. 193).

I got to know artist, midwife, writer, activist and Jewish mother Laura Godfrey-Isaacs through the same community where I met Betsy Dwek.

I learned that Laura was very knowledgeable about the placenta, and how it fits into Jewish culture. She kindly wrote about it for this book:

> I wonder, dear reader, if, after giving birth, you got sight of your placenta, and with those gathered, there was appreciation, and gratitude, for the beauty and majesty of this miraculous organ?
>
> A bit like the elegance of a seal swimming in water, contrasted with their awkward ungainly movements on land, the placenta, a beautifully constructed and engineered piece of bodily machinery, that dynamically drives the growth of a new human being during pregnancy, becomes a lumpen, inert slab of flesh after birth, holding its secrets close. Placenta, *shilya* "afterbirth" in Hebrew, means cake in Latin, *mutterkuchen* (mother cake) in German, and *plakoúnta* (flat, slab-like) in Greek.
>
> Western maternity services focus on the placenta predominantly during the antenatal period or at birth (where it can partially or completely refuse to come away). However, many myths, beliefs, and traditions center the placenta as a site of power, continuity, and connection, after birth. What happens to the placenta when separated from the mother and baby is believed by many cultures to influence the life of the child it nourishes, and therefore how we treat it, honor it, and dispose of it is linked to the child's ultimate path in life.
>
> Ancient Egyptians believed the placenta was like a child's angel or secret guardian. In Cambodia, it is deemed to be the origin of the soul. In Malaysia, for example, the placenta is often prepared with salt and tamarind and buried with books and drawing utensils under the doorway of the family house, ensuring the child will grow up to be a hardworking student. The Maori people of New Zealand use the term *Whenua* to denote placenta and land, and believe burial symbolizes a continuation of the connection between the baby and mother earth. In Bali, the tradition of enclosing the placenta in a coconut shell and hanging it in a tree in a graveyard is believed to protect the baby from illness and misfortune. The village of Bayund Gede has been designated a National Heritage Site due to the hundreds of hanging placentas found in the grounds.
>
> Western scientific understanding of the vital role the placenta plays in childbirth is, like most research into women's health, underfunded and patchy. Though developing expertise in this area, particularly from immunology, casts

new information and insights that should make us all reconsider its powerful nature and lead to a reconsideration, a reverence even for its influence way beyond the antenatal period.

So keen are we in the labor ward to dispense with the placenta that most births involve an artificial injection of oxytocin for the third stage (delivery of the placenta)—that most vital of hormones of labor, breastfeeding, and social bonding—followed by a sharp pull from the midwife, and zero effort from the birthing person. Swiftly, this is followed by cutting of the cord and in some cases the cord blood being donated to others. This cord blood contains miraculous shape-shifting stem cells that can help treat a range of diseases, such as some cancers, immune deficiencies, and genetic disorders.

If we were to incorporate current scientific research findings into the placenta's role, as well as cultural and spiritual meanings, can we imagine a change in practice that saw us treat the placenta differently? One where we give it the due care and attention it deserves, as well as create ways to preserve it for ritual or ceremonial purposes? In this way we could incorporate care of the placenta into the reclaimed fourth trimester period (the three months after birth) which centers rest, recovery, and connection. In this way we could honor the profound role this vital organ has played in our baby's life in-utero, and take time to consider its spiritual and symbolic power after birth.

One such way is to exercise delayed cord clamping—a now common, though not universal practice. We could wait at least one minute, if not till the cord was completely drained of blood or it came off in its own time (Lotus Birth). This would prioritize the baby's health in recovering the residual blood from the placenta and umbilical cord and delay severing the baby from mother, rather than rushing to cut it or donate those precious stem cells to others.

Specific Jewish traditions are few, but recorded in the Talmud, we are prescribed a practice of placing the placenta in a bowl, rubbing it with straw, salt, and oil, and burying it a few days after birth. Some believe the placenta represents the Tree of Life—a symbol found in many religions, cultures, and beliefs, which denotes our connection to the earth, knowledge, and the continuity of life. The central umbilical cord implanted into the middle of the placenta branches off into multiple vessels migrating across the surface making it appear like the stems and branches of a tree. In *Kabbalah*, the Jewish mystical tradition, an iconic tree of life with ten different spheres (*sefirot*) encompasses archetypal elements such as wisdom, beauty, mercy, and intelligence. Many people have created their own rituals around these ideas, burying their placenta in a garden, next to a favorite tree, or planting a new tree above it.

A more prosaic use of the placenta is to ingest it, much like other mammals do after birth and there are many ways of cooking and eating it. The placenta, as a by-product of the body, like breast milk or sucking bleeding gums, would not be considered forbidden, and is therefore kosher, if eaten by a Jewish person. Nor is there considered to be a prohibition against this due to *marit ayin* (the eating of animal blood which has been separated from the body). In addition, the eating of placenta could be done for health purposes, which would be permitted. Chewing on a raw piece has long been used by traditional birth attendants to stem postnatal bleeding. Drying, grinding it into a powder, and encapsulating it to ingest as pills over time is a recent possibility. Others designate recipes in order to serve it up to the mother, as a bolognese, stir-fry, or stroganoff.

Whatever ways you find to engage with your placenta, recognizing it as an important part of your childbirth journey is bound to be of value, enriching your understanding of the vital role it takes in pregnancy and birth, and providing opportunities for ritual and ceremony after birth. This miraculous, powerful cosmic body should finally be reclaimed as an important character in the story of your birth and the future health of your baby.

One parent in my research study said that they made the Jewish choice to bury the placenta, while other Jewish parents told me they variously ignored it, took a photo of it, turned it into pills, or let the hospital dispose of it.

Immediate Post-Birth Rituals

If the mother has Psalm 121 (*Shir Hamalos*) up in her birthing room, it is thought that this should be one of the first things that the baby sees when it has been born. This is so the baby can be exposed to holy writings and religious thoughts right away (Ertel, n.d., n.p.). If the psalm has not been up, the baby can be shown Hebrew letters. The Lubavitcher Rebbe, a Hasidic rabbi, was said to have explained, "It is true that the child was just born, and cannot yet distinguish between light and dark or between sweet and bitter. Nevertheless, since the child has already come into the world and possesses eyes with which to see the world, we should see to it that the first thing the child sees is the letters of the Hebrew alphabet, from whose combinations all of creation has come into being" (Weisberg, 2024, n.p.).

"Jewish tradition suggests only two brief blessings at the moment of delivery, perhaps because the moment is so overwhelming that one does not need a lot of outside words or formal rituals to be made intensely aware of God's presence. There is a tradition of saying a short blessing at the moment of delivery, a thank-you to God for having survived this most difficult time with mother and baby alive" (Falk & Judson, 2004, p. 78). Some will say *Birkat Hagomel*, to recognize that the birthing parent just went through something dangerous. This connection between birth and death was stronger in past times. "Today, an element of fear surrounds birth, but the experience of tragedy is rare enough that women do not usually believe that they will die at this time. Thus, specific prayers for childbirth are often omitted from modern prayer books, [and] we are no longer congratulated for our deliverance, only for the baby's safe arrival" (Klein, 1998/2000, p. 201).

Many people will say prayers to welcome the baby and thank God for the new little one. Those who follow tradition more closely will pray in a way that is differentiated, depending on if it is the mother or the father who is praying, and if they have welcomed a son or a daughter. The mother will always wash her hands and offer the prayer of gratitude *Shehecheyanu*, while the father will say *Shehecheyanu* for a daughter and *Ha-tov V'hameitiv* for a son. The latter prayer is different because it is thought to celebrate something that brings joy to an entire community, while the former is more about individual happiness. Obviously, some people will find this biased, so they make different prayer choices, and there is some suggestion that either prayer could be used, regardless of gender (Falk & Judson, 2004, p. 79).

CHAPTER 5

Jewish Postpartum

During pregnancy, many people only focus on the birth and tend to forget that once you have gone through labor, you actually have a baby to care for and you will also need time to recover. When I work with clients, I use a generic postpartum preferences document so we can explore their hopes and plans (see Appendix 4). This includes a range of topics, such as what foods they want to eat, who will be visiting them, how to handle issues that arise, and so on. However, for Jewish people, there are some specific aspects to this that need to be considered, such as eating kosher food, or going to synagogue. In general, "[i]f mother and baby are well, the first week after delivery is a time for celebration, and family and friends visit the new parents. The 'week of the son,' celebrated since Talmudic times, culminates with the circumcision, although Jews have also celebrated the first week after the birth of a daughter" (Klein, 1998/2000, p. 205). However, traditions have been changing over time, as will be discussed in what follows.

Jewish Postpartum Preferences

I have suggested a Jewish-specific postpartum preferences document to cover additional things that may be relevant (Appendix 5). "Traditionally, Jews have believed that childbirth depends on a partnership with God, the creator of life, who forms the infant's soul, supervises pregnancy, and determines the outcome of birth. From ancient times to the present, Jewish parents have acknowledged and confirmed this partnership through their prayers and postnatal rituals" (Klein, 1998/2000, p. xxx). In other words, how Jews experience the postpartum period may be influenced by their religious beliefs. It's also important to always keep in mind how diverse

Jewish cultures can be and how that means that each family you meet will have their own perspectives and traditions.

Foods

As expected, different Jewish groups will have varying food traditions, including during pregnancy and the postpartum period, in part because of their specific cultural heritage. A non-birth-related example is that more religious Ashkenazi Jews will not eat rice or beans during Passover, while less traditional ones and also Sephardic Jews do not consider rice or beans to be *kitniyot*, a category of foods not eaten during Passover. The keys to Jewish food preferences or traditions include kosher food and cultural aspects.

Kosher

An important aspect of Jewish food traditions to understand is kosher. Kosher, or *kashrut*, means "proper" or "fit" in Hebrew. Kosher food is sanctioned and allowed based on Jewish law. Some items have to be certified by rabbis in order for religious Jews to eat them. While there are many different aspects to get to grips with in order to follow kosher food laws some of the most important ones are which foods can be eaten, how animals used for meat need to be killed, and the separation between milk and meat.

Some people believe, based on Genesis 1:29, that vegetarianism is the ideal method of eating for Jewish people. "God said, 'See, I give you every seed-bearing plant that is upon all the earth, and every tree that has seed-bearing fruit; they shall be yours for food'" (Genesis 1:29). Keeping a vegetarian or vegan diet would certainly simplify preparing and cooking food, because some of the other laws or guidelines are complex.

For example, others use additional laws, as given in Leviticus 9:1-11:47, to argue that meat is fine to eat, as long as it falls into certain categories. For example, "any animal that has true hoofs, with clefts through the hoofs, and that chews the cud—such you may eat" (Leviticus 11:3). This would include animals such as cows and sheep, but not camels, pigs, or rabbits, among others. In addition, the Torah includes this passage: "These you may eat of all that live in water: anything in water, whether in the seas or in the streams, that has fins and scales—these you may eat. But anything in the seas or in the streams that has no fins and scales, among all the swarming things of the water and among all the other living creatures that are in the water—they are an abomination for you and an abomination for you they shall remain: you shall not eat of their flesh and you shall abominate their carcasses" (Leviticus 11:10-12). This explains why observant Jews will eat fish, but not seafood such as shrimp or lobster. There are further laws, including against eating ravens or ostriches, but as you can see, this strict categorization, which can be considered to be between animals that fall neatly into classes, and those that do not, is the basis for the prohibition against eating particular items.

Furthermore, in some countries, including here in the UK, animal welfare laws require animals to be stunned before they are killed, which is thought to be more humane (as someone who doesn't eat any animal flesh at all, I am not totally convinced by this, but that's a subject for a different book). However, Jewish slaughter does not employ the stunning method. Instead, *shechita*, or Jewish animal slaughter, starts by cutting the animal's throat. This severs the blood vessels and it is believed that animals lose consciousness quickly; some argue that this is humane (again, I won't go into any analysis of this, choosing instead to just state what people claim). Observant Jews cannot eat meat that doesn't follow kosher laws, and that wasn't killed in accordance to *shechita*, ideally by a trained *shochet*, a ritual slaughterer.

A final aspect of kosher food to discuss here is that of *milchig*, *fleishig*, and *pareve*. The phrase "You shall not boil a kid in its mother's milk" is repeated several times in the Torah (Exodus 23:19, Exodus 34:26, and Deuteronomy 14:21). Some believe this is in reference to practices that were carried out by non-Jews, and so telling people not to do it was a way of distinguishing Jews from others. Regardless of the origin or the ultimate meaning, it became the basis for the separation between milk and meat (do not cook meat in milk, which turned into the larger prohibition against serving meat and dairy together). Observant Jews therefore do not eat dairy items, or *milchig*, with meat products, or *fleishig*. In other words, steak cooked in butter or chicken covered in melted cheese would not be kosher. Nor would it be acceptable to have, say, a meat main course and a dairy dessert in the same meal. Religious Jews thus have meat meals or dairy meals, and they likewise have separate sets of plates for these different meals and have separate sinks for those dishes.

Some foods can be eaten with either meat or dairy (or, indeed, on their own), and they are called *pareve* and are considered neutral. Fruits, vegetables, grains, drinks, and ingredients such as vegetable oil or salt are among the many edible items that are classified as pareve.

Incidentally, some believe that kosher laws must be followed even by your pets, if you're a Jewish family. If you were supporting a Jewish family in the postpartum period or if you yourself are Jewish and were cooking for an observant Jewish family, you would need to ensure you were following kosher laws, so that the people could actually eat the dishes you prepared.

A mother described the food she and her husband had during and after birth:

> My daughter was born on *Shabbos* and my midwives came to my house and drove me and my husband to the birthing center. He made *kiddush* and had a meal while I was in labor. Everyone loved my challah. Right after the birth, I had brisket and *challah*. It was so filling and delicious.

Visitors

The concept of who is welcome to come visit is the same for both visits to the hospital and visits to the home. Obviously hospital rules in the former case will also apply, in terms of who can come, how many people can come, and what times they can visit. In the section on birth above, I discussed how there are varying points of view on whether a male partner should be present during birth. If someone is religious and has given birth, it is important to respect their potential distance from their husband, due to *niddah*.

One woman noted:

> All the doctors knew about how to deal with elements of Jewish law to some degree ... They didn't try to get my husband to touch me after the delivery (which I wouldn't have wanted because I was *niddah*).

Regarding other visitors, some new parents will have had a number of people present during the birth, possibly including their relatives, in-laws, and friends. Even if not, some of those people may be eager to meet the new baby as soon as possible. While this might be expected practice within some Jewish subcultures or families, it's nonetheless important to remind those who have given birth that they have a choice. If they want to be alone with their baby (and potentially their partner), that is absolutely valid. It might feel difficult to speak up and to ask people to leave, but the new mother's needs and feelings should come first. The first hour or two with the new baby—sometimes called "the golden hour"—is a really precious time, and it's fine to choose to be in a bubble, without lots of visitors.

Prayers

Some observant new parents will immediately want to pray, as discussed in the last chapter, and some fathers in particular will even want to go to shul to do so. Once the baby and mother have been checked by medical professionals and deemed healthy, praying should be encouraged for those who wish to do so.

Falk and Judson (2004) offer ideas for prayers that can be said when parents bring a new baby home as well as ones for the older sibling/s to say when they meet their new baby sister or brother. It can be difficult for an older child to adjust to this new being, so including them early on, whether through prayer or by having them get and/or receive a present for and/or from the baby, can be beneficial.

Recovery

Recovering from birth is both a physical and emotional matter. "The Rabbis of the Talmud believed that the recovery of a postpartum woman was of such importance that the laws of Shabbat could be broken" (Falk & Judson, 2004, p. 83). In regard to the physical aspects, "[t]he Talmud acknowledges that a woman who has just given birth is in mortal danger and therefore advocates treating her as an invalid for the first thirty days. In Talmudic times, she was attended by other women, who believed that her limbs were disjoined from the immense physical strain of labor and delivery. They kept her room warm, and helped take care of her baby. These women prepared food for her that was intended to reduce uterine bleeding, heal and strengthen her, and increase her supply of breast milk" (Klein, 1998/2000, p. 200). While this deep level of care and attention is, unfortunately, less likely to happen these days, it isn't out of the realm of possibility, and perhaps should be encouraged.

Even if someone is unable or unwilling to fully rest for a month, they should at least be encouraged to spend some days or weeks in or near bed, and they should ideally have others who will take care of the practical elements, such as cleaning, cooking, and changing the baby's diaper. Interestingly, more observant communities may be more attuned to this, as they tend to have a larger number of children and will understand at a cellular level how much they need to rest after birth. One parent explained as follows:

> Postpartum is a very crucial time and there is a huge lack of education about recovery. Because I live in a community where women commonly have eight children, I got much more guidance from them than any health "professionals."

Some new mothers, particularly among the more observant, go to a "recuperation home," where they "are provided with three hot meals a day and the babies are looked after in a nursery and brought to you when they need feeding. Bearing in mind some women [in the more religious communities] have babies every year, it had the feel of a holiday camp—an annual retreat for relaxation and renewal before it was time to go home and have another baby" (Fletcher, 2025, p. 140). In her memoir, Haredi woman Yehudis Fletcher describes how she was "[a]t peace" in this home, where "the women shared baby stories and laughed together, and it brought me joy every day (ibid.)." It's easier for her to be there, being looked after, than being at home with her husband, or staying in a house crowded with relatives. This may be an appealing or necessary option for some mothers and babies.

Self-Care for New Parents

In terms of emotional recovery, new parents should be supported to express their feelings. This may involve reflecting on or debriefing their birth experience (either with a friend, a midwife, a therapist, etc., or on their own), journaling, writing poetry, or similar. It could also mean doing things such as getting a postpartum massage or taking a warm shower while someone else takes care of the baby. For more observant Jews, this can also encompass prayer, whether at home or at synagogue, and, when their lochia (post-birth bleeding) has finished, going to the *mikveh.*

Stillbirth or Infant Death

In the past, Jewish law has not provided any suggestions for how to mourn an infant who was stillborn or who died soon after birth. "In Jewish tradition, parents are not obliged to observe the mourning ritual after stillbirth or the death of an infant within thirty days of birth, and therefore, in the past, it was not customary to mourn this loss formally. A baby who survived for thirty-one days and then died has always been ritually mourned, however" (Klein, 1998, pp. 165-166). It does seem rather a flaw of a framework for life that generally tries to support people through all sorts of transitions and challenges to not offer any clear traditions or guidelines for handling a situation as horrible as an infant death and also to arbitrarily act as if a baby who died before 31 days wasn't really alive. To add to the pain of this, "[i]n traditional practice, there is only the burial of the body in an unmarked grave in a special section of the cemetery" (Dickstein, 1996, p. 367).

Furthermore, "[t]raditionally, Jewish parents have not attended the burial of their newborn infant. The burial society makes all necessary arrangements, and still today many advise parents against attendance. Some Jewish burial societies bury the infant with an older person, whereas others bury the infant in an unmarked grave. Some burial societies do not inform parents where the infant is buried, others do" (Klein, 1998/2000, p. 167). On top of that, such a death was seen as a "private tragedy" (Klein, 1998/2000, p. 258) (even if it would have been talked about in the community), and since Jewish mourning practices, which are usually communal, wouldn't have been observed, the parents would have felt incredibly alone with their loss. This all seems quite cruel and wouldn't bring any sense of relief, support, or closure to the grieving parents.

"In modern times, Jews have questioned this" (Klein, 1998/2000, p. 165) so people have started make their own decisions about it. Some Conservative rabbis came together in the 1990s to challenge Jewish tradition and to recommend a change in practice (see Dickstein, 1996). "Nowadays, some Jews want social recognition of their grief when pregnancy ends in tragedy and observe all or part of the mourning cycle, or they create their own mourning ceremony" (Klein, 1998/2000, p. 58). As an example, the United Synagogue, a major British charity for Jews, recommends that fetuses who are stillborn at 21 weeks or later be buried. They write, "Any foetus which miscarries at 21 weeks or more must be buried in a Jewish cemetery. They will be attended to with dignity and tenderness, and will be placed in an area that is set aside for such purposes. In some instances, the parents choose a Hebrew name for the baby but usually the *Chevra Kaddisha* will give a name whilst preparing the remains for burial. If a male foetus is sufficiently developed a circumcision will also be carried out" (United Synagogue, n.d., n.p., sic). As mentioned earlier in the book, the *Chevra kadisha* (sometimes also spelled kaddisha) is the Jewish burial society.

Other suggested ritual responses now include reciting prayers for the recovery of the grieving parents and also for the mother herself to recite the prayer for "thanksgiving for deliverance from danger. As tragic as the loss of the baby is, she must still acknowledge that she faced physical danger and survived" (Dickstein, 1996, p. 372). "The community must respond by fulfilling its obligation for...visiting the sick...The family should be visited by close friends, meals can be provided and other services offered by the broader community" (ibid.). When they feel ready, the parents can also immerse in the *mikveh.*

Nowadays, some people also suggest a proper funeral and burial service for the baby. "There is a need to mark and mourn this potential life that came so close to being, and to respond to the loss and grief of the expectant parents and their community. As discussed above, the issue of the viability of the third trimester fetus is a significant factor. For a full response to stillbirth, we turn to the rituals associated with burial and mourning" (ibid.).

In terms of the practicalities, circumcision of a boy baby is optional (see below for much more on this topic) (Dickstein, 1996, p. 372). "The funeral should be held as soon as possible. However, to enable the mother to attend, the burial may certainly be delayed until she recovers enough physical strength to be present at the cemetery. The service would consist of prayers, psalms and other readings" (Dickstein, 1996, p. 373). It is thought that there should be no eulogy, but that the rabbi should "speak words of comfort to the family" (ibid.). The family should tear the clothes or a piece of black cloth as they would for any other death.

As for where this should take place, "[b]urial should be in a Jewish cemetery. Often, cemeteries have a special section for the graves of stillborns and infants. The stillborn may also be buried in a family plot. Many funeral homes and cemeteries reduce or do not charge a fee to bury a stillborn" (Dickstein, 1996, p. 372).

After the funeral, it is absolutely acceptable for the family to mourn. "A meal of concern should be provided by the community on the return of the family from the cemetery. The family might also light a 21-hour *yahrzeit* candle or even a Shabbat candle. When contrasted with the traditional seven-day candle, this more quickly extinguished candle symbolizes that the potential life of the baby did not come to fruition" (Dickstein, 1996, p. 373). Jews traditionally have a seven-day *shiva*, or mourning period, when the bereaved individuals do not work or leave the house, and when other people bring them food and spend time grieving with them. "The Jewish mourning ritual disrupts everyday life—work stops for a full week—and Jews clearly had to draw a line somewhere concerning the mourning of a lost baby, when this was a common occurrence. How does one not mourn a stillborn baby or an infant who survived birth and died soon after, however?" (Klein, 1998/2000, p. 166). It is suggested that in the case of stillbirth or early infant death, the *shiva* period be limited to one day (Dickstein, 1996, p. 373). I would suggest that families decide for themselves what feels right. A *shiva* of one day may not be enough. The family can also recite *kaddish*, or the mourner's prayer, and can also honor the *yahrzeit,* or anniversary, of the death (Dickstein, 1996, p. 374).

Clearly, then, traditions are being updated when it comes to the very sad loss of babies, either through stillbirth or soon after being born, and this is, I believe, positive, as it recognizes that parents cannot be expected to simply move on without acknowledgement of their bereavement.

Postpartum Depression

Another difficult experience in the postpartum period is depression. Many, perhaps most, new parents experience the "baby blues," not least due to the change of hormones in the immediate time period after birth. However, postnatal depression is a more serious and more long-lasting change to mood, and it's thought to affect at least 10% of people who have just given birth (NHS, 2022, n.p.). Signs of postpartum depression include "a persistent feeling of sadness and low mood, lack of enjoyment and loss of interest in the wider world, lack of energy and feeling tired all the time, trouble sleeping at night and feeling sleepy during the day, finding it difficult to look after yourself and your baby, withdrawing from contact with other people, problems concentrating and making decisions, [and] frightening thoughts—for example, about hurting your baby" (ibid.). If you or someone you are supporting or are close to is experiencing any of these symptoms, it is important to get help as soon as possible. Such help might include medication or talking therapies.

There is also a serious condition called postpartum psychosis, which is much rarer (only about 0.1% of newly delivered parents get this), and which often involves hallucinations, mania, delusions, and other quite serious symptoms (NHS, 2020, n.p.). Treatment options might involve in-patient therapy (usually the baby can go with the mother to these places), anti-psychotic medications, or cognitive-behavioral therapy.

There is no shame in feeling depressed or worried in the weeks or months after your baby's birth, and it is essential that you get the help you need, so you don't keep suffering. One charity estimates that 25% of new Jewish parents experience postpartum depression (Menucha, 2019, n.p.).

One new parent discussed how she had postpartum depression, but didn't get the support she needed when it came to exploring the role Jewishness might have played in it:

> I have had two years of psychotherapy. We only skirted around how being Jewish may or may not be a factor in my poor mental health. It is only later that I am learning more about inter-generational trauma. It would be good if mental health practitioners had some awareness of this.

It would be hugely beneficial for healthcare professionals, relatives, and others supporting Jewish parents in the postpartum period to acknowledge that Jews are often—though obviously not always—traumatized by what has beset them individually and as a people throughout history. This can manifest through them being fearful about the future for themselves and their babies, or worrying about food supplies and antisemitism. It can also present itself through a range of other characteristics or feelings.

Certainly, new Jewish parents can experience postpartum depression unrelated to their Jewishness, but their cultural and religious identity may be an additional factor, and it is one that should be explored.

Besides more general talking therapies, there is some specialist help for Jewish people with perinatal depression or other mood disorders, such as an organization called Menucha.

Naming

Many Jewish children receive both a name that works in the language where they live, and also a Hebrew name (sometimes this is the Hebrew version of their name, such as Deborah/Dvora). Some even get a Yiddish name too. The initial naming tends to happen after birth, with a more elaborate naming some days later. This latter naming would then include an explanation of the name and the reasons behind it.

"Traditionally, Ashkenazi Jews have not named a baby after a living relative, but after one who has died, to honor his or her memory. In contrast, Sephardic, North African, and Middle Eastern and Asian Jews have called their name after living relatives. Sephardic Jews have sometimes derived names from the circumstances of birth ... Orthodox Jews still favor the traditional naming patterns, in which family names are passed from generation to generation, fostering a sense of family continuity and tradition. When a baby is named after a well-loved relative, the child may grow up identifying with this ancestor and may be proud to continue in family footsteps. Jewish parents have never given a newborn the name of a baby who had died previously" (Klein, 1998/2000, p. 239).

Much more will be said about naming shortly, but for now, I will just note that it is important to recognize that many Jews will not name their baby right away, and they should not be pressured by the hospital or others to do so. One parent had a good experience regarding this, with the hospital respecting her heritage:

> They let me not name each child before going home, for example.

Circumcision

All right, this is a big, emotive, meaty (pardon the pun) topic, and I'm acutely aware that this brings up numerous opinions and feelings for many people. For some Jews, circumcision is just so standard and expected that there's no discussion about it. Others are adamantly against it. There's also a swathe of Jewish people who just aren't sure and who have mixed feelings, so they need more information. So let's cut (sorry again) to the chase.

Defining Circumcision

Circumcision in a Jewish context means removing the tip/foreskin of the penis. This takes place in a ceremony called a *brit milah*, or *bris,* which means "covenant of circumcision." The actual removal is carried out by a *mohel.* The Torah verses that are the basis for this are Genesis 17:10-14: "Such shall be the covenant between Me and you and your offspring to follow which you shall keep: every male among you shall be circumcised. You shall circumcise the flesh of your foreskin, and that shall be the sign of the covenant between Me and you. And throughout the generations, every male among you shall be circumcised at the age of eight days. As for the homeborn slave and the one bought from an outsider who is not of your offspring, they must be circumcised, homeborn and purchased alike. Thus shall My covenant be marked in your flesh as an everlasting pact. And if any male who is uncircumcised fails to circumcise the flesh of his foreskin, that person shall be cut off from kin; he has broken My covenant" (Genesis 17:10-14, translation from Sefaria, n.d., n.p.). Just to explain a little more, this is done because Abraham was said to have circumcised himself at the age of 99 years old as well as his sons, Isaac and Ishmael, in order to enter a covenant with God, so "undergoing this process means that [babies] are entering into a covenant between them and God" (Markovits, n.d., n.p.).

Before we get into it, I want to say that Jewish circumcision is for males only; while even male circumcision is controversial in some circles, it's really important to differentiate it from female circumcision, which is also called female genital mutilation. As you might guess from the name, female genital mutilation involves partially or completely removing the external genitals from a female baby or child (or sometimes even an adult female) and it changes the function, appearance, and sensation of their genitals drastically, not infrequently causing problems that can last for the rest of the person's life. While female genital mutilation is practiced by certain, mostly Muslim and/or African cultures, it is widely condemned around the world and many are agitating for an end to it.

Jewish or Jewish-style circumcision, on the other hand, is still provocative as a topic, but certainly not universally denounced. In the United States, for example, male circumcision rates across all ethnicities average 80%, with some variation depending on ethnicity; circumcision is even recommended as a standard approach as a way of preventing or combatting sexually transmitted diseases in some circumstances (Morris et al., 2014, n.p.). Also, other, non-Jewish peoples around the world have circumcised or continue to circumcise for ritual or religious reasons of their own.

Boys and men can get circumcised at any age by a doctor in the hospital if they have medical reasons for doing so. For instance, if they have *phimosis*, which is a tight foreskin, this can be released, or if they have an inflammation to the penis head and foreskin, which is called balanoposthitis, then circumcision might be indicated. Some people also simply ask the doctor to circumcise their baby boy at birth. This might be for cultural reasons, or because they worry about the risk of urinary tract infections, sexually transmitted diseases, hygiene, or other issues. Medical circumcision is not the exact same thing as ritual circumcision, as the latter "involves the excision of the prepuce, the tearing of the mucous membrane to expose the glans penis, and suction of the wound, followed by its dressing. Father and circumciser recite blessings. The foreskin thus removed and the flow of the infant's blood are the Jew's offerings to God. In this way, a boy is given full membership in the Jewish community" (Klein, 1998/2000, p. 211).

For it to be a Jewish circumcision, it generally needs to be carried out by a *mohel*, who is a specially trained professional, an "expert in the medical and surgical techniques of circumcision who performs the procedure for Jewish babies. However, a *mohel's* expertise goes beyond just the technical skills. A *mohel* is also knowledgeable in the customs and traditions behind *bris milah* (*brit-milah*), which represents the covenant between God and the descendants of Abraham in Jewish belief" (Markovits, n.d., n.p.) Not only is it thought to be less painful when carried out by an experienced *mohel* (Shechet & Fried, 1996, n.p.), but it also then is in accordance with Jewish law. "Thus, if you are a Jewish parent who has a child who needs to be circumcised, it is important for you to choose a *mohel* rather than a doctor due to the fact that in the Jewish belief, the act of circumcision itself, *Bris Milah* (*Brit-Milah*) is a religious observance" (USA Mohel, n.d., n.p.).

It is essential to understand that circumcision is considered a key Jewish act. "The circumcision is the most important of all the religious ceremonies after birth. Jews circumcise their baby boys on the eighth day after delivery if the infant is in good health. Jews have imbued the rite of circumcision with great spiritual significance because it maintains the Covenant between God and Abraham, between God and the Jewish people. The Bible warns that one who does fulfil this duty is 'cut off' by God from the community; he receives the ultimate divine punishment because God cuts off his soul from its spiritual source. Throughout the ages, rabbis have offered at least twenty different reasons for the importance of circumcision" (Klein, 1998/2000, p. 211). It can be stressful and can bring up many different thoughts. "Performance of this rite can make parents aware of the importance of continuing Jewish tradition, or it can become the focus of a conscious rejection of Jewish life. In addition, circumcision can be an occasion that cements family ties or an issue for family crisis. Thus, today, more than ever before, circumcision can have spiritual, religious, social, educational, and psychological significance" (Klein, 1998/2000, p. 211).

Interestingly, some less traditionally observant Jews moved away from circumcision for some time but have now moved back towards it. For example, "[i]n recent years, Reform Jews have returned to celebrating this and other religious rituals, maintaining certain major differences from the Orthodox. (One is the inclusion of women in the performance of the ritual, and another is the recognition of patrilineal as well as matrilineal descent. Thus, Reform rabbis accept that the son of a Jewish father and non-Jewish mother can be considered Jewish if both parents are committed to raising him as a Jew, just like the son of a Jewish mother and non-Jewish father.)

The Reform movement now recognizes the importance of circumcision to Jewish identity in a mixed society" (Klein, 1998/2000, p. 214).

In short, while circumcision is seen as one of the ways to physically and spiritually mark a boy as a Jew and to link him to his relatives and ancestors and community, that is not the only reason why some people choose to do it, and also, despite that, some choose not to. In other words, it is a complicated subject, so next we'll look at some of the reasons for and against it.

One parent shared a story that makes it clear how controversial or misunderstood circumcision can be:

> After my son's birth, I asked a midwife if she thought he would be healthy enough for his circumcision at 8 days old. The midwife raised a concern to Social Services due to a lack of training. The concern was quickly quashed by more experienced professionals in the maternity hospital, but it was still a bad experience for me postpartum.

Reasons for Circumcision

All right, well, obviously the key reason for circumcision for most religious Jews is that it's considered an important part of being male and Jewish. If you're observant and you believe it's part of our covenant with God, you're not really going to need more reasons than that. It would be like me asking, "What's your reason for celebrating Shabbat?" Sure, you could come up with some more reasons, like the fact that it's nice to have family time and a chance to do something other than to work, but they're all going to be secondary to the religious tenets. I already explored the covenant above, so I won't go into it more in this section. Instead, here are some additional reasons people offer.

A professor of Jewish history adds an extra question to the discussion: "Outside of ancient Israel, circumcision is usually a puberty rite, clearly related to fertility. The removal of the foreskin admits the young male into manhood by readying him symbolically for procreation. The symbol and substance are closely related and meaning is not hard to identify. In the Torah, however, the rite is relocated to the earliest stage of infancy when the child is little more than an extension of his mother. What possible connection can the rite have to fertility in this new context?" (Schorsch, 1994, n.p.). For Jews, circumcision may not traditionally be seen as a fertility rite, but some further reading suggests there is a link. At the ripe old age of 99, Abraham gets circumcised to show his connection to God. He and his wife have heretofore been childless, but Abraham's circumcision totally changes their circumstances. "Sarah becomes pregnant with Isaac only after her elderly husband has undergone the operation. Circumcision is as critical to setting human history on a new course as the original call to Abraham to leave his native land and his father's house. Fertility comes to Sarah at the age of 90 with Abraham's entry into the sacred covenant" (Schorsch, 1994, n.p.). To sum up, "circumcision as symbol goes beyond fertility. It must do justice to the reciprocal nature of a covenantal relationship. If, on the one hand, it recalls the Creator as Procreator, the Guarantor of fertility to an unsettled clan, on the other it expresses human allegiance and devotion to God" (Schorsch, 1994, n.p.). In other words, there may be some belief that circumcision can increase fertility. It would be interesting to see further research on this.

Another reason some people believe circumcision is worth doing is because it symbolically forces a separation; this can be considered an anthropological perspective on circumcision. There are a few varying separations to account for here: a division between the baby boy and his mother (i.e., her body and his), the separation between male and female (since only males get circumcised), and also literally and figuratively slicing the Jewish body so it's different from the non-Jewish one (because while some other groups circumcise, it is thought that only Jews do so because of their covenant with God). While Jewish circumcision takes place eight days after birth, it does bear some relationship to some puberty rituals in other cultures. "Puberty rituals serve to symbolically separate boys from their mother's body, as initiation and circumcision inaugurate them into the secrets of the adult man's world. As their 'last bit of femininity' is cut away, the surrounding ceremony is meant to mark their 'second' or 'real' birth—the moment they become men independent of their mothers" (Schipper, 2024, p. 106).

For some less observant Jews, it is mainly for tradition's sake or for the sense of being Jewish that they circumcise. For example, someone might be in an intermarriage and may never attend synagogue, but may still choose to circumcise because "that's what we Jews do." All this is to say that a circumcision can create a sense of community, whether it's about age, position in the world, or ethnicity/religion.

If a religious reason or community-identity reason isn't quite enough for you, however, maybe because you're secular, then why else do people circumcise? There's often a major concern about health and hygiene behind the choice. I've heard a number of people say that boys and men aren't great at cleaning around or under their foreskins. This seems to do males a disservice, by suggesting they do a shoddy job at using soap and water in the shower, but apparently "[c]ircumcision makes it simpler to wash the penis" (Mayo Clinic, 2022, n.p.). "Still, boys who haven't been circumcised can be taught to wash regularly beneath the foreskin" (ibid.)

Also, as already noted, circumcision does seem to reduce risks of sexually transmitted diseases, especially HIV (Szabo & Short, 2000, n.p.). While "[m]ale circumcision should be seriously considered as an additional means of preventing HIV in all countries with a high prevalence of infection" (Szabo & Short, 2000, n.p.), it is useful to underline the last phrase in that sentence, "all countries with a high prevalence of infection," because if you live in the West, that is not applicable to you.

Circumcision also can decrease the likelihood of penile issues, such as phimosis, where the foreskin can't be pulled back, and both penile and cervical cancer. You may be surprised by the reference to cervical cancer when it comes to men, since they don't have cervixes, but "[a]lthough cancer of the penis is rare, it's less common in men who have been circumcised… [and] cervical cancer is less common in the female sexual partners of men who have been circumcised" (Mayo Clinic, n.d., n.p.). In other words, it can keep women safe if you circumcise your son, although you won't know when he's an infant if he's asexual or homosexual, thus rendering cervical cancer irrelevant to his future. Still, some protection against penile cancer can be beneficial.

Another health reason is in relation to urinary tract infections. "The single risk factor of lack of circumcision confers a 23.3% chance of urinary tract infection during the lifetime. This greatly exceeds the prevalence of circumcision complications (1.5%), which are mostly minor. The potential seriousness of urinary tract infection supports circumcision as a desirable preventive health intervention in infant males" (Morris & Wisewell, 2013, n.p.).

Then we can add in some of the other reasons that many non-Jews offer, namely that they want their baby son to look like his father, or like the other boys in school, or that they just think circumcised penises look "tidier" or "more attractive" than the uncircumcised variety. I've heard several women comment that they themselves preferred "the look" of circumcised penises and thought other women would feel the same, so they decided to circumcise their sons for the esthetic taste of those boys' (presumed female) future partners. I'm not totally convinced that esthetics should be a major part of your decision-making process, however, and it is slightly odd, perhaps, to be thinking about the attractiveness of your son's penis.

As explained above, there is a foundation in Torah for the choice to circumcise. Interestingly, however, it is not only the covenant that some Jewish people refer to when it comes to circumcising, because some believe that Jewish texts provide other reasons. Maimonides "also said that the ritual was not performed merely to achieve bodily perfection, but also to perfect man's moral shortcomings, because removal of the foreskin counteracted excessive lust, weakened the libido, and sometimes also reduced the pleasure of sexual relations" (Klein, 1998/2000, p. 213). In this case, the idea seems to be to focus the mind on the study of Torah and the relationship to God.

It seems fair to say that for most Jewish people, religious reasons and tradition would be the key points in favor of circumcision, though some of the other potential benefits, such as a reduced risk of urinary tract infections or a lower chance of cancer, may also help sway you in that direction.

One parent explained why she decided on circumcision:

> We believe the world is not random. We were given the Torah and a way to follow a path of truth. Our children were given to us so they can grow in the way of their ancestors going back thousands of years. So of course we had a bris for both of our sons! Thank God there were no complications and it was on the 8th day.

Another added an interesting point:

> Circumcision is important to me because it is cleaner. It is also a feminist issue because if a baby boy grows up and contracts an STD, he is more likely to pass it on if he isn't circumcised.

A third parent noted an inner conflict regarding circumcision:

> We would have circumcised a boy, even though I feel like we don't do other non-necessary things to children's bodies (I didn't, and wouldn't, for example, pierce a baby girl's ears). I was not going to win that argument with my husband or my family, so I am grateful that I didn't have a boy. I don't think the consequences are so severe that I would consider myself part of the no-circ movement, but I do think it goes against our modern ideas of bodily autonomy.

Reasons against Circumcision

All that being said, not all Jews do choose to circumcise. Some really struggle with the choice and want to explore reasons for and against before deciding what to do.

It must be acknowledged that as the mother of two daughters, I have no (fore)skin in the game (sorry). However, we knew when pregnant that if either of our children ended up having a penis, we would not circumcise, and this decision was greeted with much consternation by Jewish relatives and acquaintances. They were convinced that circumcision was the right thing to do as Jews, and the right thing to do for health and hygiene purposes, and the right thing to do generally in today's society, which meant that any uncircumcised boy might feel left out. There was also some disbelief that I'd deny my relatives the dubious pleasure of a *bris.* It was though we were thought to be selfish for not wanting to circumcise this as-yet unborn child. I spent more time than I'd ever imagined having to explain and defend my thoughts about this, which is not exactly what I wanted to be doing while preparing for birth and parenthood.

I know we're not alone in being Jews who are uncertain about circumcision. As you can imagine, the basis of questioning circumcision is more or less the opposite of all the reasons for it that I mentioned in the previous section, with a few added comments and ideas.

Even from an observant point of view, I do think a case could be made that the idea of a covenant could be seen as metaphorical, or perhaps as something dating from a particular time and place that is no longer literally relevant. That is, just as rabbis have always analyzed, explored, and debated many, perhaps all, aspects of Jewish law, religion, and culture, this should and does continue today, and some rabbis may come to the conclusion that Jews can have the covenant and be fully Jewish without the need to circumcise. Maybe new traditions can be developed that involve cutting or ripping material instead of the body, or perhaps we can solely welcome new babies into Jewish life through prayer and ceremony, not surgery. It feels like people might want to consider why God would create newborn babies to look as they do, only to expect a drastic change to them almost immediately. It's a big ask, though of course those in favor of circumcision would say that that's the whole point.

Another thing to consider is that circumcision is irreversible (though I'll come back to foreskin restoration in a moment). Many parents can't imagine wanting to damage or mutilate a child at any stage of their life. The idea of forever changing what was a perfect newborn body is absolutely abhorrent to many. Some argue with this, stating, "one traditional line of Jewish thinking that says God creates man imperfect—uncircumcised—so that man must work to perfect himself," wherein circumcision helps to rectify this (Trachtman & Blustain, 1999, n.p.). If you're more of an evolutionary mindset, though, this might be harder to swallow. Incidentally, if you are of the opinion of not effecting changes to someone else's body, this should then also apply to other surgeries, such as transforming the genitalia of an intersex baby without their consent or input, and it would even apply to seemingly milder events such as piercing a baby's ears or nose. Personally, I believe in people having ownership over their own bodies, so I wouldn't want to make any drastic changes to a child's body without their understanding and consent, or without a real medical need.

There are some risks to circumcision, such as bleeding and infection (Mayo Clinic, n.d., n.p.), and, more uncommonly, issues such as the foreskin not healing properly or being too short. Another risk mentioned is when the person carrying out the circumcision is not properly trained or uses unclean tools, and this can lead to a botched procedure or to problems in the short-term and/or long-term. However, this is less likely in the Jewish community, which uses well-trained *mohels* to circumcise babies.

In terms of the arguments about cleanliness, research shows that for boys with access to clean water who are taught how to wash themselves, there is no significant health or hygiene benefit to circumcision. Normal hygiene is enough to keep an uncircumcised penis clean, and given that there are a few risks to circumcising, parents have to weigh up which risks they're willing to take. Obviously, as already mentioned, in certain situations, circumcision is a really good choice, such as in preventing the spread of HIV, syphilis, and gonorrhea (Szabo & Short, 2000), but this tends to be more relevant in certain locations, such as in less developed countries, without easy access to sex education, condoms, and clean water, and does not really apply to the majority of Jews. So it's almost as though parents need to guess whether their sons might grow up to live there and to need circumcision for this reason. Self-evidently, this is impossible to predict.

In regard to people saying they want their sons to fit in, you also have to consider where you live and what the norm is in your culture. If you live among other observant Jews, then the norm is circumcision. But most boys in the UK, where I live, are not circumcised, so a circumcised boy would stick out, as it were, more than an uncircumcised one. Being different is not a problem, of course, but given that people kept mentioning this as a reason for cutting a boy, I felt it was worth pointing out that it's not a cultural norm in many countries beyond the US, Israel, and Muslim nations. Additionally, for those who cite this reason or the concept of sons and fathers looking similar penis-wise, we could pose the question, "How often are you looking at each other's penises and comparing?" Really, are parents and children or groups of friends naked together so frequently and so concerned about having identical-looking penises that this is genuinely a reason for circumcising? Penises all look different anyway, so how important is the amount of foreskin in this regard?

I've personally been told a number of times how "disgusting" and "weird" and "dirty" non-circumcised boys are. It's sort of ironic, but those are the same sorts of terms antisemites often use to describe Jews. That alone is enough to give me pause. It's also clear that whenever a particular look or style is described as "weird" (or, on the contrary, as "attractive"), then that stems from cultural norms. A particular body part shouldn't be perceived as disgusting or pleasing in and of itself. Such a view is subjective opinion, not objective fact.

However, this book is not only about me and my more secular practices. So it's important for you to do your research around circumcision and to make your own choice. By the way, some other research suggests, "the risks [of circumcision] are small but worth considering carefully. Complications from circumcision surgery are rare, but like all surgeries, there are some risks—including bleeding, infection and injury to the penis or urethra...The foreskin is sensitive, and in adulthood, some are distressed and even angry that theirs was removed" (Levine, 2023, n.p.). Regarding the latter point, there has even been at least one court cases where a man later sued his parents for circumcising him: "This landmark case brings into question whether a physician can remove healthy, normal tissue from unconsenting minors for non-therapeutic reasons, and whether a parent can legally consent to a medically contraindicated surgery for a minor child." (Attorneys for the Rights of the Child, 2000, n.p.) On the other hand, one *mohel* argues, "And what about the trauma that circumcision inflicts on us males? I have no clue how different I would be today had I not had that trauma. Nor does anyone else" (Cartun, 2001, n.p.).

Still, "Since 2012, the American Academy of Pediatrics (AAP) has followed a policy statement that argues the medical benefits outweigh the risks of circumcision. However, it stops short of being a recommendation of the procedure" (Levine, 2023, n.p.). In other words, there are some potential benefits and some potential risks, and parents need to decide what is best for their own child, although inevitably they will be influenced by their culture and religion. "The Torah has thus transformed circumcision into a resonant symbol of Jewish destiny: a divine promise of national fertility coupled with a human commitment to live by God's law. The challenge of our egalitarian age is to shape a worthy initiation rite for our newborn daughters" (Schorsch, 1994, n.p.). We'll return to his last comment, about daughters, below. For now, however, though it is pretty accepted in American and several other cultures, this does not mean that if you live there, you have to do it. You can make an independent choice that differs from cultural norms.

Interestingly, there have been some cases where men have chosen to restore their foreskin. Obviously, you cannot find the foreskin that was cut off in infancy and simply reattach it. Instead, "[f]oreskin restoration is a process that reverses a circumcision. You won't get your old foreskin back. But you can stretch penile skin over time to create a new foreskin or surgically attach skin from another area of your body to your penis. Risks depend on the approach, but may include dissatisfaction with how your new foreskin looks" (Cleveland Clinic, 2023, n.p.).

If a Jewish patient/client or friend or relative tells you they are not going to circumcise, you should accept this decision and not badger them to change their mind, even if their choice is anathema to you. If they say they're not sure, listen to them or discuss with them the reasons both for and against provided in this book. Let them come to their own conclusions. Try not to allow your own personal views to sway them, as this could lead to discomfort and pressure, or even to a breakdown in your relationship. Circumcision is a very delicate subject, even if it seems like a foregone choice for many Jews. One mother wrote the following regarding being uncertain about circumcision:

When my husband and I were deciding whether or not to circumcise our first son, a central and often unquestioned part of the Jewish faith, our hesitancy caused a terrible conflict between me and my father. Sitting down for the weekly Sabbath meal at my parents' house when I was heavily pregnant with my first-born son, I explained to my parents that my husband and I were in turmoil over whether or not to circumcise our son, as we felt it was irrelevant to our lives as non-practicing, secular Jews. My father became angry, and I remember hearing his words, "You must respect the wishes of the parents." I looked at him, shocked, replying, "But we are the parents!" Until my son's birth, I continued to struggle with the decision of whether or not to go ahead with the circumcision. I questioned whether I wanted to bring him into a culture that demanded his injury as a method of initiation, prolonging another inter-generational cycle of violence. It was difficult to feel that I was disappointing my father, and it was even harder to feel like we were "dissenters." I worried that not circumcising him would disconnect him from the Jewish community, as well as set him apart from the family. We did end up circumcising both our first- and second-born sons and I live with messy and disjointed feelings of guilt, pride, regret, and belonging.

There is also a little story about when I first met the guy who performed the circumcision and I told him how much turmoil I was feeling about the decision, and he said to me something like, "That is the point; the parents are supposed to feel turmoil and suffering and do it anyway, for God." I remember thinking that was a really shitty response—and it actually made me feel worse! It made no sense to me whatsoever. I also reflected a lot at the time at how the circumcision really sets up a relationship based upon guilt between Jewish mothers and their sons—perhaps with a lasting attempt to over-compensate for that initial betrayal of the baby.

Another parent explained how she was against a circumcision and decided it should be a choice her sons made for themselves. Instead, she carried out another ceremony:

> We named both our children in a *brit yitzhak*, developed by Yotam Schaechter [this is a Sephardic tradition, which often involves eating sweet items and listening to a lecture or discussion on the Torah]. I was adamant that I didn't want to circumcise, and my husband originally wanted to. We discussed and argued about many options and eventually decided on this. We'll encourage our kids (both boys) to pursue circumcisions if they want to, later. I really objected to such a body-altering procedure without reason. We thought about a *brit dam*, like for a male convert [*hatafat dam brit*, a ritual drawing of blood], but realized it wouldn't count any more than not doing it at all, and would cause pain for truly no reason. But my husband wanted something that was dramatic, an act of faith rather than reason, and Yotam's ceremony satisfied it.

A third said:

> My son is not circumcised and it's something I am careful not to disclose with the Jewish community. I couldn't bring myself to do it and feel that personally, I couldn't justify making irreversible changes to his body without his consent. I don't judge those who do perform *bris* because I understand how deeply rooted this practice is. I do sometimes worry if he will have difficulties with Jewish peers when he is older because of this though as well as the fact that due to family history there is a chance he may need circumcision for medical reasons anyway—in which case, it would have been better to have a *bris* as a baby after all.

The Brit Milah

If you do decide to circumcise your baby son, what is the process? What happens and when? The ritual is called a *brit milah* (though some also call it a *bris*, as you will have seen in the past sections; this depends on your pronunciation of Hebrew and your cultural/ethnic traditions).

First of all, it has to take place on his eighth day of life. In other words, a traditional Jewish circumcision cannot happen in the hospital, a few moments after birth. Some people, such as non-Jewish Americans, may ask the doctor to circumcise at that stage, but there is a particular reason while Jews do it some days later. This long explanation is particularly interesting:

> To my mind, the key to this ever-present meaning of circumcision, as opposed to its historical content, lies in the insistence on doing it on the eighth day. There is nothing arbitrary about the selection of the day. Given the import of the symbolism, the Torah could not have chosen any other. The significance of the eighth day is illuminated by a singular prohibition in Leviticus: "When an ox or a sheep or a goat is born, it shall stay seven days with its mother, and from the eighth day on it shall be acceptable as an offering by fire to the Lord" (Lev. 22:27). In other words, no sacrificial animal is to be removed from its mother for the first seven days of its life. Divine prerogative defers for a time to the intensity of the kinship relationship. Similarly, circumcision is delayed to the eighth day, as if to say that is the very first time when the male child may symbolically be dedicated to the service of God.
>
> The rite is a pledge of fealty and the mark, a lifelong external sign of apartness. Till the eighth day the child is without its own identity, entirely in the domain of its mother. The partnership with God is not forged until the first faint signs of viability and independence. The bestowal of a name at the same time underscores the transition to individuality and responsibility. Thereafter, male Jews spend the rest of their lives moving from fate to faith, turning "the covenant in the flesh" (*brit milah*) into a testimonial of spiritual nobility (Schorsch, 1994, n.p.).

Besides the significant date, it is also important to consider who carries it out. As already noted, a circumcision isn't done by the doctor who was there when the baby was born. Instead, it is strongly recommended that a *mohel* is employed. Not only does this make the event a real Jewish circumcision, but it's also argued that a professional *mohel* will be faster than a doctor, will inflict less pain, and will be gentler. A *mohel* notes, "If you want a quick procedure done by a specialist, all the while the baby is being lovingly held instead of tied down, use a *mohel.* If you want to strap your son down for up to 10 minutes on a tray, then shoot his penis full of shots, then lay a heavy weight on his penis until you finally get around to cutting off the foreskin, use a doctor. This is, of course, all predicated on the assumption that the *mohel* is competent. You find that out by reputation. An incompetent *mohel* is not to be trusted with your son's life. The 10 minutes of discomfort a doctor would impose are small price to pay for the security of knowing your son's body is in the hands of a competent surgeon" (Cartun, 2001, n.p.).

If a *mohel* is better than a doctor, the question is why and who is this person? "Traditionally, the circumciser, *mohel*, is a pious man trained in surgical hygiene as well as the rabbinic laws pertaining to circumcision" (Klein, 1998/2000, p. 220). Furthermore, "[a] competent *mohel* is a specialist, accustomed to circumcising "under pressure" (in front of a gathering of people), as most doctors are not. A *mohel* does not usually use anesthetic, because his anesthetic is the speed with which he does the circumcision. There are new Jewish legal rulings on this issue that permit anaesthetic, but *mohelim* do not always take advantage of this ruling. In any case, it takes five seconds—I actually count every time: "one-1,000, two-1,000," etc., up to "five-1,000," and it is done—for a *mohel* to circumcise, because a *mohel* uses a Magen shield, not a clamp, and there is almost no application time for a shield. With a shield, the foreskin is grasped, usually with medical tweezers, then pulled through the slit in the shield, then sliced off with a scalpel. The shield protects the glans of the penis, which, because it is too large to fit through the slit, remains below the shield" (Cartun, 2001, n.p.). The *mohel* cited here emphasizes the speed of the surgery to try to say that the child is not in discomfort and pain, or at least not for long.

While traditionally *mohels* (okay, *mohelim* if you want the accurate plural) have been men, this is changing. "Today, there are women circumcisers only in the Reform Jewish community" (Klein, 1998/2000, p. 222). Interestingly, several decades ago, "*Brit Milah* Board, the first training program offered by any liberal Jewish institutions to train medical professionals—men and women alike—to perform ritual circumcision [was created]. Gender-blind on principle—women were already ordained as Reform rabbis—the movement didn't meditate on the intense historical chauvinism that surrounds Jewish circumcision" (Trachtman & Blustain, 1999, n.p.). They believe there is textual support for this—if not cultural support—because "[t]he *brit* is so important, Jewish texts tell us, even a woman, a minor and a slave may perform it" (ibid.) Beyond the choice of who carries out the circumcision, families also have to consider the structure and style of the event. Traditionally, "[a] quorum of at least ten men attends the circumcision, although to make it a joyous event, many guests are usually invited. Sometimes the mother does not attend the rite itself" (Klein, 1998/2000, p. 220). Among less traditional Jews, mothers are more likely to attend, but this is relatively new. "*Brit mila* always has been a boys' show: Centered on the male baby and anatomy, a male *mohel* presided, the father was toasted, and the male relatives participated in the enactment. Women stayed in the kitchen comforting the mother as she heard her baby cry in the next room. The mother entered only to receive the baby when the ceremony was over" (Trachtman & Blustain, 1999, n.p.). Some people have found this exclusionary. The mother, after all, went through pregnancy and birth, and then is left out of a key ritual, and it can be argued that this reflects the idea mentioned above, about circumcision being the way to differentiate the little baby boy from his mother.

Some people feel that traditional circumcisions are swift affairs, with prayers and the actual cutting taking place without much explanation or even care. But it is such a life-changing event that modern *mohelim*, particularly female ones, are challenging this. As well as ensuring they include both parents and other relatives and friends, "[t]hey aim at inspiration, making language more gender-neutral, adding commentary, and offering translations, all of which enrich and soften an otherwise upsetting and intimidating ritual" (Trachtman & Blustain, 1999, n.p.). A recent addition to the ceremony for some is "a prayer of thanksgiving for the parents to recite and her own blessing in honor of people lost in the Holocaust" (ibid.). A Jewish celebration isn't complete without food, of course. "After the circumcision is a celebratory feast. Whenever possible, Jews have invited the whole community to a circumcision feast, because they have considered this a great mitzvah" (Klein, 1998/2000, p. 221). Some people choose to have a smaller, family-only meal or party, however. Often, charity donations are made too, as a way of celebrating and contributing to the community.

Finally, for males who convert to Judaism, their *brit* will be significantly different than what has been described here. It is more likely to be medicalized and it generally won't involve a large family party. That doesn't mean that it shouldn't be honored and enjoyed, though, because it is a big step to accept the covenant. If they were already circumcised, such as in the hospital when they were born, they may have a *hatafat dam brit*, which involves a hopefully painless letting of a drop of blood, to symbolize the covenant.

In short, there are different approaches to the *brit*, and they continue to evolve as time passes, though obviously many still opt for the traditional *brit*. It is also true that some of the past generations of Jews may have been unable to imagine female *mohelim*, explanations of the ritual, translations of prayers, and so on, but it's important for Judaism to adapt to the Jews of today and to be a welcoming space for those who wish to participate. People who choose to have a *brit* for their son should feel able to plan the ritual in conjunction with the *mohel* in a way that best suits them. In the survey I carried out, the most common comments about circumcision were about uncertainty regarding having one and the challenge of finding a qualified *mohel* in certain communities with fewer Jews.

A family who converted to Judaism wrote this about their *brit*:

> We're a bit of a story as our sons were circumcised as part of our conversion. They were two, eight, and ten at the time. Their dad got his done six months before them because I was hesitant about the whole thing so I wanted him to

> go first. The older boys were given all the info and choice because of their age. But I suppose we directed that as it was necessary for conversion as it's commanded in the Torah and it is a sign of the covenant we made with *Hashem*. I was very nervous at the time but looking back I'm very glad we did it and medically they have no infections now too whereas they did before.

Another parent described their *brit* as follows:

> [We had a] female *mohel* (*mohelet*?) for the last one. Family party *bris*, not in hospital, in private home.

A third wrote:

> My postdoc adviser, who is a Jewish infectious diseases doctor from NYC, was able to advise me to choose only a *mohel* who did *chatzitza* [a barrier] with gauze to avoid oral herpes transmission. That screened out many NYC area *mohelim*. We ended up having a *mohel* who was a physician and even as a physician usually used a glass tube for *chatzitza*, and we had to specifically direct him to use gauze. We also had a pediatrician prescribe us EMLA cream [a topical anesthetic] that we could use at the *bris*. We had filled out the birth certificate within 12 hours of birth, but our son's name did not yet exist in the health insurance system at the time we filled the prescription, and we were never able to get that reimbursed and paid $50 out of pocket for it.

Baby-Naming, Zeved Habat, Brit Bat, and Brit Shalom Ceremonies

It has probably become very clear that a lot of attention has been paid to newborn boys in Jewish culture. In some ways, this is odd, since Jewishness generally passes down the generations through the females, so you'd think girls and women would be respected and appreciated more. But on the other hand, many cultures are patriarchal and view the birth of boys as more important and more of a blessing than the birth of girls, and Judaism has certainly fallen into that category. In recent times, however, people are beginning to push back against this and to say that there should be celebrations in honor of the birth of a girl too. "Now parents want to welcome a daughter ceremoniously and celebrate her arrival with the extended family and in the community as joyously as they welcome a boy" (Klein, 1998/2000, p. 258). Or, to put it a bit more starkly, "There is a gaping hole where a parallel, obligatory covenant for baby girls should be" (Trachtman & Blustain, 1999, n.p.).

Traditionally, "Jews have welcomed the birth of a daughter according to local customs, and different from the welcome accorded a son. Often they have done this on a Sabbath morning in the synagogue. Some communities, however, have held special home celebrations that date from medieval times and bear influences from local, non-Jewish naming ceremonies. Yet other communities have no ceremony at all" (Klein, 1998/2000, p. 227). Naming ceremonies are often called *zeved habat* (gift of the daughter) or *simchat bat* (celebration of the daughter).

In the past decades, the shape of these naming ceremonies, at least among Reform or Masorti Jews in some countries such as the UK and the US, looked as follows: "fathers were given an *aliyah* (the honor of reciting the blessing before and after a section of the weekly Torah portion was read) at the synagogue the first Shabbat after a girl was born. The child received her Hebrew name at the same time. After services, both parents were honored at a congregational *kiddush*" (Reform Judaism, n.d., n.p.). Generally, the baby's new name would be explained, such as by stating which relatives she has been named after or what the other significance of the choices is. Also, "some Jews have incorporated a Talmudic custom into a newborn girl's welcoming ceremony: they invite family and friends to join them when planting a tree, and they recite a prayer of thanksgiving and blessings for the child's future" (Klein, 1998/2000, p. 230). In other words, as one female *mohel* stated in an article about female participation in such events, "A naming for a girl has to do with welcoming the child and what you wish for the child. I think the intent of the ceremony is the same" (Trachtman & Blustain, 1999, n.p.).

The naming ceremony is fairly widespread now, but some people have gone a step further to recommend what has been called a *brit bat* service; the meaning of the phrase is "the daughter's covenant," which means that females, too, can accept their covenant with God. Some like this to take place on the eighth day of the baby's life, just as you would for a boy's *brit milah*, to show they are equal in importance. While one person suggested ceremonially nicking a girl's genitalia (Trachtman & Blustain, 1999, n.p.), this has thankfully not been accepted as part of a *brit bat* service. Activities that are options for a *brit bat* include, besides those already mentioned as part of a naming ceremony, wrapping the newborn in a *tallit*, prayers, specially chosen readings, lighting candles, holding your wedding canopy over your family, having the baby's older siblings or other relatives make art for the baby or offer blessings to her, singing, giving the baby gifts (usually Jewish-related ones), and so on.

Klein suggests that naming ceremonies were not seen as being of the same importance, symbolically or spiritually, as the *brit milah* ritual. She writes that "a naming ceremony may stress a daughter's family continuity and her link with the biblical matriarchs, as well as introduce her to the Jewish community. This ceremony is not a covenant, however, and it does not have the same spiritual significance as circumcision. Nothing marks the baby physically or symbolically in the manner of circumcision" (Klein, 1998/2000, p. 227). I would argue that this is changing because even though a girl is not literally cut the way a boy is, many Jews have begun to see that welcoming a baby girl to the community of Jews is just as important. Creating a ritual that involves naming, planting a tree, donating to charity, reciting prayers, having a special meal, or any other activity of the parents' choosing shows that these parents are as eager to celebrate the birth of their daughter and to acknowledge her as an essential member of her family and wider community. A *brit bat* is a more egalitarian approach to celebrating newborn babies.

Another option is the *brit shalom*, or the covenant of peace, ceremony. This is usually for boys who aren't being circumcised, though some people use the term to describe the events they have for their daughters too. A *brit shalom* can be a way of avoiding tricky conversations with relatives about circumcision, because it keeps your decision regarding that private and instead focuses on naming and welcoming your baby boy.

A parent wrote this about naming:

> We followed the Jewish tradition where you do not release the baby's name until 8 days after birth.

Another parent said:

> Our daughter was named at the first Torah reading after her birth. We named our children after the rebbeim and rebbetzins. We had to go through some hoops delaying writing the name on the birth certificates. But the birthing center staff was used to it.

A third wrote:

> We had a baby naming/blessing for first child but that was due to pressure from my mother. I found the process of planning with a three-month-old baby stressful. I'm glad we did something but didn't choose to do the same the second time around.

One parent decided against a naming, explaining:

> Baby namings are recent traditions, so I didn't feel that it was essential.

One parent explained their choices as follows:

> We chose for our sons not to have a *brit milah*. I come from a Reform/Liberal Jewish background and while many practices have changed with the times, including the addition of naming ceremonies for daughters, female rabbis, and same-sex marriage, the act of circumcision has remained the same, even within progressive communities. I found this clashed with my own values, in addition to those of my non-Jewish partner. While we understand how pivotal *brit milah* is as a life cycle event for Jewish people, we felt we could not make the decision to circumcise our sons without any medical reason.
>
> We consulted with two different rabbis about our views and to enquire about alternative ways to mark the boys' births and to honor their Jewish heritage without circumcision. We had a mixed response, with one rabbi being more supportive of our choice, having come across families who had also made the same decision before, while the other rabbi was more adamant that *brit milah* was vital and even suggested that our sons would not be completely Jewish without it. This was very hurtful as we had no doubt we wanted to raise them Jewish and we are active members of our community. We decided instead to have a *brit shalom* 'covenant of peace' at our home on the eighth day of life.
>
> Alternative suggestions for rituals for ceremonies include the cutting of a pomegranate, washing the baby's feet, and the lighting of candles. We chose to have a low-key family event, where we blessed our sons while they were wrapped in their great-grandfather's *tallit*, explained why we chose their names, and stated our hopes for them for their futures. It would have been nice to have celebrated the occasion more publicly but unfortunately, we are not confident we would have the full support of our community due to the idea of not circumcising seemingly remaining taboo.

Parental Relations

There are two aspects to changing parental relationships once a baby has been born. One is the emotional and the other is sexual, though obviously for many people, they will be interconnected.

In regard to the emotional, how a couple feels about one another and how they relate to each other will inevitably change with the arrival of a new baby. Going from a couple to a family (or from a family with X children to a family with X+1 children) impacts everything from the practical to the atmospheric in a household. It also affects how people see one another and themselves. For example, someone who has just birthed a baby is no longer an individual, but now also a parent, one who has been through pregnancy and childbirth. There are new tasks and changing roles that come with a baby. In more observant and traditional homes, it will be considered appropriate and right that the mother does certain things while the father does others, while in less traditional ones, roles might not be divided up along gender lines or may be more flexible.

If a couple is struggling with this transition for whatever reason—for instance, if the birthing parent felt unsupported during the birth, or if the new parents have different ideas about feeding the baby, or if one has returned to work quickly and the other feels "stuck" at home and unappreciated—it is important for them to get help. This could be through couples counselling, mediation, open discussions with friends/relatives, or by getting advice and ideas from their rabbi or a healthcare professional.

Something that some couples have differing views about is how and when to return to having sex. In the case of heterosexual relationships, it's usually suggested that they wait until the lochia (postpartum bleeding) has stopped—which is usually around six to eight weeks after birth—and until they have been checked by a doctor, but it's obviously an individual choice. No one should feel pressured to have sex before they're ready.

In more observant Jewish homes, they will wait for postnatal purification, which means not having sex until the lochia has stopped and the woman has been to the *mikveh*. Less observant Jews, including many non-heterosexual couples, generally do not follow purity guidelines, but may still enjoy going to the *mikveh*. "Reform Jews abandoned the laws relating to a woman's purity on the grounds that these were archaic and irrelevant to the modern world [and, one could add, misogynist to some extent]. Yet increasing numbers of women today in all streams of Judaism find positive meaning in these ancient laws, in terms of the physical and spiritual rebirth that they signal. Those who observe them enjoy temporary abstinence from sexual relations and they focus on nonsexual forms of marital communication at this time" (Klein, 1998/2000, p. 233).

It's important to acknowledge that relationships do change with the birth of a baby and will continue changing, and the couple or family needs to talk about this openly and honestly, and to get support if that would be beneficial.

Matrescence

Matrescence is a term that has been written about in a non-Jewish context by Lucy Jones (2024) and it describes the process of becoming a mother. Transitioning to parenthood is a big change for many people, but it's often thought to especially impact mothers, not least due to the physical changes women go through in pregnancy and birth as well as the societal beliefs specifically around what motherhood is. As examples, women may wonder what their choice to breastfeed or not signals about them as mothers, whether they should return to work after having children, how to cope with the changes wrought in their bodies through pregnancy, what sort of daycare and schools their children should go to, what values to instill in their kids, and so on. Each society, and each subsection of society, along with each individual family, has its own opinions on all these matters and many more. This in turn impacts the choices people make.

For Jews in particular, they also will reflect on what it means to become a Jewish mother and what Jewish motherhood is or could be. They will ponder many of the topics discussed in this book, such as whether to circumcise or not, how to name a child, how long to breastfeed for, and so on, as well as others not explored here, including whether to send their children to a Jewish day school, how involved to be in the Jewish community, which synagogue to go to, if any, and so forth. They will also be influenced by Jewish views of motherhood, starting with the historical matriarchs in Judaism—Sarah, Rebecca, Leah, and Rachel—and running up through Jewish jokes about mothers or how Jewish mothers are depicted in literature or movies.

Becoming a parent is not something that happens once and then is finished; rather, it's a continuing process, and people can change their views of parenting generally and themselves as parents more specifically over time. New mothers need to allow themselves time to explore the concept of matrescence and to give themselves the freedom and flexibility to become a mother in the ways that suit them best.

Adoption

I'm aware that the previous chapter focused on birth as the main way to make a family, but people create their families in a variety of ways and it is important to acknowledge that. I referred to LGBTQ+ families and also to infertility treatment earlier in this book, and I wanted to add adoption and fostering to this discussion. Since fostering is generally short-term, I won't say much about it, since Jewish families who are fostering may not want or feel able to include a non-Jewish foster child in a Jewish life; the situation will obviously be different for a foster child who is already Jewish. Adoption, however, tends to be a permanent situation.

Adoption is well respected within Judaism. "Since ancient times Judaism has valued and encouraged adoption, and some of the greatest biblical heroes—including Moses and Esther—were adopted. Given the importance the Bible placed on caring for the orphan, the rabbis of the Talmud desired to formalize and encourage guardians to provide a home for those most in need and so created a special category for them, saying that 'A person who raises an orphan in their home is regarded by Scripture as if he had fathered them.' This was viewed as a righteous deed and an act of supreme loving kindness" (Koffman, 2018, n.p.). For those who are adopted, the following is generally advised, "A child of a non-Jewish mother who is adopted into a Jewish home requires conversion to Judaism. This involves immersion in a ritual bath (*mikveh*) for girls and boys, as well as circumcision (*brit milah*) for boys. In these cases, the child is asked to affirm their commitment to Judaism at the time of their Bar or Bat Mitzvah" (ibid.). In addition, Jewish adoptive parents will want to consider many of the topics explored in this chapter on postpartum traditions and elsewhere in the book. How will you welcome your new arrival? Will the child need to officially convert? If it's a boy, will you circumcise? Will you give the child a Jewish name? What blessings might you want to say for your new baby/child and your new role? What does it mean to become a parent through adoption, and how will you recognize and honor this?

Take some time to think about Jewish traditions and consider how you can adapt them to your particular situation. An adopted child also deserves a Jewish reception and integration into their family.

Other Traditions

In the course of my research for this book, some Jewish traditions or ideas came up that I hadn't been aware of; this isn't surprising because Jews are a heterogenous group, and this means that beliefs and behaviors vary quite a lot. So in this final section on the postpartum period, I just wanted to include some information and a few quotes from my survey that reflected some of these other traditions.

One parent wrote:

> We kept rubies on our babies' bassinets.

Another parent said:

> We put a red "bendel" on the crib and/or stroller, which we do for other things, too.

A third described the following:

> I did have family members on my husband's side (from Egypt) who tied red strings on babies' wrists and hung psalms on their crib. I think I may have had Psalm 121 or 20 on our crib to make them happy.

All three of the foregoing quotes refer to the *roiteh bendel*, or red thread, which some people believe helps to protect the baby from the evil eye or other bad things. Interestingly, though this is a folk belief, some argue that Jews shouldn't do it, because it is a "heathen" practice, rather than a religious one. Still, superstitions such as putting a red thread or other red things near the baby generally don't harm anyone.

Besides the focus on red, other traditions I have read about include relatives bringing certain meals and even including the healthcare professionals in those meals, hanging up a *kimpetbrivl* (or Ashkenazi birthing amulet), giving presents to the midwife or doctor, and lighting candles. In terms of candles, "[t]he light was an expression of rejoicing, as well as a precaution against harmful demons, who worked in the dark" (Klein, 1998/2000, p. 205).

Some people who would not consider themselves observant still like to partake in Jewish traditions as a way of connecting to their ancestors and to their culture. This might mean having a *brit milah* or *brit bat* even if they are not regular synagogue-attenders or it could involve reciting particular psalms despite being atheists. "In their joyous celebration of these ancient rituals, Jews maintain age-old traditions to affirm the Jewish identity of newborns and to mark a milestone in a woman's life cycle. They have found ways of adapting these traditions to suit modern conditions, for example, by reviving old customs or writing a new blessing, song, or poem to express the spirituality a parent may feel on the occasion of the ceremony … [some secular Jews carry out traditions despite not necessarily believing in them religiously and] as modern Jews rediscover their roots, some are now finding joy and meaning in these old traditions" (Klein, 1998/2000, p. 236).

However people choose to honor their birth and new baby or to spend their postpartum period is their own choice, though many Jewish people will have Jewish aspects involved to a greater or lesser extent.

CHAPTER 6

Jewish Infant Feeding

Although it's true that breastfeeding rates have generally gone down in the West, including among some Jewish women, it's also the case that traditionally, Judaism supports and encourages breastfeeding. "Jews, like other peoples, have believed that a mother has a natural desire to nurse her baby and that any woman who is well enough should do so. In the past, however, women who were wealthy, or who had twins often hired a wet nurse" (Klein, 1998/2000, p. 193). Today, it is known that some more Orthodox communities encourage the use of bottles so that women return to fertility sooner and can therefore produce more children. "Because breastfeeding usually delays the resumption of ovulation after childbirth, it often provides a natural form of contraception for a few months. Ultra-Orthodox Jewish women who choose not to nurse conceive again quickly and have large families, fulfilling the duty of being fruitful" (Klein, 1998/2000, p. 197).

Choosing how to feed your baby is a personal one, but it is also one that is heavily influenced by the people around you. What your culture values, what you see the people around you doing, and what you are encouraged or supported to do will impact both what you feel you want to do and whether you succeed in meeting your goals. Here in the west, we live in an overwhelmingly bottle-feeding culture, so it's more common to meet people who give their babies and toddlers formula than it is to see someone breastfeeding or chestfeeding, even though as mammals we have evolved to feed our children from our bodies.

Though feeding your baby definitely counts as part of the postpartum period, there was so much to say about it that I chose to make it its own chapter. Therefore, in this chapter, I focus on Jewish guidelines and traditions around breastfeeding in particular, but I will also reference other kinds of infant-feeding. I personally became particularly interested in Jewish beliefs about breastfeeding when I was breastfeeding my older child during Friday night Shabbat services in a synagogue (not my usual one). I was quite shocked and upset when a woman who worked at the synagogue rushed over to say that they weren't "comfortable with that sort of thing," and asked me to leave the sanctuary and go sit in a cramped room to breastfeed alone. I felt embarrassed and confused, because I had thought Judaism was supportive of breastfeeding and was family-friendly, including during religious services. I eventually decided to carry out more research into it.[7]

When I spoke to other Jewish parents who breastfed, I discovered that I had been correct in my initial assumption that Judaism was breastfeeding-friendly. Other people told me that they felt very supported by Judaism to breastfeed. Some felt it was a religious requirement to breastfeed, some even said it was a key part of their spirituality, and many breastfed in synagogue without an issue. So, in my case, it is likely simply that it was that particular synagogue, or that specific woman, who had a problem with breastfeeding. But one negative experience like that can completely derail someone's desire or ability to breastfeed, and my aim as a doula and IBCLC is to ensure that clients feel empowered to do what is right for them and their baby.

I interviewed a number of people to learn more about Jewish views on feeding, particularly about more traditional beliefs and behaviors that I didn't grow up with, and while it was fascinating, I was regularly reminded of the old joke about how you can get 20 Jews in a room and end up with at least 25 distinct views on a single subject. There are certainly differences of opinion about what Jewish law and culture says about breastfeeding.

---

7 Much of what follows here is taken from an article I wrote some years ago and published in the magazine for the Association of Breastfeeding Mothers in the UK (Woodstein, 2022). I quickly found that very few breastfeeding peer supporters or lactation consultants knew much about Jews and breastfeeding, and thus they appreciated the information. Unless otherwise noted, the quotes in this chapter are from that article. I have not included the individual interviews I carried out in my references for this book.

Religious Roots to Breastfeeding

Although, as mentioned before, the rabbis who interpreted the Torah and who have provided guidance were primarily men and were thus not attuned to the experiences of women as much as we might like, there is plenty of evidence in the Torah itself for attention paid to breastfeeding, and its literal and symbolic meanings. "In the Book of Deuteronomy, there is a poetic description of God feeding God's people honey from the rock as they marched through the wilderness. The word the Torah uses though for "fed" is *vayeneikehu*—to breast-feed. God made the people suckle honey from a rock. The image is evocative, poetic, and mystical. The image is also certainly more evidence that one of the metaphors the Bible has for God is The One Who Breast-feeds" (Falk & Judson, 2004, p. 95).

Rabbi David Kimhi, a medieval biblical commentor usually known as RaDaK, wrote, referencing Psalm 8: "The first of the distinguishing marks in man after his coming into the (light and) air of the world is the power to suck." In other words, breastfeeding is one of the key characteristics for humans, and some would believe that it was designed this way by a god. Viewing sucking like this in turn impacts how Jews understand breastfeeding.

Hannah Katsman, an IBCLC in Israel with six children, notes that for Jews, caring for your children is a religious obligation (and a pleasure), and that such care includes breastfeeding. She told me, "To me and to many women, breastfeeding is an important part of our religious practice. The Torah goes to great pains to emphasize how important it was for Moshe, the greatest prophet in the Torah, to nurse directly from his mother and not from an Egyptian woman. Rulings that minimize women's role in caring for their babies, or that interfere with the connection with their babies, make me feel like my role as a Jewish mother isn't being valued."

On her website, where she writes about breastfeeding, among other topics, Katsman goes into more detail. "Two biblical stories shed light on a Jewish approach to breastfeeding. Baby Moses, hidden so he wouldn't be killed by Pharaoh's evil decree, was placed in a basket on the Nile. His sister stood by to make sure he would be safe. When Pharaoh's daughter rescued Moses, she sent for a wet nurse from the Hebrew slaves. According to the Midrash, an early compilation of rabbinic interpretations of Exodus, Moses refused to nurse from an Egyptian wet nurse. The leader of the Jewish people was nursed only by his own mother. In Judaism nursing is more than food—it plays a key role in transmitting religion, values, and culture. Hannah also nursed her son, Samuel, for several years before sending him to study under Eli and fulfill his life's mission as a prophet (I Samuel, Ch. 2). Rabbinic texts define the nursing period from between two to four or five years old" (Katsman, n.d., n.p.). There are further biblical references to breastfeeding. "Two Talmudic homilies reveal that God enables the milk to come forth. One tells that, when Abraham arranged a banquet for the weaning of Isaac, he invited many people, but no wet nurse, and a miracle happened; Sarah's breasts filled with milk, and she suckled all the babies at the celebration (proving her motherhood, to counter rumors that Isaac had been adopted). The other story describes the straits of a man whose wife had died in childbirth and who was too poor to pay for a wet nurse. God filled his breasts with milk to feed the infant" (Klein, 1998/2000, p. 194).

Rachel Neve Midbar, a Jewish mother of six, a poet, and a PhD student, reminded me that in the Torah, Sarah was 99 years old when her son Yitzhak (Isaac) was born. She breastfed him so people would know that she was the one birthed him. She nursed him for two years, which is possibly where some people get the idea that Jewish women should breastfeed for at least two years.

As mentioned, there's one story in Judaism (among other places, it comes up in the Genesis Rabbah midrash, which is a collection of analyses of the story of Genesis) about a man breastfeeding. His wife died and God then gave the man the ability to breastfeed and sustain the baby. I'd imagine there are some people who wish that it were possible for a spouse to help out in this way.

In sum, there are clear religious roots to breastfeeding for some Jews, as well as a number of references in religious texts to the act. It is also part of cultural tradition (although obviously the formula industry has impacted Jewish people as well as everyone else). Breastfeeding can thus be considered an obligation (and a joy) for the breastfeeding mother but there is also an obligation for her community to support her with it. So what should breastfeeding counsellors or IBCLCs know about Jews and breastfeeding?

Fasting

Generally, of course, someone who is breastfeeding/chestfeeding will want to eat and drink well. "Through the ages, Jews have insisted that a nursing woman maintain a good, healthy diet" (Klein, 1998/2000, p. 194).

However, as in some other religions, there are a number of fast days for Jewish people. There are several major fast days, such as Yom Kippur (the Day of Atonement, which is part of the Jewish New Year, in the autumn), and Tisha B'Av (a day of mourning), and a bunch of minor fast days. Fasting means abstaining from both food and drink, unlike in some other religions, where drinking is allowed. It is a general expectation (and a halachic, or religious, obligation) that everyone will fast, unless there is a medical reason. However, the people I spoke with when researching this topic noted that in actual fact, there is some flexibility around this.

Some recommended that a pregnant or breastfeeding woman speak to her rabbi, doctor, or lactation consultant about her individual situation. Medical opinion is mixed about what could happen to the fetus if you fast during pregnancy and of course milk supply might decrease. In an academic piece by Maharat Ruth Balinsky Friedman (Maharat is her title, as she is ordained), she writes that pregnant or breastfeeding women who feel a "craving" do not have to fast (Friedman, 2013, n.p.). In the Talmud, the rabbis say that the pregnant or breastfeeding woman should have what she craves; amazingly, this is considered the case even if the craving is non-kosher (Falk & Judson, 2004, p. 9). Friedman suggests asking pregnant or lactating women what they themselves want to do about fasting and then finding a solution or plan that works for them, while not endangering their health or their baby's health (Friedman, 2013, n.p.).

Modern Orthodox, feminist Rabbanit Leah Sarna (Rabbanit is her title because she is ordained) said that, "Yom Kippur is one of the most important parts of our religious practice" and requires 25 hours of fasting from food and drink. If a woman fasts for 25 hours, her supply may dip and she might need to give her baby pumped milk or formula." Leah told me, "A huge number of women do a modified fast." Such a modified fast would include "one cheekful (half a mouthful) of liquid every nine minutes (or one fluid ounce of solids)," to ensure they kept up their supply and could take care of their baby.

A number of people referenced the concept of *pikuach nefesh*, which has already been discussed, and which means that saving a human life takes precedence over anything else, even if one has to break religious or other laws. It is considered that if a woman feels she needs to eat or drink in order to best care for herself and/or her baby, then that is what is most important. The Talmud, which is the book that describes Jewish law, includes the concept, "Whoever saves a single life is considered by scripture to have saved the whole world." Each life truly matters. So if a woman needs to eat so her breastmilk supply doesn't decrease or so she doesn't feel unwell, then this matters more than fasting on a particular day. Hannah Katsman, the IBCLC in Israel quoted earlier, told me, "rulings that obligate a mother to fast for as long as she can, and only to break her fast once the baby has shown distress, have caused a lot of grief and ended many nursing relationships. The *Chazon Ish* has a ruling stating that babies shouldn't get formula if it might upset their stomach, and that avoiding this situation is considered *pikuach nefesh*. That is a ruling that shows sensitivity to babies. Fortunately, more and more rabbis are ruling more leniently regarding fasting."

Shoshana Pritzker, a registered dietitian nutritionist and a Jewish, breastfeeding mother in the US, wrote the following to me, "Breastfeeding is highly demanding on the body when it comes to calorie needs and hydration of the mother. Moms need an additional 700 calories per day when breastfeeding. That's 700 calories OVER their daily required calorie intake. So if your body needs 1800 calories per day, you now need to eat 2500 calories per day to provide sufficient calories to produce milk and provide ample nutrients for yourself. If you are breastfeeding twins, or more than one child at a time, you need an additional 1000 calories per day. When fasting your body ends up in a deficit and utilizes stored body fat and muscle to keep you alive. If you're breastfeeding, your body is going to use a lot more of your stored energy sources (fat and muscle) to continue production. Studies have shown that during a short fast, milk supply will not decrease. However, nutritional status of the mother will suffer and essential minerals found in breastmilk are reduced. Plus, the mom is at risk for vitamin and mineral deficiencies and dehydration. During a fast, your body will make sure baby is getting what they need (whether pregnant or breastfeeding). However, it's at the expense of the mother." Shoshana Pritzker suggested that Jewish women who are pregnant or breastfeeding, and who want to fast first talk to their doctors or lactation consultants, and also ensure that they drink at least one glass of water an hour. Some people do experience a drop in supply, but Pritzker felt it didn't happen to everyone and said mothers shouldn't worry about it. "Less stress is best!" she said.

Some women do like to fast on the Jewish holidays. Meira E. Schneider-Atik, a mother of three, told me, "I breastfed all three of my children and I loved it. It was good for me and for them. I fasted on Yom Kippur and Tisha B'Av with no issues even while pregnant and nursing. My doctor and my rabbi worked together with me and we came up with a plan that allowed me to fast. I prepared and hydrated beforehand, and I stayed home from shul and rested. My husband was a huge help (he always is)."

Not everyone feels able to do this. Shoshana Pritzker concluded, "If you experience mom guilt over not fasting during Jewish holidays, remember that Jewish law exempts anyone whose health may even be slightly harmed by it, and that includes pregnant and nursing mothers." Clearly, fasting, as with much else in Judaism, will vary depending on a woman's level of religiosity and the support she receives from her rabbi, physician, spouse and community.

Menstruation

For many people, one of the benefits of breastfeeding is lactational amenorrhea, where you do not get your period. This is generally useful as a way of preventing another pregnancy too soon, if you are in an opposite-sex relationship (you can, however, still ovulate, so it isn't fail-safe). For religious Jewish women, the time spent without menstruating has additional positive outcomes. The key point here is that lactational amenorrhea allows for a couple to have more physical contact, because menstruation forces a separation between spouses.

Rachel Neve Midbar, who specializes in menstrual poetry, talked to me about Jewish family purity laws and the connection to breastfeeding. She referred to the *mikveh* and noted that in her experience, one of the purposes of the *mikveh* is to separate life from death; if someone touches blood or death, they must clean themselves ritually. This could be if they killed a fly or if they visited a graveyard, for instance. They must then go to the *mikveh* to divest themselves of the link to death.

When a woman menstruates, Rachel explained, it is considered that she is touching death, because the egg, which once had the possibility of life, is now dead. So Jewish law states that when a woman is done menstruating, she must wait until absolutely no more blood comes (she can test this by inserting a white cloth inside herself and she can show it to her rabbi, if she feels she needs an outside opinion), then seven days later she goes to the *mikveh* to separate herself from her menstruant status. She enters the mikveh, recites prayers, and then is ritually cleaned.

When a religious woman is *niddah*, or experiencing a discharge of blood, she is not supposed to touch her husband, sleep in the same bed as him, or even pass him anything. This means that for around two weeks per month, a married couple have to keep their distance from one another. For some couples, this might be a challenge. So exclusive breastfeeding and the concomitant lactational amenorrhea extends the time without blood, and without the enforced separation, and allows the closeness that some people might prefer to have. (We can note that some people might like having less physical contact and instead prefer to rely on emotional and verbal connections.)

Rachel Neve Midbar argued that these rules are "not about cleanliness but about ritual purity," and instead are about separating life from death. So a menstruating woman (or a woman who has lochia after birth) is not dirty or impure but rather considered to be touching death. However, I must point out that not everyone agrees with her interpretation (remember what I said about Jews loving to discuss and argue?). Other people I spoke to felt that a woman was in fact "impure" while menstruating, and that being close to death had nothing to do with all this. In other words, even religious perspectives are mixed. One reminded me that the *mikveh* is used in other circumstances, to purify the person, such as before marriage, or at conversion, or before prayer, and so on. Clearly, opinions differ on the concept of purity.

While there is more to be said about this, the most important part to understand is that breastfeeding not only can extend time between children, which could be beneficial in a community that often has quite a few children, but also potentially allows for more connection between spouses.

Modesty

For observant Jews, there are also issues of modesty. As with some better-known groups, such as religious Muslims, some Jewish women dress modestly, cover their hair, and do not show their bodies in public. This would potentially include not breastfeeding in public, but it may also mean not breastfeeding at home if it's in front of male relatives (father, father-in-law, brothers, and so on) or male friends.

In addition, Jewish women who exclusively pump or who pump while at work would be concerned about privacy and modesty. Depending on where they live, they may need support in talking to their employers about this.

In an article on breastfeeding, Rabbi Ysoscher Katz writes the following: "There is a fantastic description in the Gemara (Sotah, 30b) of the people of Israel, men and women, reciting the "Song of the Sea" after the amazing miracle of the splitting of the Sea of Reeds. The Gemara says: "How did they recite the "Song of the Sea"? The baby was placed on the knees of his mother and nursed from her breasts. When they saw the Shekhinah, the baby lifted his neck, detached from his mother's nipple, and said: 'This is my God and I will adore Him, as it says: from the mouth of babies and infants you have become fortified with strength.'" Here, in the middle of nursing, a baby removes his mouth from his mother's breasts and, in close proximity to exposed breasts, recites the song and, in so doing, mentions the name of God when he says, "this is my God and I will adore Him."

Of course, we do not learn *halakha* from narrative stories, but this nevertheless serves as a complement to the proof that we have already stated: minor and brief nakedness is not considered *gilu'i ervah*, exposure of nudity, and it is therefore permissible to pray and discuss issues of holiness in the presence of a nursing woman" (Katz, n.d., n.p.).

In other words, a religious story shows a baby breastfeeding then referring to God while still at the breast, and this implies a clear link between breastfeeding and spirituality. More relevantly to this section on modesty, it also suggests that exposing the breast is not necessarily immodest. It is not seen as nakedness in all contexts and some Jewish women will therefore feel able to breastfeeding in front of others.

Breastfeeding in Shul

So here was my original sticking-point, the thing that turned me off Judaism for a while: breastfeeding in shul. Imagine my surprise when parents from across the Jewish spectrum told me that they breastfed in synagogue without anyone saying a negative word to them. It turns out that my experience was probably due to me being in a slightly more religious synagogue that was in the US, a country that often struggles with breastfeeding in public. Indeed, on that particular trip, I had people constantly telling me to sit in cars to breastfeed (in Chicago during the winter!), or to face the wall, or to go to a room by myself, so clearly it wasn't just the synagogue.

Meanwhile, here in the UK, I breastfed in our synagogue multiple times, and even during Hebrew school classes or festival celebrations, and it was absolutely fine.

It's important to note that the more traditional congregations are segregated by gender, so women and children sit upstairs, while the men are downstairs, which means women have no issue latching babies and children on because they are in a female-only space. In more modern and less traditional synagogues, people are in mixed-gender areas and this means that they are sometimes more hesitant to breastfeed. Many such people recommended speaking to the rabbi or using some sort of cover, but everyone I spoke to noted that there is no actual prohibition against breastfeeding in shul.

Rabbanit Leah Sarna told me that more synagogues are trying to become more breastfeeding-friendly. And Rabbi Ysoscher Katz wrote in his article, "it is not merely permissible to bring young children and nursing babies to the synagogue, it is also a *mitzvah* [good deed]" (Katz, n.d., n.p.).

Everyone I spoke to said that breastfeeding should be welcomed in shul and that it could be done discretely/modestly, as preferred by the woman and her particular congregation.

Pumping

As with other breastfeeding/chestfeeding parents, many Jewish mothers return to work after having their babies (note: this is less common among the ultra-Orthodox). So pumping is likely to be a significant part of their lives for that reason, or, of course, for any of the other myriad reasons that some parents express milk, such as having a baby who is not well enough to latch. Rabbanit Leah Sarna mentioned how in the US, where she is located, pumps are covered by health insurance and most women work, so owning and using a pump is really common. The issues are that some women may not recognize that they would need to pump every day and would assume they could take the Sabbath off or that non-Jewish IBCLCs who work with them might not know that they need to find solutions to the problem of pumping during the Sabbath, when you aren't supposed to work.

For observant Jews, there is a prohibition on working during Shabbat (the Sabbath, from Friday sundown to Saturday sundown). In this context, working means doing something for a purpose. If a woman were to hand-express or use a manual pump, this would be considered work and she would have to discard the milk, because otherwise it would be employed for its purpose. For this reason, an electric pump is to be preferred, because the breastfeeding parent is not doing the work. But a traditionally observant Jewish woman cannot turn the pump on and off herself.

Leah, who also teaches the Talmud to teenage girls, and who is writing a book on the *halakhah* (religious laws) of pregnancy, birth, and early parenting, told me that there were some electric pumps with Shabbat timers. However, she noted that they aren't necessarily the best quality pumps, and some aren't commercially available at the moment. The best thing, of course, would be to feed the baby directly at the breast, but if a mother usually pumps, or if she is away from her baby or otherwise has to pump during Shabbat, Leah said, "I'm advocating that the better thing to do is to choose where you're going to pump on Shabbat, keep it plugged in, and use your elbow to turn it on. That's the *halakhic* option." The pump does the work, and you're indirectly turning it on in this case (switching the electricity on would be considered work).

Of course, if a woman happens to have a non-Jewish friend, neighbor, nanny/au pair, or someone else who can turn the pump on and off when needed, that is also a solution since it is fine for non-Jews to do work on Shabbat. Most people probably do not have this option, however.

A Jewish mother wrote:

> When my first son was born, I used a manual pump on Shabbat. I remember hearing some time later that there was some question about whether using a pump was allowed, but I wasn't aware of that at the time. When my second son was born, I still pumped sometimes during the week, but I was able to set things up so that I was with him on Shabbat and didn't use the manual pump. It was just more trouble than it was worth.

If you're supporting a Jewish woman who pumps or who needs to be away from her child on Shabbat, it's important to help her find a solution that will fit within her religious framework. In general, using an electric pump is more acceptable, but the woman will have to find a way of indirectly turning it on and off, such as with her elbow, as Rabbanit Leah Sarna suggested.

Length of Breastfeeding

The World Health Organization recommends exclusively breastfeeding infants on demand and then breastfeeding older children "up to 2 years of age or beyond," alongside other foods and drinks (Shrimpton, 2017, n.p.). Interestingly, even though that's modern medical advice, in Jewish culture, it's traditionally been the case to breastfeed for that amount of time. "Throughout the ages, the usual duration of breast-feeding was eighteen months to two years, but often longer, sometimes even five years; Jewish women traditionally nursed a sickly child for longer and weaned boys earlier than girls" (Klein, 1998/2000, p. 195).

I have heard that two years is a good amount of time in part because a two-year-old will be a lot sturdier, thanks in part to the breastmilk they have received, and thus better able to survive, and also because many women will have returned to fertility around fourteen or fifteen months postpartum, so they may well be pregnant or about to get pregnant when their child is two or thereabouts. Obviously, you can breastfeed through pregnancy, and you can tandem-feed, but perhaps this hasn't been as recognized or encouraged in Jewish culture.

For the more observant, *halachic* guidelines suggest, "Breastfeeding is *halachically* encouraged, especially for the first two years of life. Nursing may be continued until the child's fourth birthday (or if the child particularly needs it, the fifth birthday). Up to the age of two, if a child has ceased nursing, he may resume breastfeeding even if he has only nursed for a few months. However, if a healthy child above the age of two does not wish to nurse for 72 hours, breastfeeding may not be resumed. A child under two years old may begin breastfeeding even if he has never nursed. An older child may not" (Nishmat Yoatzot Halacha, 2023, n.p.). One mother in my survey wrote:

> I feel passionately about the importance of breastfeeding and doing so for as long as I feel happy to (2 years+).

Another was more specific about the way her Jewishness influenced her choice about the length of breastfeeding:

> Some of [my] beliefs are found within Judaism, [such as to] breastfeed for 2 years.

Other Ideas About Breastfeeding

Some Jewish ideas about breastfeeding seem to be inaccurate, and perhaps should be put in the category of folk beliefs rather than evidence-based knowledge.

"The medieval rabbis advised that a woman begin nursing with her left breast rather than her right, because the left breast is nearer the heart, the seat of wisdom" (Klein, 1998/2000, p. 194). When I was very active as a breastfeeding counsellor and IBCLC, I'd heard from others in the breastfeeding-support community that left breasts had better blood supply and therefore better milk supply, but actually, research doesn't seem to bear this out (e.g., Engstrom et al., 2007).

Another incorrect piece of information is, "For almost two thousand years, most Jews maintained that a mother who was breastfeeding a child should stop if she conceived, because her milk would be affected by pregnancy and could harm the nursling" (Klein, 1998/2000, p. 195). This is also simply not true. Many people breastfeed through pregnancy and then go on to tandem-feed, and there is no evidence whatsoever that this is harmful to the fetus/baby, the older child, or the breastfeeding parent.

Weaning

When I put a call out for people's personal stories about breastfeeding and being Jewish, a few told me that how they fed their children had nothing to do with their religion, but the great majority connected feeding to their spirituality. For a number of Jewish women, the choice to breastfeed had to do with being Jewish. They breastfed because they felt Jewish guidelines encouraged it and their community supported it. For others, how they behaved during the breastfeeding relationship was influenced by—and in turn then influenced—their religious beliefs and actions.

I have sometimes talked about weaning celebrations, and jokingly wondered what Jewish-specific ones could be called. One possibility inspired by Judaism is a bar/bat breastvah (the name inspired by the Jewish coming-of-age ceremonies bar/bat mitzvah). It turns out that I was right that there were Jewish approaches to weaning ceremonies. For example, some people told me that they had weaning ceremonies in the synagogue. This provided a meaningful end, and also signal to themselves, their nurslings, and their community that this part of their relationship was over. I was told that in the Tanach, there are references to celebrating the breastfeeding relationship and weaning, so there is some precedent for this. Rabbanit Leah Sarna said that a good example was Genesis 21:8, where Abraham throws a party for Isaac's weaning. As Michele Klein writes, "Abraham made a great feast on the day that Isaac was weaned, and Hannah offered a prayer of thanksgiving after weaning Samuel, but these customs never became part of Jewish ritual, although they were practiced in some communities. An infant was weaned only when he or she was strong enough to cope with ordinary food, and not if the child was sickly. When a mother weaned her infant, she often expected another pregnancy soon afterward" (Klein, 1998/2000, p. 235).

Others said that they went to the *mikveh* (the ritual bath) in order to mark the end of breastfeeding and they explained that using the *mikveh* was a way of separating themselves from breastfeeding. "In recent years, some non-Orthodox Jews have celebrated weaning as a life-cycle ritual. They have created a new ceremony and have linked it to Abraham's ancient banquet. This ceremony focuses on the nurturing roles of the parents and the joys of the child's independence. Some mark the occasion by giving charity to the hungry" (Klein, 1998/2000, p. 236).

Whether at two years old or earlier or later, weaning is significant for many nursing dyads (the baby/child plus the person feeding the baby/child), and there are some Jewish ways of marking this. It is also a concept that is in transition, so people who feel so moved can develop their own weaning traditions. For instance, I've had breastmilk jewelry made for both me and my children, and I have also produced photo albums dedicated specifically to our breastfeeding journeys, which they can look at any time they want to. The jewelry and photo albums are not particularly Jewish, but they might be useful approaches for other people to try. I've heard of other people having parties, sometimes even with breast-shaped cakes or cupcakes, as a way of marking the end.

Bottle-Feeding

Much of the foregoing was about breastfeeding, but of course some Jewish people bottle-feed or combi-feed too. Sometimes this is for medical reasons, such as someone taking medication that isn't safe for the baby. There might also be psychological reasons, such as that they were abused and it's triggering to have someone touch their chest. It could also be that it's their personal choice for other reasons, or they might receive pressure from their spouse or others to "share" the feeding of the baby, although obviously if it's a situation of pressure, then they should be given support to counteract that.

There is nothing in Judaism against using formula milk. "The Jewish Talmud allowed babies to be fed by a female animal if the wellbeing of the child depended on it" (Schipper, 2024, p. 162). On the other hand, some Jewish subcultures encourage the use of formula for reasons other than the wellbeing of the child, such as the desire to have more children at a quicker rate. It is important to note that not all formula milks are certified kosher, so if you are working with an observant Jewish family that keeps kosher and plans to use infant formula, they will want to ensure their formula has been produced in accordance with kosher regulations and under the observation of a rabbi.

One person in my study wrote:

> The Orthodox aren't supported to breastfeed and are encouraged to bottle-feed. They're also exhausted from having so many children. They give a lot of bottles. Israelis are more likely to breastfeed, but here in the UK, we're such a bottle-feeding culture and that affects Jews too. There's not much exclusive breastfeeding anymore. They need bottles to help them cope with the exhausting lives they lead. They can't afford to see a lactation consultant.

Clearly, such mothers may want or need support in order to breastfeed, and to slow down their production of children, even if this is not encouraged by their subculture.

Another mother wrote:

With our first child, our daughter, I bowed to pressure postpartum to give formula, but weaned off it very quickly once at home. With our son, I was confident enough to insist on only breastfeeding.

In other words, while there are times when bottle-feeding is best for the parent and/or the child, and Jewish writings understand this, sometimes it's poverty (so people cannot afford the help they need) and/or exhaustion and/or a heavy emphasis on fertility that leads to bottle-feeding. Since it is known that not breastfeeding for as long as they want to can lead to years of breastfeeding grief (Brown, 2019), it would be ideal if Jewish parents—and non-Jewish ones too—were given the support they desired and needed in order to meet their breastfeeding goals.

Experiences

To close, here are a couple of quotes from people about their experiences breastfeeding as Jewish women.

One said:

I am in public health, and I chose to breastfeed. I feel very strongly about breastfeeding, and I also feel strongly that a lot of women don't get the support they need early on to make it successful. If your baby is eating 10-12 times a day, and you can't feed one of those times, then it can easily start to go downhill.

A second wrote:

I didn't think about breastfeeding as a specifically Jewish act initially, but I came to realize that it's in line with my Jewish values. For example, I believe in lovingkindness, bonding with your children, educating your children, giving to others, and so on, and those are all things that you offer (and receive) through breastfeeding. I'm really proud that I, as a Jewish woman, have breastfed my children.

As this chapter has shown, opinions and practices differ among Jewish women in regard to feeding, but there are a number of key points to consider when working with Jewish mothers on their breastfeeding journeys, namely fast days, menstruation, pumping, modesty, breastfeeding in synagogue, and weaning.

Jewish mother and poet Rachel Neve Midbar sums it up well when she says, "Jewish law sees breastfeeding as a natural function. Breastfeeding takes precedence over almost everything else, because it's about the life of a child." As has been seen in this chapter, there are distinct Jewish roots to, and beliefs around breastfeeding, and Jewish parents should be supported to breastfeed for as long as they want to.

CHAPTER 7

Jewish Parenting

Once you have a baby, you need to think about how to raise them. You'll be pondering a whole range of topics, including what foods to offer, which schools they should attend, whether they should learn an instrument and/or a sport, what sort of neighborhood would be best for them to grow up in, when they can start dating, how late their curfew should be, and so on. Frankly, the worrying and the considering starts as soon as you begin discussing the concept of pregnancy and it never really seems to end, as there's always something that hasn't occurred to you or that you'd like to improve about your parenting. If you belong to a specific religion or ethnic group, your culture may influence your decisions or give you additional issues to consider.

Naturally, Jewish people have some distinct beliefs and traditions when it comes to parenting. Like everything else, these vary. "In studying Jewish attitudes towards childbearing, we have also seen how high Jews have traditionally set moral and ethical standards for their communities. However, this aspect of Jewish tradition, like others, reflects patterns set long ago and that are fast disappearing outside Orthodox circles" (Klein, 1998/2000, p. 251). I'm not sure I totally agree with the second part of this quote. From my discussions with many non-Orthodox parents, I've come to understand that even if someone isn't that religiously observant, their experiences as a Jewish person still affect their "moral and ethical standards," as Klein puts it, and their choices in regard to their children.

In this chapter, I'll explore some of the key Jewish values that parents may choose to incorporate into their parenting.

One parent summed up Jewish parenting as follows:

There's an emphasis on tradition, community and family involvement, education and arts, and also on integrity and generosity as central personal and family values.

The Jewish Mother

Before we go too much further, I think I need to address what might be an elephant in the room: the stereotypical idea of the overbearing, overly anxious Jewish mother. I referred to this early, how there are many jokes about Jewish mothers, and while some of them seem over the top, others might hit a bit too close to home. There is a "widespread stereotype of Jewish mothers as the original helicopter parents: clingy, needy, guilt-mongering hovercraft who always believe their precious spawn are perfect" (Ingall, 2016, p. 7). While there isn't enough space here to explore exactly where this idea come from—Ingall argues it is a "confluence of factors," such as American Jews beginning to move to the suburbs, which were previously not places where Jews lived, and the exclusion and culture shock that that involved, plus, more importantly, mothers getting even more worried about their children in the aftermath of the Holocaust (Ingall, 2016)—the truth is that most stereotypes have some elements of truth, even if they are exaggerated and then used as a reason for mockery and discrimination. In the case of the Jewish mother concept, if you add in some portions of antisemitism and misogyny, you end up with a stereotype that is viewed as being extremely negative, and even damaging.

So what is a Jewish mother really? Obviously, there are as many types of Jewish mother as there are Jewish mothers themselves. But if I had to offer a definition of some kind, I'd say an archetypal Jewish mother is one who cares deeply about her children, dotes on them, wants the best for them (and maybe expects the best from them as well), and perhaps sometimes is a bit more into their business than they'd like. In other words, this definition could very well be true of the vast majority of mothers, Jewish or not.

Still, the stereotype seems to be living on. If you want to say that a Jewish mother is one who adores her children and would do anything to help them be safe, healthy, and happy, then it's a stereotype I'd happily claim.

One mother in my study wrote this:

> I think I have elements of being a neurotic Jewish mother. I worry a lot about the safety of my children and have been told I am overprotective. I have fairly high expectations when it comes to academic study and want them to achieve to their best ability—I hope without putting unnecessary pressure on them though.

Key Jewish Values

There are many ethical aspects of Judaism, as well as ideas that Jewish people tend to value highly. In this section, I will focus on a few of the big ones, though I want to acknowledge that other people might disagree with my choice of values, and may think I've missed out on some of the important ones. Still, these are the values I've tried to prioritize in my own life, including in my parenting.

Chesed

Chesed is often described in English in a one-word phrase that is useful even if it doesn't really cover it all: "lovingkindness." *Chesed* refers to a quality that involves compassion, empathy, generosity, altruism, respect, and, of course, love and kindness. It is thought to describe the way God created the world. In return, this is how people should behave towards themselves, one another, God, and all other beings.

The concept of *chesed* is featured regularly in the Torah and it describes altruistic acts but is more encompassing than charity. It's more about the giving of yourself to others. It can be a guiding principle in terms of how we interact with other people.

A parent wrote:

> In terms of parenting, I think it is both implicit and explicit in the things that we do, such as observing holidays, but also in what we think of as the Jewish values that matter to us: community, *chesed*, social justice, respecting elders, etc.

A Jewish midwife said:

> Definitely some chesed going on in terms of why I chose to be a midwife! Certainly I think there's something in there about a culture that values helping others. On the downside, this includes the part of *chesed* where it can involve not having the best boundaries.

Tzedakah

Tzedakah is another fundamental Jewish concept, and it means "justice." It covers both giving money to charity and actually doing things to help other people.

In an article I published (Woodstein, 2016) a number of years ago (when we only had one child, so hence the singular in the article), I described how I wove *tzedakah* into my parenting:

> We give money to various charities on a monthly or yearly basis, and [t]hen there's the actual doing of volunteer work, rather than simply financially supporting charities. Children can both see their parents carrying out volunteer work and be involved in doing it themselves, such as at a homeless shelter, or by tutoring peers or younger children.
>
> We also try to sometimes pick up some extra items when we go grocery shopping, and then we take those boxes of cereal or cans of tomatoes, and drop them off in a collection for a food bank. It's very simple to explain that we're giving the food to people who don't have as much as we do, and it's also fun for our daughter to help hunt for these objects on the shelves in the store.

Tikkun Olam

Tikkun olam is another of our core Jewish ethical values. It refers to "repairing or healing the world," and it encourages people to choose to care about social responsibility and social justice and to take social action. It means to carry out deeds to better the world, not to just to think, or hope, or pray for things to improve. Interestingly, originally *tikkun olam* meant to do something that improved society, but gradually the phrase became connected to the physical, actual building of a better world (Abramowitz, 2017).

Noa Tishby defined the four pillars of Judaism as being "religion, peoplehood, *tikkun olam*, and nationhood" (Acho & Tishby, 2024, p. 22). In other words, healing the world is as important to Jews as the religious commandments and as being an ethnic group with its own country. The following quote is about Reform Judaism in particular but really could refer to any subset of Jews: "Central to Reform Jewish beliefs is the idea that all human beings are created *b'tzelem Elohim*, in the image of God, and that we are God's partners in improving the world. *Tikkun olam*, the repair of our world, is a hallmark of Reform Judaism as we strive to bring about a world of justice, wholeness, and compassion" (Reform Judaism, n.d., n.p.).

You may have heard the term *mitzvah* in the phrase "doing a *mitzvah*." Often, this refers exactly to someone performing an act of *tikkun olam*, whether on a small scale (visiting a housebound and ill person) or a large scale (helping to build homes for refugees). Some people also consider Torah study as being a way of repairing the world. Carrying out such deeds is good for the world, but it is also good for you, because it makes you feel useful, since you can see you're contributing to society.

One parent said:

> I try to impart values, such as *tikkun olam*, the importance of education, and asking questions. I also incorporate holidays and send them to religious school. I do, however, teach them that the Torah is fiction, but we can still learn from it.

Being a Mensch

Another Jewish value is aspiring to be a *mensch*. The word *mensch* comes to us from Yiddish, and originally from the German word for "person." But a *mensch* is way more than a regular person. It's someone who is decent, ethical, polite, honest, and caring. A *mensch* is an upright human being, a role model. They do what's right because it feels good to do it, not because they've been told to do it or because they think they ought to. When they have done something good or right, they would never brag about it or try to get credit for it.

One parent said their aim was:

> Raising them to be happy, healthy *menschen* who are productive members of society.

Other Values

Here, I just want to sum up a few other points that often influence how Jews live.

Pikuach nefesh, which has been referred to above, is the principle that states that saving someone's life should come above all else. That is why, for example, abortion would be considered acceptable in some circumstances. *Kavod habriyot* is respect for human beings and means that we should acknowledge other people's individuality, dignity, and humanity, and treat them with kindness, compassion, and respect. The Hebrew word *shalom* means "peace," and *shalom bayit* is a concept that refers to peace in the home. In a broad sense, *shalom bayit* suggests that in relationships, we should communicate with openness and honesty and should listen to and care for one another. Finally, *hachnasat orchim*, which means "welcoming guests," extends the idea of peace in the home to hospitality in a general sense.

I would argue that all Jewish values boil down to consideration for our fellow human beings, other creatures, and the planet.

Living in a way that follows all these values would mean a person is carrying out *mitzvahs*, or good deeds. As a parent said about their belief regarding parenting:

I believe every child that I have is a *neshama* (a soul) entrusted to me by *HaShem* to raise in the path of Torah and *mitzvahs.*

Education and Questioning

It is a stereotype that Jewish people love to study, but I think this is a stereotype we should be proud of. Studying has always been a priority for Jewish people. It's true that early on, this mainly applied to males, but mothers have been recognized as the educators in the home, and before long, both girls and boys were educated. I must acknowledge that in more observant communities, however, the genders do get different types and levels of education. In less traditional groups, everyone is equally educated.

Education for many Jews is both secular and religious. Torah study is a pillar for observant Jews. The study of the Torah requires literacy. People were expected to be able to read holy teachings themselves, and to be able to analyze them independently. This is different from some other religious groups, where one leader/priest was said to be responsible and to be the only one who could access the texts. For this reason, some groups became literate much later than Jews, as only the leader (always a man) needed to be able to read the religious texts. Studying the Torah was thought to offer guidance and to help people live moral and useful lives.

"The major themes throughout Judaism are that God is one, that life has a purpose, and that purpose is to live a good and moral life. However, life is very confusing and filled with potential conflict. The essence of orthodox Judaism is that only through intense and relentless study involving argument and counterargument via logic and extrapolation, can Jews be guided through this confusion into leading the proper life. Therefore, the orthodox Jewish essence is that one must study Torah from the earliest years with all their intellectual might. The purpose is to try to figure out through logic and introspection, debate and counter debate, all based on Torah, what it is that God expects of us. Only through critical study of Torah can orthodox Jews figure out how to manage every single detail of living" (Silber, 2010, n.p.).

Of course, education happens everywhere, not just in *cheder* (religious school) or at synagogue, and education isn't always religious in content or purpose. "It's not magic. It's not genetics. It's that Talmudic mandate to be a light in the world—learning, practicing, teaching" (Acho & Tishby, 2024, p. 147). This love of learning is partly why Jews survive and thrive.

It is really important to note that this isn't just rote learning we're talking about, though. Education demands questioning, analyzing, and debating. In other words, you should think for yourself and consider different perspectives, rather than simply accepting everything you've been told. "Even the most fundamentalist orthodox Jewish viewpoint maintains that Torah and science do not conflict. Humankind must use its creative intelligence to resolve conflict and to figure out from the "basic" principles of Torah what is right and never to be blinded by dogma… The orthodox view of the most respected rabbinic minds is that Torah should be a window to view the universe with an open mind and should not be a wooden shutter" (Silber, 2010, n.p.).

Jewish parents will need to make decisions about whether to send their children to a full-time Jewish school, or to a mainstream school plus a weekend/evening Jewish school (generally referred to as Hebrew school or *cheder*), or only to a mainstream school, or to home-educate them, or something else altogether. Whatever their decision regarding formal education, they will generally also always encourage discussion and analysis in the home. One parent wrote:

> [My child] is at a Jewish school and we do holidays at home/on the road, etc. It's important for me as a Jew abroad to put in the effort to educate her on what it means to be Jewish.

It is probably due to this emphasis on education that many academic and professional fields have a disproportionate number of Jews in them. It's not some conspiracy on the part of Jews. Rather, it's a hunger to learn, to think, and to contribute to the world.

Knowledge of Judaism

In terms of education, many also believe that knowledge specifically of Judaism should be offered to children. I already mentioned how some people choose a Jewish day school or send their children to religious school on the weekends, often in preparation for having a bar or bat mitzvah one day (a coming-of-age ceremony, where they become a "child of the commandments"). Besides that, a majority of Jewish families tend to teach about Judaism by honoring the holidays. As noted earlier, you will find Jewish people who celebrate the holidays despite not considering themselves religious, or even being atheist. For many Jewish parents, a way of passing on Jewish culture is through this recognition of the key holidays and the stories and values that those holidays commemorate.

One parent said:

> I'm not religious. We don't go to synagogue, and my kids aren't particularly steeped in Judaism. But it is very important to me that they understand their heritage and our history as a people especially since so many people still hate us today. The ways I parent as a Jewish person are constantly evolving.

Another wrote:

> [I] focus on Jewish culture and customs, particularly holiday traditions. I think it's important to maintain Jewish traditions for future generations and pass on Jewish history.

A third said:

> It was important to me that my kids decide about their own Judaism based on knowledge and not ignorance. Therefore, it was important to me that they be able to read Hebrew, follow a service, chant Torah, etc. They have their own *tefillin* (that they don't use) and their own *tallitot* (that they do use when they go to *shul*). It isn't so much about Judaism being better than anything else, but about feeling like I have an obligation to pass on our own history and background, because no one else will do it for us.

For these and other parents, regardless of their level of religiosity, they want to pass on knowledge about Jewish history and traditions, and they often encourage their children to decide for themselves as they get older how much of that they wish to carry on.

Family

Amidst the education, the charitable work, and all the other values and habits that are considered vital parts of Jewish parenting, I probably would be remiss in not adding that family tends to be quite important to Jews. Friday night Shabbat dinners are often big family affairs; these regular meals may also include friends, neighbors, colleagues, and random people someone's met at synagogue or while volunteering, because coming together for food and companionship is so prized. I've heard some Jewish people express surprise at the way Americans celebrate Thanksgiving or how many families have large Christmas feasts, because those are just annual events, whereas Jewish families tend to meet weekly.

Psalm 128:6, or "'May you live to see your children's children,'" has been a favorite Jewish blessing since antiquity. It expresses the hope that a person will live a long life, long enough to welcome the arrival of grandchildren. Jewish tradition regards this as a blessing" (Klein, 1998, pp. 256-257). Family is prioritized and treasured. Some Jews say they are happiest when eating a meal together, debating the news or some finer point from the Torah or even gossiping about friends or just sharing titbits of information from their day, and basking in the glow of togetherness and intimacy.

Appreciation for Life

Jews tend to highly appreciate and value life. Instead of saying "cheers", we say *l'chaim*, which means "to life". Also, we say *Am Yisrael chai*, or "the people of Israel live." Some might wear a necklace with the word *chai*, or "life," on it in Hebrew. Life is precious and should be valued and honored.

A mother shared how, despite the desperately sad loss of her son, she and her family aimed to be thankful for everything they have and to honor life in all its forms. She wrote:

> We are a traditional Jewish family and raise our kids to love Jewish festivals and Jewish traditions, and to follow the precepts of *Pirkei Avot* (The Ethics of the Fathers).
>
> Tragically, my son died at age 12 from a rare form of brain cancer. On his grave are engraved the words, אֵיזֶהוּ עָשִׁיר? הַשָּׂמֵחַ בְּחֶלְקוֹ–Who is rich? Those who are happy with what they have.
>
> I believe it is important to raise kids to be kind and respectful to all human beings. This isn't specifically a Jewish precept.

A Jewish Household

So, given all the vital Jewish values and beliefs, how, then, does this affect approaches to parenting? In short, parents may choose to imbue their household with Jewish actions, such a going to synagogue or giving to charity, and Jewish ethics, including being as good a person as possible or showing consideration for the planet, and the people and animals that live here. It is also suggested that Jewish parents "are obligated to bring their children into the covenant through a public ritual; provide them with clothing and shelter, teach them Torah, teach them to read, counsel them towards higher education and employment, teach them that their job is not only what they do during world but their job is also to make the world a better place, foster their self-esteem, and some say teach them to swim" (Falk & Judson, 2004, p. 48). The swim part might seem a bit random among all those other guidelines, but it can be a matter of safety. Many schools now have a swim requirement, showing that it's viewed as a sensible idea.

One parent said that this is how they have a Jewish household (they mention swimming too, but in a metaphorical sense).

We read Jewish story books, celebrate Jewish holidays, go to synagogue, etc. I can't speak generally about it but we have a Jewish house—it's just how we live, it's the water we swim in. Our older child goes to a Chabad daycare in addition to the YMCA. It's important that we use Hebrew and Yiddish terminology, teach Yiddish songs, celebrate Shabbos every week (even though we're not fully observant), find ways to bring our kids into the holidays. We also live in an area with few Jews, and even fewer observant ones, so we think a lot about how we want our kids to present themselves and Judaism to their peers, how we want to explain others' holidays to them, etc.

When asked what they do to parent Jewishly, another replied:

Everything! From singing Jewish bedtime songs and saying *Shema* every night to my son wearing a yarmulke, we try to surround our children with a pride and love of their identity as Jews. We try not to expose them to the toxic or meaningless values of the secular world so they only watch Jewish, Chassidic videos, and we do not own a TV. We turn to Jewish educators for parenting guidance because it is important to us to recognize the inherent Godliness within our children and use that as a guide.

A third, with now-grown children, described as follows:

We sang *Modeh Ani* and washed our baby's hands every morning, sang Jewish songs throughout the day, and we sang *Shema* at bedtime. It says a couple times in the Tanach that God blessed Avraham's descendants because He knew Avraham would teach his children to love God and follow in His ways, and my husband and I very much believe in that. All of our kids spent at least some time in Jewish day school. We tried to use trust in *Hashem* as a way for our children to offload some of their anxieties ("We do our best and let *Hashem* handle the rest," I'd sometimes tell them.) We modeled gratitude both to *Hashem* and to the people around us all the time. We have a kosher and *Shomer Shabbos* home and this was discussed with our kids and modeled in age-appropriate ways all along.

A less religiously observant parent said:

> We don't keep kosher or go to synagogue every single week. We don't even believe in God, and the kids know it. But we do celebrate all Jewish holidays and talk about being proud of our Jewish heritage. The children go to Hebrew school so they can meet other Jewish people their age, and they are encouraged to learn about and participate in Judaism to whatever extent they want to. We are clear with them that we're culturally Jewish, and that this matters.

In short, there are many ways to have a Jewish household and to be a Jewish parent, but instilling children with knowledge about their Jewishness, and pride in their identity, while also trying to teach them to be good people, seems to be the overarching thread that connects many, perhaps most, Jewish parents.

CHAPTER 8

Supporting Jewish People in the Birth World

If you are reading this and you are a healthcare professional or other person who regularly comes in contact with Jewish colleagues or clients or patients, then I hope by now you have learned quite a lot about Judaism, and about Jewish birthing and parenting practices and beliefs. In this final chapter, I'd like to focus more specifically on how we can make the birth world a more inclusive place for Jewish people. Certainly, all the foregoing information and ideas will help, because the more you know, the more you can adapt or adjust as needed, but I also think some very practical tips might be beneficial. As Jewish midwives Laura Godfrey-Isaacs and Jessica Falk Perlman (2025) point out in a talk they held at a maternity and midwifery conference, "Jewish communities have been neglected and overlooked regarding health inequality." It's time for this to change.

Combatting Antisemitism in the Birth World

First of all, the birth world, like every other field or institution, is not free of antisemitism. And yes, I can just as easily note that it's not free of any kind of racism or prejudice, because frankly, these problems are everywhere. We're all prey to biases and preconceptions that sometimes make us treat others in a way that isn't as impartial, respectful, or caring as they deserve or require. But since this book is about Jews, let's focus on antisemitism.

All institutions and all individuals should do their best to educate themselves about Jews, Judaism, and the specific needs of Jewish people, and they should apply what they learn. Institutions and organizations need unambiguous policies that state how they will handle any form of antisemitic harassment, discrimination, or other such issues. It also needs to be clear who people should turn to when they have heard or experienced antisemitism. There should ideally be several named managers or administrators who are available for discussing and dealing with any concerns or complaints; patients, clients, and employees should all have access to such people's name and contact details. They should also know exactly what will happen once a concern has been raised. This includes the timeline for how promptly the situation will be investigated, what steps will be taken, what the potential outcomes might be, and what will happen if the results are unsatisfactory.

Additionally, everyone would ideally be trained in how to have difficult conversations and how to speak up when they hear something inappropriate. In other words, if someone is telling a "Jewish joke," or making a nasty comment about Jews, other people need to know what to do and to feel confident doing it. It isn't always so easy to say, "Sorry, but I don't think that's acceptable," or "We don't talk about each other like that in this workplace," or "I think you might need to educate yourself a little more," and yet doing so is exactly what's necessary. People should feel able to speak calmly and politely in response to prejudice, while knowing that the rest on the institution will back them up. It may be that offering continuing education classes in unconscious bias, having challenging conversations, or even discussing taboo topics can help.

Perhaps most importantly, a workplace or institution needs to create an atmosphere of trust and no tolerance of discrimination. Having policies and encouraging people to speak up will mean nothing if this isn't followed through with. People need to feel safe and accepted, and they need to see managers or others acting in a determined way to ensure that everyone is treated respectfully, and that any issues are dealt with assiduously and efficiently. It may go without saying that improving inclusion and respect for one group of people will actually offer benefits to everyone; respect isn't a pie that shrinks if you give a piece to one person or group. On the contrary, showing a commitment to equality and inclusion and refusing to accept prejudice of any kind will improve things across the board for all. Another way of saying this is that giving a piece of respect pie to, say, Jews will make the pie grow ever bigger and tastier. It will help nourish everyone.

In short:

- Offer training on Jews and Jewish practices.
- Have clear policies regarding how antisemitism will be handled.
- Make the chain of command known, so people understand who to go to.
- Train staff in having difficult conversations.
- Create a workplace that is safe and free of discrimination.

Treatment of Jewish Birthing People and Families

The chapters before this one aimed in part to offer information about Jewish birth and perinatal practices, with the hope being that more knowledge might lead to more understanding and compassionate treatment of Jewish patients and clients.

To sum it up, however, we can say that serving and treating Jewish people means being considerate of their beliefs and traditions. For instance, although there are varying views on circumcision, even among Jews, if a family opts for it, you should respect it. Recall the story mentioned earlier about a family that was reported to social services for planning a circumcision. In addition, it's important to recognize that many Jewish people have experienced trauma, whether historical, generational, or individual, and they may need additional support. Know where to signpost them so they can receive the information or care they need. For some Jews, their first or most important point of contact may be their rabbi. One mother wrote:

> One thing I will say is that sometimes less religious but knowledgeable Jews will tell me a medicine is okay to take, or okay for my kids, but I prefer to ask a *Rav* [rabbi] first.

That is to say, even if a medical professional tells her something, she will want to check with her rabbi about it as well. Working in the birth world means being empathetic and seeing all clients or patients as individuals who are shaped by the culture they come from and live in. One Jewish midwife noted:

> If I were to care for a more religious family then I would ensure to be respectful around beliefs and being conscious of different practice (e.g., not asking about the name until after the *bris*, being understanding if the husband does not want to be in room at the time of birth, etc.).

Another thing to consider is whether you could run Jewish-specific antenatal or postnatal classes or groups, or whether you could signpost patients or clients to such activities. Observant Jews will already likely be linked to a synagogue and/or Jewish school (as one person told me, "Participating in the local synagogue is a way to quickly integrate into a community"), but less observant Jews might not, and regardless of that, they may not be aware of other opportunities aimed particularly at Jews. Developing such groups or events or finding out about them and signposting your patients to them, plus trying to build connections between Jews where possible, will also help improve outcomes for Jewish families.

The National Health Service in the UK recently produced a report entitled, "A review of NHS Health Communications with (and for) Jewish Communities" (Ingold, Rianjongdee, & Carrington-Elson, 2024). While this report is not specifically about birth and is more generally about communication rather than particular treatments or services, it also offers some tips. They recommend building trust, being inclusive, considering your language, thinking through the imagery you use in publications or elsewhere, analyzing the "complex barriers or challenges [Jews may have] in accessing care & trusting services," and how to overcome them, consulting with rabbis, and planning which channels to employ to communicate with Jewish communities" (Ingold, Rianjongdee, & Carrington-Elson, 2024, n.p.). They are focused more on strictly Orthodox individuals and families, but these ideas are worth keeping in mind when working with all Jews.

What Jews Wish Healthcare Professionals Did or Knew

I asked Jewish people what they wish healthcare professionals would say, do, or know to better help their Jewish patients or clients. Many simply wished non-Jews would better educate themselves so they weren't offering unsuitable care or making inappropriate comments. Examples would be not to give non-kosher food to those who keep kosher or to expect a husband to touch his laboring wife if they observe *niddah* or to schedule routine appointments on key Jewish holidays.

Here is a selection of comments:

- Stop blessing me and my kids [i.e., some, usually Christian, healthcare professionals offer Christian blessings and prayers, which may be well-intentioned, but this is not appreciated by Jews].
- I have found that many professionals don't recognize Jewish as being an ethnicity, and not just a religion.
- Not to make assumptions, but to open a dialogue. Also, if they live in an area with a lot of Jews, get training and also don't assume all Jews are the same.
- I do think it's important for them to be aware of some of the basic customs, like *Kashrut* and *Shabbat*.
- More understanding and knowledge of *bris* on day eight rather than hospital circumcision during hospital stay.
- Someone posted online that Jewish women give birth quickly because they have a specific kind of pelvis, which is total nonsense.
- Where to even start? There isn't much knowledge of Jewish practices. More education would help.

In short, don't assume, try to learn more, and ask if you're unsure.

Treatment of Jewish Applicants or Staff

A few years ago, shortly before October 7, 2023 (when Hamas attacked Israel), I carried out a study into antisemitism in the workplace. My findings did not surprise me at the time. Over half of the 120 Jewish people who replied stated that they had experienced antisemitism at work. By causal antisemitism, they referred to jokes, comments, and myths (such as the blood libel). In terms of more formal prejudice, they also noted that their names/identities were mixed up with those of other Jews in the workplace (as if Jewish employees were interchangeable); that they had swastikas graffitied on their office doors or drawn on papers; or that they were passed over for deserved promotions for reasons that seemed clearly linked to their ethnic and/or religious identity. This means that many people in my survey experienced both casual and formal antisemitism. All of these examples are upsetting and some are illegal, depending on the context and country.

I have not carried out another academic study since October 7, 2023, but I have spoken to many people informally, and also read articles, and I get the impression that if I did produce another proper study, the results would show that way more than half the people have experienced antisemitism in the workplace now. Besides the kinds of antisemitism referred to in the foregoing paragraph, people have noted high levels of graffiti, both swastikas and words/phrases, on their personal offices or in other spots at their place of employment. They have also heard more negative comments about Jews and Israel; have felt excluded from workplace events, both social and professional; and have had to hear about colleagues going to protests against Israel, or have even had to walk through such protests to get to work. Certainly, people are entitled to whatever political beliefs they want, and free speech generally is an important right, but that doesn't need to be at the expense of those who are trying to do their jobs. Sometimes free speech slips over into discrimination and harassment.

The same issues can happen to Jewish people applying for roles in workplaces. They should be considered without bias for jobs they are qualified for and, if they are invited to an interview, they shouldn't have to walk through protests or be subjected to nasty comments when they are going through the interview process. As some research notes, "[a] recent survey found that a quarter of American hiring managers and recruiters wanted fewer Jewish people in their industry and/or are less likely to advance Jewish applicants. Among the top reasons given: perceptions that Jewish people have too much power and wealth already and don't need their job" (Acho & Tishby, 2024, p. 109).

Jewish applicants and employees have the right to be treated impartially and respectfully, just as anyone else does. Workplaces that are hiring, promoting, simply retaining staff, or even making them redundant need to keep this in mind and to consider their approaches. A workplace should be safe for all employees, including the Jewish ones.

A Jewish employee said:

> My former workplace was rife with antisemitism. I had colleagues make jokes about how greedy Jews are, and one time when we were going to hire a new staff member, our manager refused to interview an Israeli applicant who was very well qualified. The manager said, "We don't need any more Jews here. You know what they're like." Then she laughed and looked pointedly at me. I finally went to HR about all this, but they didn't see the problem.

As a final note, while I was talking mainly about employees and applicants in this section, I should acknowledge that there are Jews who are not official employees but who nonetheless work, sometimes temporarily, in the birth world. Examples would include doulas, independent midwives, lactation consultants, and others. They too should be treated with consideration, even if they are not salaried employees in the same way that a doctor or full-time midwife might be. No one should be facing discrimination while trying to do their job.

Equality, Diversity, and Inclusion in the Workplace

Here in the UK, improving equality, diversity, and inclusion (EDI) is treated as a pretty positive and standard thing to do. In the US, where the words are usually put in a different order and called DEI, it's looked upon with much more suspicion, especially now that there has been a change to the political leadership. As I write, the current government is dismantling EDI policies and taskforces. I'm not completely sure why, but I think some of it has to do with complicated and painful discussions about challenging topics such as reparations and affirmative action or positive discrimination. In the US, many people are against these things, sometimes just because they don't understand what is meant by these terms. My experience (as someone who consults in EDI and is therefore biased about it) is that in the UK and other parts of the world, EDI is mostly viewed as a way of trying to make institutions, organizations, and workplaces more inclusive. It involves learning about different groups of people and thinking about how to ensure that workplaces are diverse and supportive, rather than homogenous places that expect everyone to be the same. For example, in the UK, making a workplace friendlier towards, say, autistic employees is broadly considered to be a vital thing to do that benefits everyone, not just autistic people. In the US, such a move is viewed with more suspicion.

I wanted to mention the difference in attitude towards EDI/DEI because some of my suggestions in this section might seem offensive to people in the US, who have a more negative view of DEI, whereas they might appear to be really obvious to folks in the UK, who are very accustomed to EDI.

Education and Policies

The starting-point for EDI should be better education (about all ethnicities, religions, sexualities, genders, classes, abilities, neurodiversities, and so forth). It does not have to be complicated or expensive to offer the occasional lunchtime lecture or workshop on topics such as identifying and fighting antisemitism, or Jewish birth practices, or Jewish holidays, or whatever else. Where possible, such training should be run by Jewish people themselves, but this should not add to their emotional or actual workload and they should be given time in lieu if they expend significant hours and effort on educational contributions.

Training should be followed up with strong policies that clarify how people in a workplace—including, say, a hospital, doctor's office, or birthing center—should expect to be treated and should be expected to treat one another, plus what will happen when those expectations are not fulfilled. There should be a firm antiracism policy that explicitly mentions antisemitism, and every workplace should develop and encourage a culture where people speak up against jokes, derogatory comments, isms, and so on.

When people have concerns, those concerns should be investigated promptly. It's also worth noting that while workplaces generally can't control what employees post on social media on a personal level, they should have a policy around expectations for when people are posting in a professional capacity. They may wish to state rules around that, or else they run the risk of employees inadvertently (or possibly on purpose) getting a workplace into hot water by posting racist or stereotyped material (e.g., Glynn & McIntosh, 2025, regarding the highest-paid BBC presenter who shared antisemitic content and had to leave his job).

One Jewish lactation consultant said:

> I had to leave social media groups, and even IBCLC groups, because they have turned radical. They post anti-Jewish stuff and are even against male circumcision.

Although this example is about groups that often can't be policed, except for official IBCLC groups, such as the Lactation Consultants of Great Britain, it still shows how upsetting and insulting posts on social media can be. Workplaces need to ensure that their physical and virtual spaces are not filled with vitriol and that such issues are taken seriously and handled with urgency.

Committees and Staff Networks

In addition, for workplaces that have EDI committees, they should ensure that those committees include Jewish members of staff (and if you're at a workplace without such a committee, you could recommend that they start one). EDI committees can write position papers, have working parties to tackle particular issues (such as racism generally, or antisemitism specifically), organize events or training, and state actionable outcomes, so there is an unmistakable direction and focus for their work.

Larger workplaces might also consider having affinity networks (such as an LGBTQ+ staff network). If so, a Jewish staff network would be beneficial, as a way for Jewish staff members to meet, to discuss their specific needs and desires, and to positively contribute to their institution, organization, or company. At one job, I started and helped run a Jewish staff group, and it ended up being quite an important safe space as well as a place where we could develop new ideas and make contributions to the workplace.

Inclusive Language, Imagery, and Scheduling

A workplace should also be inclusive when it comes to language, imagery, and scheduling. I remember reviewing a company's antiracism pamphlet and being bemused to note that all the pictures in the pamphlet showed white-presenting people. That's not the way to prove that a workplace is tackling racism.

Rather, images should show a range of skin tones, abilities, genders, religions, and so on. This may sound like a comment that is encouraging tokenism, i.e., a tick-box exercise where a workplace can happily feel that they are inclusive in their imagery if they feature, for example, one person in a wheelchair, a woman in a headscarf, and one non-white-presenting person, but ideally real effort would be put into thinking through who is depicted, and how they are depicted. Also, the vast majority of Jewish people are not old men with big beards, despite what the media might have you believe, so although featuring one such person might lead a workplace to feel like they can happily tick the "Jewish box," that might not be the best approach.

In addition, language should be inclusive where possible. It isn't necessary to use terms such as "Christmas break" or "Easter break" in organizational documentation, for the simple and obvious reason that not everyone celebrates Christmas or Easter. It's just as easy and much more inclusive to refer to the "winter break" or "spring break," or to wish someone "happy holidays" if you aren't sure which, if any, holidays they celebrate. Some people argue that this "erases" Christianity, but that isn't the case at all. If you are sure someone is Christian and commemorates Christian holidays, then by all means wish them "merry Christmas" or a relaxing "Easter break". But if you aren't sure, you can use more general terms. Using generic phrases might take some getting used to, but they include more people. Christianity is still the biggest religion in the world, in terms of the number of adherents, but Islam and Hinduism aren't that far behind, and unless a workplace is specifically a Christian one (or a Muslim one, and so on), then the fact is that you will have employees of many faiths or no faith at all.

Finally, inclusive scheduling means retaining flexibility around scheduling as well as in regard to absence policies. Here in the UK, most workplaces and schools give time off for Christmas as a matter of course. I've always been glad to have time off, but I don't actually celebrate Christmas. It would be much more useful for people to be given a set number of days that they could use throughout the year for whichever festivities or other occasions they wanted. This would also ensure that staffing is available even on some of the holidays considered universal. For a volunteer role I carried out, people always appreciated that I took on more work at Christmastime so everyone else could enjoy the holiday with their families.

Another factor related to scheduling is how certain events regularly are scheduled for times Jewish people can't make. Many Jewish college/university staff have been dismayed by the way the autumn semester tends to start around Rosh Hashanah, the Jewish new year, which means they either have to miss the first day of classes or meetings, or else skip synagogue; this is not a choice people should have to make. Someone in my survey pointed out, "All conferences are on Shabbat. We're such a minority." It's difficult to attend continuing professional development, such as conferences or colloquia, if they are always on a Saturday. It might be helpful to mix things up and sometimes have, say, midweek conference instead.

Furthermore, workplaces should consider whether they can be flexible on timing during the week. I spoke to one person whose workplace had a regular meeting on Friday afternoons, which is when she needed to get home before sundown for Shabbat. It would have been better to move the meeting to the morning or to another day altogether, and it would have felt more inclusive and understanding. This is true of the application process as well. If a Jewish candidate is coming for an interview, be sure that the time and date don't conflict with Shabbat or with Jewish holidays.

Celebrations and Commemorations

I want to end this section on equality, diversity, and inclusion in the workplace with a more positive note. Workplaces should honor and recognize Jewish celebrations where possible. If you would wish people a happy Easter or Diwali in your staff newsletter or in your weekly meeting, do the same for Jewish holidays. If you offer a Christmas lunch or Chinese New Year meal in your staff canteen, you could consider having the occasional Jewish dish.

If your workplace is one that puts up posters, or has parties or events to acknowledge holidays, then do the same for Jewish ones. There are many heritage months (Asian American and Pacific Islander Heritage month, for example) or other special occasions (such as LGBTQ+ Pride) that some workplaces mark with reading lists, film screenings, brown bag lunches, and so forth, so it is important that Jewish holidays and Jewish contributions to your field or workplace are not forgotten.

Many places do nod to Holocaust Memorial Day, and that is really important, but it's also essential to remember that though the Holocaust looms large for Jews and other groups, there is much more to being Jewish than the Holocaust. Someone in HR could develop a list of the key Jewish holidays and also some major Jewish people who have worked in your field, and they could come up with plans to celebrate those people and events too.

Avoid Politics

It should go without saying that politics don't really belong in the birth world. Yes, the body is a political space in some ways, and the personal is political, and giving birth is a feminist issue, and fill-in-the-blank here for any other relevant slogan. Those things are true and there's a time and a place for discussing all of them. However, your own political views should absolutely not negatively impact the care you provide someone.

I've read or heard about increasing numbers of healthcare professionals who are wearing badges that identify their political beliefs, or who are actually speaking to and in front of patients about attending rallies or about agreeing or disagreeing with certain politicians, or about supporting or hating particular countries, all of which is not only unprofessional and irrelevant in a work setting but also can make people extremely uncomfortable.

Not only can it make people feel awkward, but it can also be scary. To experience that sort of thing—for instance, seeing someone wearing a symbol of a group that is vocally against you—in a setting where you are expecting unbiased medical care takes it to another level. In those circumstances, we don't feel like we can be ourselves. We don't know whether we're going to receive the care we need. We don't know whether there's a chance that we won't survive whatever it is we're going through, all because of the prejudiced or stereotyped beliefs that the nurse or doctor or doula has. It shouldn't be like that. It's shocking to think that at times the birth world—a place supposedly dedicated to supporting people through one of the most vulnerable times in their lives—could be so prejudiced and cruel.

As such, I'd like to suggest a couple of things. First of all, doctors, nurses, midwives, doulas, lactation consultants, and other healthcare professionals: keep your politics out of your work as much as you can. Don't scare your patients by stridently announcing your views, because you don't necessarily know what they believe and how what you are saying will impact them. There's room in society for those conversations, but the hospital or the doctor's office isn't it. Also, if you feel you have a bias against a certain group, take the time to educate yourself. Read, attend a talk, sign up for training, request a workshop at your workplace. Whatever you can do to check your bias will be well worth it.

Second, if you, as a patient, experience discrimination of any kind, report it. I know it's not fair for you to feel that the burden of such emotional and practical labor is on you, but I'm afraid that things won't change unless people are called to account for what they say and do. You can write a letter to the practice or contact patient advice services or call the human resources department. You can also request a change to the team that is working with you. If you have a partner or doula or other friend/relative with you, you can ask them to do some of this work, so you can focus on giving birth. They can be your gatekeeper as needed.

Third, for all of us, if we witness something, even if it's not aimed at us, we should speak up. It can be scary of course, but we have to do it, for the sake of society. You can say something at the time or you can report it later, depending on your comfort level.

Finally, we should all do better. We should all learn more about other people, other places, other beliefs. We should aim to see our fellow humans as, well, just that: fellow humans. We're not types, we're not stereotypes, we're not just our religion or ethnicity or ability or class or profession, etc. We're complicated individuals, in all the fullness of that word.

Of course what's happening in the world matters and it impacts everything, sometimes subtly and at other times in very blatant ways. But to whatever extent possible, we need to avoid politics in the birth world, especially when supporting people as they give birth and become parents.

Summary

Noa Tishby offers a useful list of what allies can do to support Jews: "Adopt the IHRA Definition of Antisemitism …Do your homework [learn more and make new diverse friends]…Ask your Jewish friends or colleagues to be invited for Shabbat…Go analog, not digital [i.e. be an ally in life, not just online]…Loud and proud [stop hiding, be proud of who you are]" (Acho & Tishby, 2024, pp. 221-224). Those are all excellent ideas as a starting-point, but the birth world—where people work and give birth, and come for both professional and personal support—should go further than that. Here's how:

- Antisemitism must be rooted out, challenged, and combatted.
- Jewish families and individuals giving birth should be supported to give birth in an environment free from prejudice, and with deference to their specific needs.
- Workplaces should commit to inclusivity, by which I mean they should offer further training and support for all staff members and should have clear policies dedicated to equality, diversity, and inclusion.
- Jewish staff and applicants should be treated fairly.
- Jewish contributions and holidays should be celebrated and recognized the way non-Jewish ones are.
- Politics should be avoided to whatever extent possible.

This might seem like a lot to ask, but vowing to treat Jews equitably is only ethical and fair, plus doing so would in fact improve the birth world for everyone.

CHAPTER 9

Conclusion

My intentions with this book have been three-fold. Firstly, I hope that Jewish people will have felt seen and acknowledged and maybe even will have gotten some inspiration regarding being a Jewish parent. Secondly, I hope that non-Jewish people—especially those in the birth world—will have learned something and received some insight into what it means to be Jewish during the antenatal, labor, and postnatal periods, and that this may impact in a positive way how they work with Jewish patients and clients. Finally, I would like to believe I have offered some ideas about how the birth world could be made more inclusive towards Jewish employees, applicants, and families. As such, we have covered a lot of ground, ranging over defining Jews, Jewish ideas about sex, reasons to have children, genetic testing, funeral rituals for stillbirths, kosher food, circumcision and baby-naming, breastfeeding, values to pass on to children, making workplaces more inclusive, and much more. I'm sure there are additional topics I could have included. I'm also certain that some Jewish people will disagree with certain points in this book, because there are many different ways of understanding Judaism and being Jewish. Nonetheless, I'd like to think that this has been a useful introduction to Jewish beliefs around pregnancy, birth, and parenting.

For observant Jews, "[n]ew life is celebrated and sanctified within the framework of God, Torah, and community. All Jewish attitudes towards birth rest on these three central pillars of Jewish life" (Klein, 1998/2000, p. xxix). Jewish people who are less religious or not at all religious might feel differently about God and Torah, but they will probably find that their Jewish background and community does influence how they produce and celebrate the next generation.

"A Jew's beliefs and values mold his or her religious experiences. Thus, someone who accepts the yoke of Torah finds Torah in everyday life as well as in the special experience of bringing a child into the world. In addition, for such a person the prayers, the blessings, duties, and rituals associated with childbearing are all regarded as religious experiences. On the other hand, for many secular Jews, any spiritual feelings associated with childbearing remain amorphous, emotional, and difficult to verbalize. Secular Jews may acknowledge their Jewish feelings only when choosing a name for their newborn, or not at all" (Klein, 1998/2000, p. 253). This quote may do a disservice in its description of secular Jews, but nonetheless, we could sum up the idea by paraphrasing a well-known saying: if you've met one Jew, well, you've met one Jew (you could replace "Jews" in that sentence with any other subgroup). Jewish people's traditions and habits will depend on their ethnic background, their level of religiosity, the customs of their people, and their own feelings and choices. This means that some Jewish people—whether in your family, your friendship group or community, or those you are serving as a healthcare professional—will treat childbirth and childrearing in a profoundly religious way, considering it to be sacred fulfilment of commandments. Others maybe feel Jewish only in a cultural sense but will still carry out Jewish traditions. Even that might be a step too far from some Jews. Still others may disavow their Judaism altogether. It's important for us to understand the wide variety of Jewish beliefs and traditions and then to respect individual choices when it comes to birth, infant-feeding, the postpartum period, and parenting.

Jews are traditionally told to be fruitful and multiply. My profound wish is that with this book, I can make it easier and more comfortable for Jewish people to do so, because they will know that there is knowledgeable and caring support available to them.

I hope this book has offered some new information and ideas and helped make Jewish issues more visible. Whether you yourself want to be fruitful or you want to support those who do, thank you for reading this book.

References

Abramowitz, J. (2017). *You are probably using the term* 'tikkun olam' *incorrectly.* Jew in the City. https://jewinthecity.com/2017/06/you-are-probably-using-the-term-tikkun-olam-incorrectly/.

Abramowitz, J. (2022). *What is modern orthodoxy?* Jew in the City. https://jewinthecity.com/2022/03/what-is-modern-orthodoxy/.

Acho, E., & Tishby, N. (2024). *Uncomfortable conversations with a Jew.* Simon and Schuster.

Ahuvia, M. (2016). *Who are Jews? An overview of Jewish history from ancient times on, and the origins of antisemitism.* UW Stroum Center for Jewish Studies. https://jewishstudies.washington.edu/who-are-jews-jewish-history-origins-antisemitism/.

American Jewish Committee. (2021). *A guide to recognizing when anti-Israel actions become antisemitic.* https://www.ajc.org/sites/default/files/pdf/2021-10/A%20Guide%20to%20Recognizing%20When%20Anti-Israel%20Actions%20Become%20Antisemitic.pdf.

Anne Frank House. (2024). *Antisemitism in secondary education: Summary of the survey research.* https://www.annefrank.org/media/filer_public/5c/27/5c27eec6-c18b-44d0-a41e-deeb529a6082/antisemitism_secondary_education_-_summary_2023.pdf.

Antidefamation League. (2023). *U.S. antisemitic incidents hit highest level ever recorded, ADL audit finds.* Antidefamation League. https://www.adl.org/resources/press-release/us-antisemitic-incidents-hit-highest-level-ever-recorded-adl-audit-finds.

Antidefamation League. (2024). *Antisemitism in the classroom.* Antidefamation League. https://www.adl.org/antisemitism-classroom.

Attorneys for the Rights of the Child. (2000). *Man sues for being circumcised as an infant.* Attorneys for the Rights of the Child. https://www.arclaw.org/press-releases/man-sues-for-being-circumcised-as-an-infant.

Aziz, A. (2022). *Why are there so many Jewish Nobel winners?* The Jewish Chronicle. December 8. https://www.thejc.com/opinion/why-are-there-so-many-jewish-nobel-winners-ctycke48.

Baddiel, D. (2021). *Jews don't count.* TLS Books.

Bahrampour, T. (2018, Feb 6). *They considered themselves white, but DNA tests told a more complex story. Washington Post.* https://www.washingtonpost.com/local/social-issues/they-considered-themselves-white-but-dna-tests-told-a-more-complex-story/2018/02/06/16215d1a-e181-11e7-8679-a9728984779c_story.html.

Bashiri, A., Neumann, L., Maymon, E., & Katz, M. (1995). Hyperemesis gravidarum: Epidemiologic features, complications and outcome. *European Journal of Obstetrics & Gynecology and Reproductive Biology, 63*(2), 135–138. https://doi.org/10.1016/0301-2115(95)02238-4.

BBC. (2009). *Judaism: Contraception.* BBC. https://www.bbc.co.uk/religion/religions/judaism/jewishethics/contraception.shtml.

BBC. (2024, Jul 11). *'Wave of Antisemitism' in EU influenced by Israel-Gaza war.* BBC News. https://www.bbc.co.uk/news/articles/c147w9572dvo.

Ben Ari, L. (2024). *'A great loss': Yemen bids farewell to one of its last remaining Jews.* Y Net Global. https://www.ynetnews.com/jewish-world/article/sj7dfbxic.

Blady, R. (2023). *Birth ritual.* Sefaria.org. https://www.sefaria.org/sheets/413801.1?lang=bi.

Board of Deputies. (2025). *Workplace antisemitism.* https://bod.org.uk/wp-content/uploads/2025/04/Workplace-Antisemitism-Survey.pdf.

Boteach, S. (2023). *Kosher sex, 2nd edition.* Gefen.

Boyd, J. (2024). *Antisemitism in the aftermath of October 7.* JPR. https://www.jpr.org.uk/reports/antisemitism-aftermath-october-7-what-do-data-tell-us-and-what-more-do-we-still-need-know.

Brown, A. (2019). *Why breastfeeding grief and trauma matter.* Pinter & Martin.

Cahill, T. (1998). *The gifts of the Jews.* Nan A. Talese.

Cambridge Dictionary. (2024). *BAME.* https://dictionary.cambridge.org/dictionary/english/bame.

Cartun, A. (2001). *Which one is better — Doctor or mohel?* JWeekly. https://jweekly.com/2001/03/23/which-one-is-better-doctor-or-mohel.

Chabad. (2004). *The shir lamaalot.* Chabad. https://www.chabad.org/library/article_cdo/aid/217669/jewish/The-Shir-Lamaalot.htm.

Chana. (2018a). *Chana charity Ltd.* Chana. https://www.chana.org.uk/.

Chana. (2018b). *Judaism, halacha, assisted reproductive technology: Everything you wanted to know about fertility but were afraid to ask.* Chana. https://www.chana.org.uk/webinars/v/62kd8h5f9ca8mxm9py3dlfek98zwrr?categoryId=63343f2e7d9ea100edd03b5d.

Cleveland Clinic. (2023). *Circumcision restoration.* Cleveland Clinic. https://my.clevelandclinic.org/health/treatments/25139-foreskin-restoration?utm_source=Savage+Love&utm_campaign=6e6d9c4434-Savage_Column_09-03-24&utm_medium=email&utm_term=0_-8251e0513b-%5BLIST_EMAIL_ID%5D.

Colino, S.H.S. (2021). Reproductive problems in both men and women are rising at an alarming rate. *Scientific American.* https://www.scientificamerican.com/article/reproductive-problems-in-both-men-and-women-are-rising-at-an-alarming-rate/.

Community Service Trust. (2024). *117% Increase in campus antisemitic incidents.* https://cst.org.uk/news/blog/2024/12/09/117-increase-in-campus-antisemitic-incidents.

Danailova, H. (2024). Combating the shocking rise of antisemitism in health care. *Hadassah Magazine.* https://www.hadassahmagazine.org/2024/10/31/combating-the-shocking-rise-of-antisemitism-in-health-care/.

Danon, D. (2018). *What do you know? Sephardi vs. mizrahi.* Herbert D. Katz Center for Advanced Judaic Studies. https://katz.sas.upenn.edu/resources/blog/what-do-you-know-sephardi-vs-mizrahi.

Diamant, J. (2021). *Jews in U.S. are far less religious than Christians and Americans overall, at least by traditional measures.* Pew Research Center.: https://www.pewresearch.org/short-reads/2021/05/13/jews-in-u-s-are-far-less-religious-than-christians-and-americans-overall-at-least-by-traditional-measures/.

Dickstein, S. (1996). *Jewish ritual practice following a stillbirth*. https://www.rabbinicalassembly.org/sites/default/files/public/halakhah/teshuvot/19912000/dickstein_stillbirth.pdf.

Doherty, R. (2021). Help at hand for pregnant women with rare disorder. *The Jewish Chronicle*. https://www.thejc.com/news/community/help-at-hand-for-pregnant-women-with-rare-disorder-fh75zo8n.

Dolan, P. (2019). *Happy every after*. Penguin.

Encyclopedia Judaica. (2008). *Barrenness and fertility*. Jewish Virtual Library. https://www.jewishvirtuallibrary.org/barrenness-and-fertility.

Engstrom, J.L., Meier, P.P., Jegier, B., Motykowski, J.E., & Zuleger, J.L. (2007). Comparison of milk output from the right and left breasts during simultaneous pumping in mothers of very low birthweight infants. *Breastfeeding Medicine, 2*(2), 83–91. https://doi.org/10.1089/bfm.2006.0019.

Epstein, B.J. (2013). *Are the kids all right?* Intellect Books.

Ertel, C.L. (n.d.). Divine Labor. *Mikveh*. https://www.mikvah.org/article/divine-labor.

Falk Perlman, J., & Godfrey-Isaacs, L. (n.d.). *Antisemitism and inclusion: Towards Jewish cultural safety in maternity care*. https://vimeo.com/1053703106?share=copy.

Falk, S., & Judson, D. (2004). *The Jewish pregnancy book*. Jewish Lights Pub.

Farley, H. (2022, Feb 10). Anti-semitic hate incidents at new high in 2021. *BBC News*. https://www.bbc.co.uk/news/uk-60322106.

Feld, M. (n.d.). *Healing after a miscarriage*. Sinai Memorial Chapel. https://www.sinaichapel.org/tools-resources/additional-poems-mourners.aspx.

Fingerman, J.J. (2019, April 24). *dispelling the myth about jews and poverty. Jewish Journal*. https://jewishjournal.com/commentary/columnist/297539/dispelling-the-myth-about-jews-and-poverty/.

Fischel, E. (2020). *B'sha'ah Tovah and superstition during my pandemic-era pregnancy*. The Forward. Available at: https://forward.com/community/447749/bshaah-tovah-and-superstition-during-my-pandemic-era-pregnancy/.

Fletcher, Y. (2025). *Chutzpah*. Doubleday.

Freeman, T. (2001). *Why Is conversion to Judaism so hard?* Chabad. https://www.chabad.org/library/article_cdo/aid/3002/jewish/Why-Is-Conversion-to-Judaism-So-Hard.htm.

Freeman, T., & Shurpin, Y. (2007). *Why Is Jewishness matrilineal? Maternal descent In Judaism*. Chabad. https://www.chabad.org/library/article_cdo/aid/601092/jewish/Why-Is-Jewishness-Matrilineal.htm.

Friedman, R. (2013). *Fasting on Yom Kippur by Pregnant or Nursing Women*. Available at: https://www.yeshivatmaharat.org/scholar/friedman/ruth.

Gechter, E. (2013). *A pregnant pause*. Mayyim Hayyim. https://www.mayyimhayyim.org/a-pregnant-pause/.

Gersen, J.S. (2024). Converting to Judaism in the Wake of October 7th. *The New Yorker.* https://www.newyorker.com/magazine/2024/12/09/converting-to-judaism-in-the-wake-of-october-7th?fbclid=IwY2xjawG_xvNleHRuA2FlbQIxMAABHXWmE55KxY6D0BivMh-kvaSqHzrc32saqoWGJzbJIC-lfJjRrBpN9fDhcQ_aem_JtF_xuXzRBzMbQKuaX2QZA.

Glynn, P. & McIntosh, S. (2025, May 19). *Gary Lineker to leave BBC after social media 'error.' BBC News.* https://www.bbc.co.uk/news/articles/c79e37nld1no.

Gov.UK. (2024). *Writing about ethnicity.* Gov.UK. https://www.ethnicity-facts-figures.service.gov.uk/style-guide/writing-about-ethnicity/.

Haberman, M. (2018). *How to create a spiritual birth plan.* Ritualwell. https://ritualwell.org/blog/how-create-spiritual-birth-plan/.

HG Help. (2021). *HG Help.* https://hghelp.co.uk/.

Hillel. (n.d.). *Antisemitism on college campuses: Incident tracking.* https://www.hillel.org/antisemitism-on-college-campuses-incident-tracking/.

Hirsh, A.V. (1998). Infertility in Jewish couples: Biblical and rabbinic law. *Human Fertility, 1*(1), 14–19. https://doi.org/10.1080/1464727982000198041.

Horn, D. (2021). *People love dead Jews.* W. W. Norton & Company, Inc.

Horn, D. (2023). *Is Holocaust education making anti-semitism worse? The Atlantic.* https://www.theatlantic.com/magazine/archive/2023/05/holocaust-student-education-jewish-anti-semitism/673488/.

Human Rights Campaign. (n.d.). *Coming home to Judaism and self.* Human Rights Campaign. https://hrc-prod-requests.s3-us-west-2.amazonaws.com/files/assets/resources/Coming_Home_Judaism.pdf.

Human Rights Campaign. (n.d.). *Stances of faiths on LGBTQ issues: Reconstructionist Judaism.* Human Rights Campaign. https://www.hrc.org/resources/stances-of-faiths-on-lgbt-issues-reconstructionist-judaism.

Human Rights Campaign. (n.d.). *Stances of faiths on LGBTQ Issues: Conservative Judaism.* Human Rights Campaign. https://www.hrc.org/resources/stances-of-faiths-on-lgbt-issues-conservative-judaism.

Human Rights Campaign, (n.d.). *Stances of faiths on LGBTQ issues: Reform Judaism.* Human Rights Campaign. https://www.hrc.org/resources/stances-of-faiths-on-lgbt-issues-reform-judaism.

Ingold, J., Rianjongdee, S., & Carrington-Elson, J. (2024). *A review of NHS health communications with (and for) Jewish communities.* NHS – Race and Health Observatory. https://nhsrho.org/research/health-communications-report-and-resources-to-improve-access-to-nhs-services-for-jewish-communities/.

Ingall, M. (2016). *Mamaleh knows best.* Harmony Books.

International Holocaust Remembrance Alliance. (n.d.). *International Holocaust Remembrance Alliance.* IHRA. Available at: https://holocaustremembrance.com/.

Ivry, T. (2013). Halachic infertility: Rabbis, doctors, and the struggle over professional boundaries. *Medical Anthropology, 32*(3), pp. 208–226. https://doi.org/10.1080/01459740.2012.674992.

JewFAQ. (n.d.). *Kosher sex.* JewFaq. https://www.jewfaq.org/kosher_sex.

Jewish BRCA. (n.d.). *Jewish BRCA.* https://jewishbrca.org/.

Jewish News. (2023). 4.5% of Jews in England and Wales identify as LGB+ according to latest census data. *Jewish News.* https://www.jewishnews.co.uk/4-5-of-jews-in-england-and-wales-identify-as-lgb-according-to-latest-census-data/.

Jewish Virtual Library. (n.d.). *Issues in Jewish ethics: 'Kosher' sex.* Jewish Virtual Library. https://www.jewishvirtuallibrary.org/quot-kosher-quot-sex#5.

Jnetics. (n.d.). *Jewish genetic disorders.* Jnetics. https://www.jnetics.org/jewish-genetic-disorders/.

Jones, L. (2024). *Matrescence.* Pantheon.

Katsman, H. (n.d.). *Breastfeeding.* A Mother in Israel. https://www.amotherinisrael.com/breastfeeding.

Katz, Y. (n.d.). *Breastfeeding and showing affection in shul.* YC Torah. https://library.yctorah.org/lindenbaum/breastfeeding-and-showing-affection-in-shul/.

Klein, M. (1998/2000). *A time to be born: Customs and folklore of Jewish birth.* Jewish Publication Society.

Koffman, L. (2018). *Jewish perspectives on reproductive realities.* https://www.ncjw.org/wp-content/uploads/2018/02/Jewish-Perspective-on-Reproductive-Realities-FORMATTED11.pdf.

Kolatch, A.J. (1995). *The Jewish book of why.* Jonathan David Publishers.

Kolirin, L. (2021). *Factsheet: Haredi Jews.* Religion Media Centre. https://religionmediacentre.org.uk/factsheets/factsheet-haredi-jews/.

Kraft, J. (n.d.). Creating the Jewish pregnancy. *My Jewish Learning.* https://www.myjewishlearning.com/article/creating-the-jewish-pregnancy/.

Kutner, R. (2025). *The Jews.* Wicked Son.

Kveller. (2019). *What to expect at a Bris.* Kveller. https://www.kveller.com/article/what-to-expect-at-a-bris/.

Levine, N. (2023). *Snip or skip: Helping parents decide the circumcision question.* Cedars Sinai. https://www.cedars-sinai.org/blog/is-circumcision-good-or-bad.htm.

Liberal Judaism. (n.d.). https://www.liberaljudaism.org/.

Linzer, D. (2018). *May a husband give his wife supportive touch during childbirth? – Part 2.* YC Torah Library. https://library.yctorah.org/2018/04/may-a-husband-give-his-wife-supportive-touch-during-childbirth-part-2/.

Lipka, M. (2016). *Unlike U.S., Few Jews in Israel identify as reform or conservative.* Pew Research Center. https://www.pewresearch.org/short-reads/2016/03/15/unlike-u-s-few-jews-in-israel-identify-as-reform-or-conservative/.

Lovy, H. (2020). God bless sex, says Dr. Ruth. *Publishers Weekly.* https://www.publishersweekly.com/pw/by-topic/industry-news/religion/article/84165-god-bless-sex-says-dr-ruth.html.

Lovy, H. (2024). *Dr. Ruth: 'In the Jewish Tradition, Sex Has Never Been a Sin'.* Howard Lovy Substack. Available at: https://howardlovy.substack.com/p/dr-ruth-in-the-jewish-tradition-sex.

Luck, F. (2024). *Hospital investigating claims 'visibly Jewish' nine-year-old child 'mistreated by pro-Palestine nurses'.* LBC. https://www.lbc.co.uk/news/jewish-child-hospital-nhs-treatment-pro-palestine-manchester-rachel-rile/.

Malul, C. (2023). *'Bless the mother of the child with a maid and a servant': Birthing songs of Yemen's Jewish women.* The Librarians. https://blog.nli.org.il/en/yemen_childbirth_songs/.

Markovits, N. (n.d.). *Why a* mohel*? The role and benefits.* USA Mohel. https://www.usamohel.com/why-a-mohel.

Mashiah, D., & Boyd, J. (2017). *Synagogue membership in the United Kingdom in 2016.* Institute for Jewish Policy Research. https://www.jpr.org.uk/sites/default/files/attachments/Synagogue_membership_in_the_United_Kingdom_in_2016.pdf.

Mason-Barkin, S. (2016). *The timeless pain of experiencing infertility.* Jewish News of NorthernCalifornia.https://jweekly.com/2016/11/11/torah-the-timeless-pain-of-experiencing-infertility/.

Masorti Judaism. (2021). *What is Masorti Judaism?* Masorti Judaism. https://masorti.org.uk/articles/what-is-masorti/.

Mayo Clinic. (2022). *Circumcision (male).* Mayo Clinic. https://www.mayoclinic.org/tests-procedures/circumcision/about/pac-20393550.

Mazzig, H. (2019, May 20). No, Israel isn't a country of privileged and powerful White Europeans. *Los Angeles Times.* https://www.latimes.com/opinion/op-ed/la-oe-mazzig-mizrahi-jews-israel-20190520-story.html.

McCallum, S., & Tidy, J. (2023, Dec 5). *23andMe: Profiles of 6.9 million people hacked.* BBC News. https://www.bbc.co.uk/news/technology-67624182.

McSorley, C., & Dunkley, E. (2024, Feb 15). UK antisemitic hate incidents hit new high in 2023, says charity. *BBC News.* https://www.bbc.co.uk/news/uk-68288727.

Menucha. (2019). *Menucha.* https://www.menucha.info/.

Mitchell, T. (2016). *Israel's religiously divided society.* Pew Research Center's Religion & Public Life Project. https://www.pewresearch.org/religion/2016/03/08/israels-religiously-divided-society/.

Morris, B.J., Bailis, S.A., & Wiswell, T.E. (2014). *Circumcision rates in the United States: Rising or falling? What effect might the new affirmative pediatric policy statement have? Mayo Clinic Proceedings, 89*(5), 677–686. https://doi.org/10.1016/j.mayocp.2014.01.001.

Morris, B.J., & Wiswell, T.E. (2013). Circumcision and lifetime risk of urinary tract infection: A systematic review and meta-analysis. *Journal of Urology, 189*(6), 2118–2124. https://doi.org/10.1016/j.juro.2012.11.114

My Jewish Learning. (n.d., n.p., a). *Ask the expert: Baby showers.* My Jewish Learning. https://www.myjewishlearning.com/article/ask-the-expert-baby-showers/.

My Jewish Learning. (n.d., n.p., b). *Creating the Jewish pregnancy.* My Jewish Learning. https://www.myjewishlearning.com/article/creating-the-jewish-pregnancy/.

NHS. (2020). *Postpartum psychosis.* NHS.: https://www.nhs.uk/mental-health/conditions/post-partum-psychosis/.

NHS. (2022). *Postnatal depression.* NHS. https://www.nhs.uk/mental-health/conditions/post-natal-depression/overview/.

Nirenberg, D. (2013). *Anti-Judaism.* Head of Zeus.

Nishmat Yoatzot Halacha. (2023). *Breastfeeding in halacha.* Nishmat Yoatzot Halacha. https://www.yoatzot.org/624/.

Nishmat Yoatzot Halacha. (2025). *Nishmat yoatzot halacha.* https://www.yoatzot.org/.

Office of Institutional Equity. (n.d.). *Protected class definitions.* https://equity.osu.edu/training-and-education/protected-class-definitions.

Paloma-Elbaz, V. (2015). *Jewish Saharans singing to birth.* Ya Lalla. https://yalalla.org.uk/.

Pew Research Center. (2016). *Identity.* Pew Research Center's Religion & Public Life Project. https://www.pewresearch.org/religion/2016/03/08/identity/.

Pew Research Center. (2021). *Jewish demographics.* Pew Research Center's Religion & Public Life Project. https://www.pewresearch.org/religion/2021/05/11/jewish-demographics/.

Posner, K.E. (2019). *An interview with Rabbi Angela Warnick Buchdahl.* Nourish Co. https://nourish-co.com/journal-all/2019/5/16/rabbbuchdahl.

Posner, M., & Shurpin, Y. (2015). *How to convert to Judaism – What to expect at a conversion.* Chabad. https://www.chabad.org/library/article_cdo/aid/2972927/jewish/How-to-Convert-to-Judaism.htm.

Rabbinical Assembly. (n.d.). *Conservative/masorti.* The Rabbinical Assembly. https://www.rabbinicalassembly.org/about-us/conservative-masorti.

Rankin, J. (2024). Europeans are experiencing a 'wave of Antisemitism', Survey Finds. *The Guardian.* https://www.theguardian.com/news/article/2024/jul/11/europeans-are-experiencing-a-wave-of-antisemitism-survey-finds.

Reconstructing Judaism. (2016). *Who is a Reconstructionist Jew?* Reconstructing Judaism. Available at: https://www.reconstructingjudaism.org/article/who-reconstructionist-jew/.

Reform Judaism. (n.d.). B'rit Bat*: Ceremony for welcoming a baby girl.* Reform Judaism. https://reformjudaism.org/beliefs-practices/lifecycle-rituals/birth-rituals/brit-bat-ceremony-welcoming-baby-girl.

Reform Judaism. (2010). *Reform Judaism.* Reform Judaism. https://reformjudaism.org/.

Rich, D. (2024). *Shifting the goalposts of genocide.* Everyday Hate newsletter. https://everydayhate.substack.com/.

Rosner, F. (1998). Judaism, genetic screening and genetic therapy. *Mt Sinai Journal of Medicine, 65*(5-6), 406–413.

Schipper, M. (2024). *The shrinking goddess.* Saqi Books.

Schorsch, I. (1994). *The power of circumcision.* Jewish Theological Seminary. https://www.jtsa.edu/torah/the-power-of-circumcision/.

Schorsch, I. (2003). *Genesis and infertility.* Jewish Theological Seminary. https://www.jtsa.edu/torah/genesis-and-infertility/.

Sefaria. (2015). *Genesis 17:14.* https://www.sefaria.org/Genesis.17.14?lang=bi&with=all&lang2=en.

Shechet, R.J., & Fried, S.M. (1996). Traditional Jewish circumcision technique of *bris. American Family Physician, 53*(4), 1070–1072.

Sherwood, H. (2023, Apr 17). *UK progressive Judaism bodies merge to give movement more reach and voice. The Guardian.* https://www.theguardian.com/world/2023/apr/17/uk-progressive-judaism-bodies-merge-to-give-movement-more-reach-and-voice.

Shrimpton, R. (2017). *Continued breastfeeding for healthy growth and development of children.* World Health Organization. https://www.who.int/tools/elena/commentary/continued-breastfeeding.

Silber, S.J. (2010). *Judaism and reproductive technology. Cancer Treatment and Research, 156,* 471–480. https://doi.org/10.1007/978-1-4419-6518-9_38.

Silberberg, C.S. (2008). *What's wrong with pre-marital intimacy?* Chabad. https://www.chabad.org/library/article_cdo/aid/628782/jewish/Whats-Wrong-With-Pre-Marital-Intimacy.htm.

Society for Humanistic Judaism. (2018). *What Is Humanistic Judaism?* Society for Humanistic Judaism. https://shj.org/meaning-learning/what-is-humanistic-judaism/.

Society for Humanistic Judaism. (2024). *Becoming a Humanistic Jew.* Society for Humanistic Judaism. https://shj.org/living-humanistic-judaism/radical-inclusion/becoming-a-humanistic-jew/.

Swan, S. and Colino, S. (2021). Reproductive problems in both men and women are rising at an alarming rate. *Scientific American.* https://www.scientificamerican.com/article/reproductive-problems-in-both-men-and-women-are-rising-at-an-alarming-rate/.

Szabo, R. and Short, R. (2000). How does male circumcision protect against HIV Infection? *British Medical Journal, 320*(7249),1592–1594. https://doi.org/10.1136/bmj.320.7249.1592.

Trachtman, I., & Blustain, S. (1999). When the *mohel* is a woman. *Lilith Magazine.* https://lilith.org/articles/when-the-mohel-is-a-woman/.

United States Religion Census. (2010). *Single year report: All denominations.* https://www.usreligioncensus.org/report1.php?year=2010.

United Synagogue. (n.d.). *A guide for the Jewish parent on miscarriages, stillbirths & neonatal deaths.* United Synagogue. https://theus.org.uk/assets/uploads/2023/12/still-birth-singles.pdf.

Vinokor-Meinrath, S. (2024). *What does it mean to bring a Jewish baby into this world?* Kveller. https://www.kveller.com/what-does-it-mean-to-bring-a-jewish-baby-into-this-world/.

Weisberg, C.J. (2024). *Auspicious practices (segulot) for the 9th month and birth-Jewish mom.* Jewish Mom. https://jewishmom.com/pregnancy-inspiration/inspiration-for-pregnancy/inspiration-for-birth/auspicious-practices-segulot-for-the-9th-month-and-birth/.

Williams Institute. (2024). *More than 2.5 million LGBTQ adults are parenting children under the age of 18.* Williams Institute. https://williamsinstitute.law.ucla.edu/press/lgbtq-parenting-2024-press-release/.

Wodziński, M. (2019). *Studying Hasidism: Sources, methods, perspectives.* Rutgers University Press.

Woodstein, B.J. (2014). *In the UK, my Jewish ethnicity is a mystery.* Kveller. https://www.kveller.com/in-the-uk-my-jewish-ethnicity-is-a-mystery/.

Woodstein, B.J. (2015). *How I learned to embrace my big Jewish nose.* Kveller. https://www.kveller.com/how-i-learned-to-embrace-my-big-jewish-nose/.

Woodstein, B.J. (2016). *How I'm trying to teach charity to my toddler.* Kveller. https://www.kveller.com/how-im-trying-to-teach-charity-to-my-toddler/.

Woodstein, B.J. (2022). *Breastfeeding and Judaism.* Academy of Breastfeeding Medicine. https://abm.me.uk/breastfeeding-information/breastfeeding-and-judaism/.

World Jewish Congress. (n.d.). *India.* World Jewish Congress.: https://www.worldjewishcongress.org/en/about/communities/IN.

Zaklikowski, C., & Zaklikowski, D. (n.d.). *Are there Jewish customs for pregnancy and birth?* Chabad. https://www.chabad.org/theJewishWoman/article_cdo/aid/484409/jewish/Are-There-Jewish-Customs-for-Pregnancy-and-Birth.htm.

Zoll, K. (2011). *The infertile women of the Torah: Infertility in Biblical Judaism.* The Infertility Voice. Available at: https://theinfertilityvoice.com/2011/05/infertile-women-of-torah-ongoing-series/.

Zupan, J. (2015). *Ask a rabbi: Can Jews Have Baby Showers?* Jewish Boston. https://www.jewishboston.com/read/ask-a-rabbi-can-jews-have-baby-showers/.

Appendices

Appendix 1: Birth Preferences

Some things to include in your birth preferences document:

- Your name.
- Your partner's name, if applicable.
- Address.
- Phone numbers.
- Names of people who will be at the birth (including partner, a doula, any relatives or friends, any older children, etc.) and their phone numbers.
- Names of people you do not want at the birth (for example, if you don't want students present, or if there is a relative who you anticipate might try to join in but whose presence is not desired).
- Where the birth will take place.
- Your preferred language (for example, if you want people to say "surges" and not "contractions", or "chestfeeding" instead of "breastfeeding").
- The sort of atmosphere you want to have (consider candles, lighting, aromatherapy, music, images, and so forth).
- If there is anything important for the people present to know about you medically (such as allergies, epilepsy, diabetes, etc., even if this is already listed in your notes).
- If something happened during a previous experience giving birth that is relevant (such as a tear that means you need extra perineal support or a trauma that you wish to avoid repeating).

Any techniques or approaches you would like to use during the birth (such as hypnobirthing or a TENS machine or back massage).

Whether you want internal examinations and/or fetal monitoring and whether you want to be told what the findings are.

What positions you might like to use.

Whether you want to use a birth pool, a birthing stool, a shower, a birth support rope, and so on.

What sort of pain relief you want, if any, and whether you want to be offered it or if you prefer to ask for it yourself.

If you are open to the use of forceps or vacuum/ventouse.

Who can speak for you if you feel unable to speak.

Who you would like to receive the baby (in the absence of a medical emergency).

Whether you want someone to announce the baby's sex and, if so, who.

When you would like the umbilical cord to be cut and by whom.

How you want to birth the placenta (if you want the injection, for example) and if you want to keep the placenta for encapsulation or burying.

What you would like to happen immediately post-birth (for instance, a "golden hour" where you are skin-to-skin with the baby, or support with latching).

Whether you want the baby to be given vitamin K and, if so, whether orally or by injection.

How you plan to feed your baby.

Anything else that you want people to know about your ideal birth.

Appendix 2: Jewish Birth Preferences

These are some additional things to consider for a Jewish birth:

Whether your partner will be present and, if so, whether they will touch you.

Whether you plan to recite prayers or have someone else do so.

If there are any religious items that you plan to have with you or to hang up in the room.

If you want a rabbi or another spiritual leader to visit you.

What sort of food you want to eat and who will provide it.

What your arrangements are for travel on Shabbat or other festivals.

If you will feel able to press call buttons or do other such things if you are giving birth on Shabbat and, if not, who will do it for you.

Whether you mind if other people carry out work on Shabbat or other festivals beyond the strictly necessary.

What your plans are in regard to naming, circumcision, or other ceremonies.

If there are other relevant spiritual aspects to your birth preferences.

Appendix 3: Hospital Bag

Your own hospital bag might include:

- Your hospital/doctor's notes.
- Your birth plan/preferences.
- Multiple changes of clothing (for labor, for recovery, for going home).
- Multiple changes of large, comfortable underpants.
- Bikini top for the birthing pool, if desired.
- Hair bands or clips, as needed.
- Maternity pads.
- Dressing gown and slippers.
- Shampoo, conditioner, soap, lotion, deodorant, lip balm, toothbrush, toothpaste, and other toiletries.
- Towels.
- Books, magazines, music.
- Phone and charger.
- Camera.
- TENS machine, if using.
- Food and drink.
- Silicone or bamboo straws and sports-type bottle.
- Breastfeeding tops and bras.

Breast pads.

Fan.

Pillows.

Candles, photos, aromatherapy oils, or any other items to relax you or remind you of home.

Your partner or other support person's bag might include:

A copy of the birth plans/preferences.

Phone and charger.

Camera.

Multiple changes of clothing.

Swimsuit (if they plan to get into the birthing pool, as relevant).

Toiletries.

Food and drink.

Money.

Books, magazines, music.

Phone numbers of people you might need to call to share news with.

The baby's bag might include:

- Diapers (cloth or disposable).
- Cloths or wipes or cotton wool.
- Muslins.
- Multiple changes of clothing (including vests, bodysuits, sleepsuits, etc.).
- Warm cardigan or coat for going home in.
- Blanket.
- A car seat.

Also, there may be some specifically Jewish items:

- Siddur or other religious books or readings.
- Psalm 121 to hang up.
- *Tallit* or other religious items.
- Mezuzah and/or *shviti* and/or amulets (such as a *kimpetbrivl* or a *hamsa*).
- *Roiteh bendel*, or red thread.
- Kosher food or other specific food or drink.

Appendix 4: Postnatal Preferences

Some things to include in your postnatal preferences document:

Your name.

Your partner's name, if applicable.

Address.

Phone numbers.

Names of people who may visit you or even stay with you after the birth (including partner, a doula, any relatives or friends, etc.) and their phone numbers.

Names of people you do not want visiting you.

Any relevant information about your plans for parental leave (such as the length of your leave or any keeping-in-touch days at work).

Any information about how long your partner will have for parental leave.

How you plan to feed your baby and any information about support you may want with that.

Your plans for recovering physically and emotionally from the pregnancy and birth, including getting rest.

Any cultural or religious traditions that will be important to you after the baby's birth.

Any foods or drinks you would particularly like to have in the postnatal period.

Items for a postpartum kit that would suit you (for instance, absorbent pads, breast/chest pads, laxatives, pain relief, a small jug, a pump, and so on).

The kind of support you would like to have postnatally (for example, grocery delivery service, friends preparing meals for you, massages, physiotherapy, help with cleaning, etc.).

Anything you can do in advance to make postnatal life easier (such as preparing multiple baby-changing stations around your home or freezing portions of meals or booking a cleaning service).

A list of books, magazines, TV shows, films, podcasts, and so forth that you might like to enjoy while recovering and managing babycare.

Any activities you would like to do, either alone or with your baby (such as baby swim class, or baby-friendly cinema, or walks, and so on).

Any useful contact information for people, healthcare professionals, organizations, websites, or charities you could contact if you needed extra support.

Other thoughts.

Appendix 5: Jewish Postnatal Preferences

These are additional things to consider for the postnatal period for a Jewish family:

Which prayers will be recited and when.

If you want a rabbi or another spiritual leader to visit you.

What sort of food you want to eat and who will provide it.

If you are formula-feeding, you may wish to look into formula that is certified kosher.

What your arrangements are for travel on Shabbat or other festivals.

If you will feel able to press call buttons or do other such things if you are in the hospital or birthing center on Shabbat and, if not, who will do it for you.

Whether you mind if other people carry out work on Shabbat or other festivals beyond the strictly necessary.

What your plans are in regard to naming, circumcision, or other ceremonies.

Where you plan to stay while recovering from birth.

If there are other relevant spiritual aspects to your postpartum preferences.

www.ingramcontent.com/pod-product-compliance
Lightning Source LLC
LaVergne TN
LVHW010055110826
845155LV00028B/344